Attitudinal Decision Making
in the Supreme Court of Canada ....

Law and Society Series
W. WESLEY PUE, GENERAL EDITOR

The Law and Society Series explores law as a socially embedded phenomenon. It is premised on the understanding that the conventional division
of law from society creates false dichotomies in thinking, scholarship,
educational practice, and social life. Books in the series treat law and
society as mutually constitutive and seek to bridge scholarship emerging
from interdisciplinary engagement of law with disciplines such as politics,
social theory, history, political economy, and gender studies.

A list of the titles in this series appears at the end of this book.

Attitudinal Decision Making
in the Supreme Court of Canada

C.L. Ostberg and Matthew E. Wetstein ......

UBCPress · Vancouver · Toronto

15 14 13 12 11 10 09 08 07   5 4 3 2 1

Printed in Canada on ancient-forest-free paper (100% post-consumer recycled) that is processed chlorine- and acid-free, with vegetable-based inks.

Library and Archives Canada Cataloguing in Publication

Ostberg, C. L. (Cynthia L.), 1963-
  Attitudinal decision making in the Supreme Court of Canada /
C.L. Ostberg and Matthew E. Wetstein.

(Law and society, 1496-4953)
Includes bibliographical references and index.
ISBN 978-0-7748-1311-2 (bound); 978-0-7748-1312-9 (pbk.)

  1. Judicial process – Canada. 2. Canada. Supreme Court. 3. Conflict of judicial decisions – Canada. 4. Political questions and judicial power – Canada. I. Wetstein, Matthew E., 1963- II. Title. III. Series: Law and society series (Vancouver, B.C.)

KE8244.O88 2007   347.71'035   C2006-906158-0
KF8764.ZA2O88 2007

Canadä

UBC Press gratefully acknowledges the financial support for our publishing program of the Government of Canada through the Book Publishing Industry Development Program (BPIDP), and of the Canada Council for the Arts, and the British Columbia Arts Council.

This book has been published with the help of a grant from the Canadian Federation for the Humanities and Social Sciences, through the Aid to Scholarly Publications Programme, using funds provided by the Social Sciences and Humanities Research Council of Canada.

UBC Press
The University of British Columbia
2029 West Mall
Vancouver, BC V6T 1Z2
604-822-5959 / Fax: 604-822-6083
www.ubcpress.ca

This book is dedicated to our parents
Rosemarie Ostberg, Paul and Kate Wetstein,
and in loving memory of Donald Ostberg

Contents

Tables and Figures

FIGURES

Acknowledgments

It is frequently said that no person is an island, and a similar comment applies to those who endeavour to write a book. We have benefited from the assistance of many individuals during the course of our work, and we owe a debt of gratitude to them. For important financial support, we gratefully acknowledge the University of the Pacific for several grants, including a Scholarly Activities Grant in 1997 (The Supreme Court Data Base Project) and two Eberhardt Faculty Research Grants in 2000 and 2004 (Leadership on the Supreme Court of Canada, and Economic Liberalism and the Business Decisions of the Supreme Court of Canada). We also benefited from the generous support of the Government of Canada's Department of Foreign Affairs through its Faculty Research Award program. Their funding supported our travel to Winnipeg and Ottawa to collect data on newspaper accounts of the ideology of Supreme Court nominees in the summer of 2004. We extend special thanks to Daniel Abele, the program officer for the Canadian Embassy, in Washington, DC, for his efforts in support of our work. As is customary with any grant project, the findings that we present represent our own views and should not be attributed in any way to the granting institutions.

We are grateful for the permission from several journals to reprint portions of our previously published material. Chapter 4 presents some updated findings from our prior work on search and seizure cases: Matthew E. Wetstein and C.L. Ostberg, "Search and Seizure Cases in the Supreme Court of Canada: Extending an American Model of Judicial Decision Making across Countries," *Social Science Quarterly* 80 (1999): 757-74. Other significantly revised portions are derived from the following publications: C.L. Ostberg, Matthew E. Wetstein, and Craig R. Ducat, "Leaders, Followers, and Outsiders: Task and Social Leadership on the Supreme Court of Canada in the Early

Nineties," *Polity* 36 (2004): 505-28; Matthew E. Wetstein and C.L. Ostberg, "Strategic Leadership and Political Change on the Canadian Supreme Court: Analyzing the Transition to Chief Justice," *Canadian Journal of Political Science* 38 (2005): 653-73; C. L. Ostberg and Matthew E. Wetstein, "Judicial Behavior on the Canadian Supreme Court: Attitudinal Conflict in Right to Counsel Cases, 1984-2001," *Political Science Quarterly* 121 (Winter 2006-07), and C.L. Ostberg, Matthew E. Wetstein, and Craig R. Ducat, "Attitudinal Dimensions of Supreme Court Decision Making in Canada: The Lamer Court, 1991-1995," *Political Research Quarterly* 55 (2002): 237-58.

During our periodic trips to Canadian universities and research centres, we received extraordinary assistance from many dedicated librarians. We want to thank in particular several of the staff at Carleton University, including reference librarians Michelle Atkin, Heather Berringer, and Nancy Peden, for their help in tracking down news stories on the nominations of Canadian Supreme Court justices. We also received assistance from the staff of the National Library of Canada and the University of Manitoba in the course of that data collection. Daniel Jutras, former executive legal assistant to Chief Justice Beverley McLachlin, also took time out of his schedule to correspond with us and provide information on oral arguments of the Supreme Court. We also benefited from the gracious help of Judith Rubin, who worked for many years as a reference librarian at the Supreme Court of Canada. At UBC Press, we want to thank Darcy Cullen and Frank Chow for their efforts in the editing and production of the book. In addition, Randy Schmidt served as a tremendously helpful editor. We enjoyed collaborating with him, and the periodic ability to exchange communiqués on hockey life in Kelowna, British Columbia, and Stockton, California.

Many colleagues have offered commentary and advice on our research as it has been presented at conferences and in the "seminar through the mail" of the peer review process. We are particularly grateful to Christopher Manfredi of McGill University for his constant willingness to read our work and find some merit in its rough edges. Likewise, we would like to thank Jim Kelly of Concordia University and Lawrence Baum of Ohio State University for their helpful and insightful comments on our work. A few of the arguments advanced in this book represent the fruits of our collaboration with Don Songer at the University of South Carolina, and Susan Johnson at the University of North Carolina, Greensboro. We are grateful for their willingness to work with us, and for their help in honing some of our thoughts about the attitudinal model. We have also benefited from the advice and commentary of a number of scholars in the course of presenting our findings at conferences and in the manuscript review process. In this regard, we extend thanks to Peter Russell, University of Toronto; Neal Tate, Vanderbilt University; Roy Flemming, Texas A&M University; Ted Morton, University of Calgary; Matt Hennigar, Brock University; Ian Green, York University; Carl Baar, York University; Steve Wasby, University at Albany, State University of New York, Mark Rush, Washington and Lee University; Bob Dudley, George Mason University; Charles Epp, University of Kansas; Herbert Kritzer, University of Wisconsin; Wayne McIntosh, University of Maryland; and countless others who have anonymously read our work.

At our home universities, we have been fortunate to find supportive colleagues (and students) who do not mind occasional discourses on Canadian judicial politics. Our research has benefited from the University of the Pacific's Department of Economics Social Science Colloquium, which provided an informal forum to present some of this research for the first time. Bill Herrin was always willing to schedule our presentations to the colloquium, and the pointed questions and comments of our peers always served to improve our work. We also want to extend thanks to Donald DeRosa and Phil Gilbertson, whose unwavering commitment to the teacher-scholar model has enabled this book to come to fruition.

We would like to acknowledge the support of some of the faculty in the political science department at Northern Illinois University who played a pivotal role in our early development in the field. Mike Wyckoff's tutelage in empirical research was so sound that we often hear his voice in the background reminding us to always start from sound hypotheses. Likewise, we thank Bob Albritton for his words of encouragement regarding our research on the Canadian Supreme Court. Additionally, Lettie McSpadden was a helpful mentor during our graduate studies.

Special thanks must be reserved for our mentor and friend Craig Ducat of Northern Illinois University, who played a critical role in developing the initial database that served as a springboard for this research. Craig has been a wonderful colleague with whom to collaborate, mainly because he has the uncanny ability to ask the right questions, provide the right phrasing when needed, and prod for more clarity and zip in the writing. It also helps that Craig always knows the best restaurants in town, whether it is in Chicago, Boston, Quebec, Ottawa, or Sherbrooke. We are certain he will not agree with all that we have written here, but we also know that he will tell us in due time how far we have strayed from his guidance.

Finally, we would like to thank our family and friends for their patience and forbearance during the writing process. Specifically, we would like to thank Mike Duveneck, who supported our endeavour through thick and thin; Scout, who sat at our table providing daily support; and our parents, to whom the book is dedicated.

Attitudinal Decision Making
in the Supreme Court of Canada

1
Models of Judicial Behaviour and the Canadian Supreme Court

Twenty-five years after the addition of the *Canadian Charter of Rights and Freedoms* to the Constitution, academics, politicians, and Supreme Court watchers continue to debate the impact that the document has had on the high court and Canadian society. One ramification that is not disputed, however, is that the *Charter* has clearly placed the Court centre-stage in some of the most dramatic policy debates pertaining to issues such as gay rights, Aboriginal territorial claims, abortion, health care, and minority language rights. Given the Court's enhanced role in the political process, it is not surprising that justices on the bench are frequently at odds over how to resolve some of these high-stakes policy issues.

A prime example of judicial disagreement emerged in June 2005, when the Court released a divided ruling in a bitterly contested dispute over the constitutionality of Quebec's prohibition on private health insurance programs (see *Chaoulli v. Quebec (Attorney General)*, [2005] 1 S.C.R. 791 [*Chaoulli*]). The justices on the seven-member panel that decided the case took three distinct stances on the legal issues. Writing for the majority, Justice Deschamps struck down the Quebec ban because it forced citizens to endure extensive waiting periods in Canada's national health care program, thus infringing the right to life and personal inviolability guaranteed in Quebec's *Charter of Human Rights and Freedoms*. Three of her colleagues – Chief Justice McLachlin and Justices Major and Bastarache – would have gone further by ruling that the ban not only violated the provincial charter but also the citizens' rights to life, liberty, and security enshrined in section 7 of the *Canadian Charter of Rights and Freedoms*. Justices Binnie, LeBel, and Fish, in dissent, concluded that Quebec's private health care ban did not violate notions of fundamental justice because the waiting periods were not arbitrary in nature, and went on to suggest that the Court should not meddle in an affair that had already been resolved through protracted debate in various provincial and federal elections (see *Chaoulli* at 860-61). Ultimately, the disagreement that emerged in this case reflects a larger trend of conflict that has become more common-place in the post-*Charter* Court as it becomes increasingly embroiled in highly contentious issues that have a profound impact on the larger Canadian body politic.

If one analyzes the case from a political science perspective, one might ask: What was it about the *Chaoulli* case that triggered disagreement among the Canadian justices? Were their opinions animated by differences over the appropriate legal interpretation to give section 7 of the *Charter* when deter-mining what constitutes a reasonable waiting period for publicly funded health care? Or were the justices at odds because they held differing ideologi-cal policy stances on the kinds of health care services that should be pro-vided to Canadians? Or, alternatively, did some of the justices engage in strategic activity behind the red velour curtain that might have been critical to the development of the fractured ruling handed down by the Court? Clearly, each of these possibilities provides a viable explanation for the roots of the discord surrounding the health care debate that has emerged in the modern Canadian Supreme Court. Only further systematic research on the under-lying sources of judicial conflict will reveal the degree to which each explana-tion provides an accurate account of the motivating forces behind such disagreements.

The *Chaoulli* case is just one example in a long line of contested rulings that has prompted at least one member of the high court to publicly com-ment on the rifts within the Court. In a speech commemorating the twenti-eth anniversary of the *Charter*, Justice Iacobucci called on public law scholars to devote more attention to exploring the patterns of judicial conflict that have emerged on the Court in the post-*Charter* era (Iacobucci 2002). Since members of the Canadian Supreme Court have maintained a traditional al-legiance to a norm of consensus, it is important to explore what factors have led to an increase in disagreement among the justices in recent years. The significance of Justice Iacobucci's request cannot go unnoticed, especially in light of the increasingly prominent role that the justices have come to play in the policy process. We believe that an understanding of how the justices ar-rive at their decisions, particularly highly contentious ones, is worth investi-gating because their rulings have such a dramatic and lasting impact on Canadian society. In addition, how the Court resolves a given dispute is criti-cal because that ruling can have a dramatic impact on the way that similar legal disputes are framed in the lower courts, and how policy debates unfold in provincial legislatures and in Parliament. Scholars should also explore the roots of judicial disagreements because it might help the Court, as an institution, understand how to cope with or limit potential strife in the future. Such analysis could also result in a reduction in divided rulings, which in turn can help shore up the Court's legitimacy and stature in a democratic society that is currently debating the appropriate role of the Court in a system predicated on parliamentary supremacy. More broadly, we believe that if researchers have a better understanding of what fosters conflict in the post-*Charter* era, it might provide a significant contribution to the development and refinement of a more global theory of decision making that is aimed at explaining judicial behaviour beyond the confines of a particular nation.

We believe that an examination of conflict in the post-*Charter* Court takes on even greater significance when viewed in light of a larger global transformation that is taking place on courts in a multitude of countries and those that decide transnational issues. According to Tate and Vallinder (1995) there is a "judicialization of politics" that is occurring in high courts around the world, putting them centre-stage in the resolution of significant policy disputes. These scholars contend that the global transformation of courts is due to a number of factors, including the fall of communism, movement toward democratization by various states, and the increased influence of American legal jurisprudence on these emerging democracies (5, 2-3). They stipulate that this worldwide phenomenon constitutes "one of the most significant trends in late 20th and early 21st Century government" (5). Given the heightened profile of courts, it is not surprising that citizens have increasingly used them as a forum for settling divisive individual rights claims that necessarily have important political, social, and moral ramifications for society as a whole. Since high courts are becoming central institutions of policy-making power, it is imperative that comparative scholars systematically analyze what creates, exacerbates, and diminishes strife among members of these institutions. In short, the political, social, and institutional roots of conflict that divide high court justices should become a prominent subject of inquiry for comparative scholars worldwide.

The global trend toward more politicized and powerful courts raises a critical theoretical question: Do high courts of common law heritage have similar decision-making patterns? This question deserves careful examination and scrutiny because if so, then perhaps one overarching theory of judicial behaviour may be developed that can systematically explain the bulk of conflict that emerges between justices within and across a myriad of democratic high courts. In order to explore this question, one must assess the current literature to determine whether any theoretical paradigms exist that might facilitate such a cross-cultural analysis. We believe that the attitudinal model of judicial behaviour might serve as a viable overarching theory to explain decision making across a multitude of high courts because a number of comparative studies throughout the years have successfully demonstrated the validity of its components in a sporadic fashion outside the US setting. No comparative research to date, however, has presented a systematic test of the model across multiple issue areas while simultaneously controlling for case facts, legal factors, and other rival variables. Our study represents a first step in this effort, and was motivated by the goal of testing the applicability of the attitudinal model in the Canadian context. Given the global judicialization of politics, we think it is crucial for comparative law scholars to begin conducting such systematic tests in high courts of other countries in an effort to develop a more complete and comprehensive theoretical model of judicial activity. In the pages that follow, we outline the contours of the attitudinal model and discuss rival theories of judicial decision making. We also provide a detailed sketch of the book and document some of the major findings of the study, most notably that patterns of ideological decision making in the Canadian Supreme Court have more complex, nuanced, and less polarized characteristics than the patterns found in its southern counterpart.

Competing Theories of Judicial Decision Making

Over the last fifty years, the attitudinal model has become one of the most prominent theoretical explanations for how justices arrive at their decisions (see Segal and Spaeth 1993, 2002). It draws its intellectual origins from rule skeptics, who, at the turn of the twentieth century, began questioning the long-held legal claim that justices merely find the law, rather than make it (Holmes 1881, 1897; Frank 1930; Fisher et al. 1993). In essence, these legal scholars believed that the written opinions of judges, which seem to follow the norms of precedent and the plain meaning of legal texts, simply act as a rationalization for advancing the justice's own beliefs and values in the cases they decide (see Llewellyn 1931, 1237; Segal and Spaeth 1993, 66). Ultimately, these legal realists called on social scientists to carefully analyze judicial rulings in order to better understand and predict the direction the law would take in the future (see Holmes 1897).

The behaviouralist revolution that took hold in the 1940s enabled political scientists to show that judicial policy preferences were critical factors that explained the rulings of individual judges. Pritchett's seminal work (1941, 1948) on the Roosevelt Court in the US stands as a hallmark of this early research; he demonstrated that political attitudes largely explained the non-unanimous decisions that were handed down by that court. His findings stimulated other behavioural pioneers, such as Schubert (1965, 1974), to utilize psychological scaling techniques on judicial votes to identify distinct underlying ideological dimensions at work in the decision-making process operating in two key areas of law. Schubert (1965, 122-23, 142-43) found that US Supreme Court justices followed a predictable ideological pattern of voting in economic cases that pitted economic underdogs against affluent interests – which he labelled the E-scale of ideological votes – and predictable lines in civil liberties cases that juxtaposed individual liberty claims against government's interest in maintaining traditional norms of social behaviour – which he labelled the C-scale of ideological votes.

Building on this foundation, subsequent attitudinalists, such as Spaeth and Peterson (1971), Rohde and Spaeth (1976), and Segal and Spaeth (1993, 2002), developed more comprehensive and coherent theoretical arguments for determining the extent to which political attitudes influence the judicial decision-making process. Like their predecessors, they believed that "the primary goals of Supreme Court justices in the decision making process are *policy goals*," and that "when the justices make decisions they want to approximate as nearly as possible [their own] policy preferences" (Rohde and Spaeth 1976, 72). These scholars subsequently extended attitudinal theory by characterizing judicial outcomes as not only the product of the ideology of individual justices but also the result of attitudinal responses to specific case facts that can be triggered in different areas of law (Segal and Spaeth 1993, 73). Their analysis of US search and seizure cases from 1962 to 1989 indicated that measures of ideology and attitudinal responses to case facts could collectively predict 74 percent of the justices' votes in this area of law (Segal and Spaeth 1993, 230). Beyond this most explicit test of the attitudinal model, Segal and Spaeth (2002, Chapter 8) present a wealth of aggregate data that reinforce the idea that modern US justices are influenced by their ideology and that their voting patterns are relatively constant throughout their careers. Clearly, the various behavioural studies discussed above have gone a long way toward debunking the pervasive myth that judges simply rely on legal texts, precedents, the intent of the framers of the Constitution and the toolbox of law school training to guide their judgments and written opinions.

The work of scholars like Schubert, Spaeth, and Segal has generated a virtual cottage industry of attitudinal studies exploring the significance of judicial ideology within different US courts and appellate courts around the world. Some of the earliest comparative attitudinal court scholarship was conducted by Schubert himself (1969a, 1969b, 1977, 1980), who was able to document ideological decision making in the high courts of Switzerland, Australia, and South Africa. His findings motivated other researchers, who have successfully shown that ideological conflict was evident in other court settings as well, including the Philippines (Samonte 1969; Flango and Schubert 1969; Tate 1995), Italy (DiFrederico and Guarnieri 1988); Japan (Dator 1969; Kawashima 1969; Danelski 1969), and Australia (Blackshield 1972; Galligan and Slater 1995; Power 1995). In Canada, Peck (1967a, 1967b, 1969) and Fouts (1969) published the first quantitative attitudinal studies demonstrating that the same kinds of liberal/conservative ideological dimensions at work in the US were also prominent on the Canadian high court. Subsequent behavioural scholarship by Tate and Sittiwong (1989) demonstrated that in addition to ideology, there were a host of judicial background characteristics that could explain judicial votes in economic and civil liberties disputes prior to the *Charter*'s adoption. Not surprisingly, the addition of the *Charter* has inspired a host of new studies exploring how the document has transformed the Supreme Court of Canada's institutional role in the Canadian policy process, and several of these studies are discussed further in Chapter 2. For present purposes, it is sufficient to say that this post-*Charter* research has documented an increase in attitudinal conflict between the Canadian justices, and suggests that attitudinal behaviour continues to operate unabated on the Court today (Songer and Johnson 2002; Ostberg, Johnson et al. 2004; McCormick 2000; Manfredi 1993, 2001; Epp 1998; Hausegger and Haynie 2003; Ostberg et al. 2002). Collectively, these comparative efforts have provided political scientists with a wealth of data demonstrating that attitudinal decision making occurs across time and place, and thus has real potential to serve as the core element in the development of a more global theory of judicial decision making in the future.

Despite the growing body of literature suggesting that ideological factors are at work in appellate courts outside the US context, the evidence has been compiled in a rather sporadic fashion in disparate issue areas across various time periods and cultural contexts. Unfortunately, these studies, although fruitful, have given little or no consideration to systematically testing the viability of what we would call the *full-fledged* attitudinal model that simultaneously controls for the ideology of justices and specific case facts. If nothing else, Segal and Spaeth's prior research (1993, 2002) has shown us the importance of taking into consideration both the ideological leanings of the justices and the fact patterns that trigger attitudinal responses in order to more fully understand the situational dynamics that influence judicial rulings. The consideration of case facts, an element that is so integral to the application of their theory in different areas of law, has been largely ignored in the comparative public law literature and in most of the Canadian scholarship to date (for an exception, see Wetstein and Ostberg 1999). Given this lacuna in the literature, we believe that a systematic test of the full-fledged attitudinal model needs to be conducted in democratic courts around the world before it can achieve the status of a more global theory of judicial decision making. As it stands, many US scholars simply assume that the attitudinal model is a viable theory for explaining judicial behaviour in democracies outside the confines of the US, given the strength of its explanatory power in one of the most powerful democracies in the world. Our research begins to fill this gap in the literature by systematically testing the impact of fact patterns and ideology in six distinctive areas of law on the post-*Charter* Canadian Supreme Court. Our findings suggest that the attitudinal model provides a persuasive account of judicial decision making in Canada, which bodes well for its applicability in other democratic high courts around the world.

Although this book explores the relevance of the attitudinal model in Canada, we acknowledge that other theories of judicial behaviour may help explain how justices determine case outcomes. Two rival theories that deserve some comment are the legal model and the strategic/rational choice depiction of appellate court decision making. Advocates of the legal model, largely affiliated with law schools, claim that when justices engage in judicial review, they should abide by the plain meaning of the text of the constitution or statute in question, and not simply follow their own particular policy preferences (Ducat 2004; Segal and Spaeth 1993, 2002). Advocates of this perspective argue that justices remain untainted by political considerations because they simply apply rules in the constitution to the facts of a particular case. If justices are unable to decipher the plain meaning of the text, advocates of the legal approach claim that they should turn to the intent of the framers for further constitutional and legal guidance. Moreover, supporters of the legal model contend that appellate justices should follow the legal norm of *stare decisis*, which ensures they adhere to legal rules established in prior cases containing similar factual circumstances (see Ducat 2004; Segal and Spaeth 1993, 2002; Esptein and Knight 1998). They claim that justices follow precedents in order to ensure that some consistency is maintained in the law. Ultimately, there is some legitimacy to particular aspects of the legal model, especially when precedents provide a clear roadmap for how a particular case should be resolved. If justices were to hand down inconsistent rulings in cases involving similar fact patterns, the public would no longer view justices as fair and unbiased arbiters of the law who are above politics; this, in turn, could undermine the legitimacy of the court. As such, precedents can serve as an important constraint on legal rulings because justices are wary of substituting their views when clear guidelines exist, and, as Epstein and Knight (1998, 45) point out, a "general norm favouring precedent exists in society at large."

Despite the foregoing discussion of the importance of abiding by precedent, one should note that first-level appellate court justices are far more likely to be constrained by previous rulings than their colleagues on courts of last resort, because of their institutional position in a hierarchical system of justice. Even though first-level appellate judges largely serve an error-correcting function, they are more likely to be norm enforcers because they are required to apply legal principles established by higher courts (see Songer et al. 1994; Neubauer and Meinhold 2004, 425). Moreover, since these judges hear cases that are largely a product of their mandatory jurisdiction, they often deal with relatively routine appeals that are fairly easy to resolve. According to Baum (2001, 274), "judges on these courts frequently express the view that most of their cases are easy to decide because the merits clearly lie on one side ... in effect, these judges are saying that the law is the dominant element in the courts' decision-making: most of the time, only one result can be justified under the law." In contrast, second-level appellate justices are not as readily constrained by the norm of precedent because their docket is mainly discretionary in nature (Baum 2001, 274-75). This, in combination with pressures from their heavy workload, makes them more likely to agree to hear more difficult cases that typically feature legitimate precedents on both sides of a given dispute. As Baum points out (2001, 275), "the law and the environment leave judges on second level courts with considerable freedom to take the directions they wish in their decisions." Since cases that reach the Supreme Court contain precedents on both sides of the legal issue, attitudinalists have argued that US Supreme Court justices are free to simply select precedents that reflect their own point of view (Spaeth and Segal 1999, 290). The point to be drawn from this is that while matters of law remain dominant in determining the outcome of relatively easy first-level appellate court cases, attitudinal theorists would contend that policy preferences provide a more accurate account of the decision-making activity of justices serving on the highest court of the land.

A third theoretical model of judicial decision making that has gained prominence in recent years focuses on the relative importance of strategic interactions that take place between appellate justices during the decision-making process. According to advocates of this theory, since high court justices work in a small-group environment, their rulings are necessarily a product of justices engaging in a collegial bargaining process with eight other justices on the bench (see Epstein and Knight 1998, 10-18; Maltzman et al. 2000; Murphy 1964; Manfredi 2002). These scholars contend that justices must act strategically in relation to each other and relative to other political actors in the system if they are going to achieve their policy objectives. This theory is based on the assumption that in an effort to advance their own policy goals, high court justices must often accommodate the preferences of other members of the court. Since these justices usually need four other members to join their opinion to prevail in a case, they often engage in a calculated bargaining process in an effort to build a winning coalition (see Epstein and Knight 1998; Maltzman et al. 2000). This model recognizes that justices will often be forced to sacrifice their own ideal policy position in a case in order to persuade other justices to move in the direction of their preferred position (Maltzman et al. 2000, 17-18; Epstein and Knight 1998, 13). From a strategic standpoint, this approach recognizes that it is better for justices to win half a loaf than to lose the entire loaf. Ultimately, advocates of this theory, unlike attitudinalists, acknowledge that justices do not blindly pursue their own policy outcomes with a devil-may-care attitude; rather, they are more sophisticated actors in a small-group environment who must take into consideration the preferences of other actors in the decision-making process.

Collectively, these theories constitute three of the most prominent accounts used in explaining judicial decision making and conflict in US appellate courts. Although advocates of each theory might contend that their perspective provides the best description of judicial behaviour, we believe that each of the approaches can be perceived as different layers of a large onion, with each sheath providing an added element of explanation for how justices arrive at their final legal outcomes. Along these same lines, Baum (1997) has suggested that each approach may explain to some extent the multiple and varied goals that US justices pursue. We believe that, like their US counterparts, justices of the post-*Charter* Canadian Supreme Court are bound to be influenced by both the strategic environment in which they work and a conscious desire to write opinions that are consistent with accepted legal doctrines. However, given the dominance of attitudinal theory in the US context, and the sporadic efforts to validate its presence in other high courts around the world, we believe that this model could play a central role in explaining judicial conflict within the post-*Charter* Canadian Court. As such, this book presents a systematic analysis of the full-fledged attitudinal model in multiple issue areas, not only to document its distinctive relevance in the Canadian context but also to advance the proposition, with some qualifications, that the model could serve as a viable link in the construction of a more global theory of judicial decision making.

There are several reasons why testing the applicability of the attitudinal model in the post-*Charter* Canadian context makes intuitive sense. First, the addition of the *Charter of Rights and Freedoms* to the Canadian Constitution in 1982 provided a unique and timely opportunity to analyze whether attitudinal decision making appears in a host of complex, highly charged areas of rights litigation that are winding up on Canada's high court docket. Second, given the host of similarities between Canada and the US, the Canadian Supreme Court represents an obvious first test case for systematically assessing the attitudinal model outside the confines of the US. The logic of this argument rests on the fact that since the two high courts have parallel institutional rules and norms, possess similar degrees of judicial independence within the broader political structure, and protect similar core rights provisions, attitudinal decision making is as likely in the Canadian context as it is in the US setting. We expand upon these themes more extensively in Chapter 2, and discuss various factors that might theoretically suppress attitudinal decision making in the Canadian high court as well. Despite the cultural and institutional differences between the two courts, we believe that the many similarities between the two institutions help explain why the attitudinal model has been a useful theoretical framework for describing decision making in the post-*Charter* era. Our findings indicate that its applicability in the Canadian context, admittedly one of the easiest test cases, holds promise for its utility in more diverse democratic cultural settings.

As one might expect, some public law scholars have expressed concern over simply trying to import the liberal/conservative ideological divide that attitudinalists have found operating in US courts to assess decision-making patterns in disparate issue areas and in other court settings (see Ostberg et al. 2002, 236-37; Flango and Ducat 1977; Dudley and Ducat 1986; Ducat and Dudley 1987). One cannot assume that justices deciding cases in two distinct areas of law or in two different countries will necessarily be motivated by the same left/right dimensions of conflict. Given this valid criticism, some scholars have attempted to avoid this theoretical pitfall by utilizing factor analytic techniques to help identify the underlying values that trigger attitudinal disagreement in the US Supreme Court in economic cases (see Dudley and Ducat 1986; Ducat and Dudley 1987). Using this unique approach, these scholars let the majority and minority voting patterns in cases sort the justices' records on two different dimensions, and then identify the source of conflict underlying each dimension based on the patterns in the cases and the values that appear in the justices' opinions. Ultimately, this methodological approach prevents scholars from falling into the convenient trap of simply imposing the liberal/conservative construct so prominent in some areas of US law on the voting patterns in other areas of law, or on justices in high courts in other cultural settings. In light of this potential shortcoming, we initially conducted a prior factor analytic study on the *Charter* rulings of the Lamer Court (1991-95), and found that two of the three principal dimensions of conflict operating in *Charter* cases were rooted in a liberal/conservative divide between the justices (Ostberg et al. 2002, 251-52). In a subsequent study examining both *Charter* and non-*Charter* cases heard by the Lamer Court between 1993 and 1997, we demonstrated that a liberal/conservative divide was in fact the most important dimension of conflict between the justices in the three distinct areas of law analyzed in this book, namely, criminal, economic, and fundamental freedoms cases (Ostberg et al., n.d.). Taken together, these recent studies suggest that the same liberal/conservative tensions that are so prevalent in the US are also salient in the modern Canadian Supreme Court. Thus, it is not surprising that this book documents that ideological differences animate much of the decision making that takes place in several critical areas of law. Having said this, our most direct tests of the attitudinal model indicate that its applicability is less definitive and more subtle in the Canadian context than in the US Supreme Court.

Research Questions and Organization of the Book

Since we are examining the significance of the attitudinal model in the post-*Charter* Canadian context, the overarching research question for this book boils down to the following: What role do judicial ideology, case facts, and other control variables play in explaining the votes of justices, in both unanimous and non-unanimous cases, in distinct areas of law argued before the Court in the 1984–2003 period? More to the point, does judicial ideology play a more prominent role than other variables in our examination of judicial behaviour in the Supreme Court of Canada? Other significant research questions addressed in this book include: What areas of law spark the most attitudinal conflict in the Court? Do the justices from different ends of the ideological continuum respond differently to particular case facts? Do they exhibit stable and consistent ideological voting patterns over time and across issue areas? Are activist judges more likely to be found on one side of the ideological spectrum? Who acted as the intellectual leaders in the post-*Charter* era, and who were content to simply follow the lead of others? Conversely, who were the outsiders on the Court and were more willing to blaze their own legal trails? Does the gender or private legal experience of the justices influence the votes they cast in particular areas of law? What significant differences are found in the aggregate voting behaviour of the first three post-*Charter* courts? Answers to these questions are explored in detail in four key chapters (Chapters 4, 5, 6, and 7).

We chose to test the applicability of the attitudinal model in the 1984-2003 period because it comprises the first twenty years of rulings under the *Charter* and was a period in which greater rates of conflict emerged in the Canadian Supreme Court. Chapters 4, 5, and 6 analyze patterns of judicial behaviour in three distinct areas of law: criminal, civil rights and liberties, and economic cases, respectively. These areas of law were chosen because they represent obvious demarcations of prominent and distinct legal categories, and because they constitute the bulk of the Court's post-*Charter* docket. Each of these substantive chapters is divided into two main sections. The first is devoted to general statistics on *all* cases in a particular area of law, while the second provides an in-depth statistical test of the attitudinal model in two specific subfields of law, analyzing both unanimous and non-unanimous cases.

The test of the attitudinal model in these chapters involved the use of a mathematical equation estimating the probability that a justice would cast a liberal vote in a particular case. We were interested in determining the relative importance of two key sets of variables – namely, the impact of a justice's perceived liberalism, and responses to case facts – while controlling for other variables in the model. The model included other potentially significant variables that assessed the influence of litigants, intervenors, and different periods of the post-*Charter* Court. The mathematical equation took the following form:

Probability of liberal vote = Constant + b_1 (justice's perceived ideology) +
$\quad$ b_2 (other justice characteristics: gender, private practice) +
$\quad$ b_3 (set of case facts) +
$\quad$ b_4 (set of parties and intervenors) +
$\quad$ b_5 (court control variables, e.g., McLachlin Court) +
$\quad$ e (unexplained variance)

This logistic regression model recognizes that judicial votes may be the product of various factors, and provides a sophisticated attempt to measure the extent to which justices' ideological values influence their votes while taking a host of other variables into consideration. When the justice-level ideology measure (b_1) has a statistically significant impact on the dependent variable (the probability of a liberal vote), then the model provides compelling evidence that attitudinal decision making is at work in the Supreme Court of Canada. When it is not significant, then ideological attitudes have less relevance in explaining judicial behaviour in a particular area of post-*Charter* litigation. The model also enabled us to test whether justices register attitudinal responses to the stimuli that case facts present. For example, in a criminal case, a justice might be more prone to cast a liberal vote in favour of the criminally accused in a circumstance where no right to counsel warning was given, as opposed to a case where officers gave proper notice of this procedural safeguard. Likewise, in the economic area, a justice may be more likely to favour union arguments in a situation where management has engaged in unfair labour practices, in contrast to a case lacking this factual circumstance. The equation also takes into consideration the effect of court control variables in order to test for differences between the Dickson, Lamer, and McLachlin Courts. Finally, the equation estimates the impact of particular litigants and intervenors, such as the Women's Legal Education Action Fund (LEAF), to determine whether their presence might sway the justices to vote in a particular manner. We included these five sets of variables in the regression models in Chapters 4, 5, and 6 whenever it made theoretical sense to do so in order to explore the utility of the full-blown attitudinal model in the modern Canadian context.

As mentioned earlier, Chapter 2 presents an extensive theoretical discussion of why we believe attitudinal decision making may or may not be relevant in the Canadian context. Specifically, this chapter examines the various political, institutional, cultural, and legal forces that may foster or mitigate the appearance of attitudinal conflict in the post-*Charter* era. For example, we contend that the Canadian Court's enhanced power of judicial review, its increased volume of *Charter* cases, and its institutional independence all work to support the contention that Canadian justices are as likely to engage in attitudinal decision making as their US counterparts. We acknowledge, however, that other factors, such as the cultural and historical legacy of parliamentary supremacy, the institutional norm of collegiality, and recent criticism of activist rulings, to name a few, help suppress attitudinal decision making by the post-*Charter* justices. Even though we conclude that attitudinal behaviour is prominent in the modern Court, we argue that the countervailing forces at work in Canadian society help foster a more nuanced and less predictable pattern of attitudinal expression than is found in the US setting. The theoretical argument advanced in this chapter is critical because it suggests that attitudinal behaviour may be prominent within high courts but at the same time may be diminished by the unique institutional, political, and cultural structures found in different countries. Ultimately, we believe that the more muted attitudinal findings in the Canadian Court have profound implications for how the attitudinal model may perform in disparate cultural settings and for the development of a more global theory of judicial behaviour.

Chapter 3 focuses on constructing a measure of judicial ideology that a justice had before he or she was appointed to the Court in order to test the attitudinal model in the Canadian context and to provide a viable indicator of judicial liberalism for future research. Since Court nominees shy away from disclosing their beliefs in public discourse, and researchers therefore lack direct knowledge of a justice's ideological views before they join the Court, we provide a comprehensive discussion of the utility of applying four different indirect measures of liberalism in Canada that have been prominent in prior US research. We ultimately employ two of the four measures in subsequent chapters because they were not highly correlated with each other, they tap distinct latent dimensions of judicial ideology in the Canadian setting, and they hold the most promise for correlating with the ideological voting patterns of the justices. The first measure is derived from the party of the appointing prime minister, while the second parallels Segal and Cover's indicator (1989), which is based on multiple newspaper accounts of a nominee's ideology at the time of his or her appointment. The inclusion of these two indicators in our subsequent statistical models highlights compelling distinctions between the prominence of both measures in the US context as opposed to our finding that only the newspaper indicator performs well across disparate issue areas in the post-*Charter* Canadian Court. In order to address possible criticisms that might be levelled at the newspaper ideology measure and advance our belief that it is the most viable a priori predictor of judicial liberalism in the Canadian setting, Chapter 3 presents multiple tests of internal and external validity to demonstrate its overarching power. We believe that this new ideological measure will have broad appeal for court watchers and researchers both within and outside of Canada, because of its potential use in future studies of the Canadian Court and its ability to be replicated in other advanced democratic societies.

Chapters 4, 5, and 6 present a three-pronged examination of attitudinal conflict and consensus that has emerged in the criminal, civil rights and liberties, and economic cases in the first twenty years under the *Charter*. Each chapter is divided into two main sections. The first is devoted to documenting the number of cases decided in an area of law, the percentage of the docket devoted to each issue, the frequency of non-unanimous rulings, patterns of ideological voting, case participation, opinion authorship, activism, and ideological voting stability. The second section addresses the applicability of the attitudinal model in two subfields of law: right to counsel and search and seizure disputes in Chapter 4, equality and free expression controversies in Chapter 5, and union and tax cases in Chapter 6.

The results in Chapter 4 indicate that panel sizes and rates of consensus in the Canadian Supreme Court in the criminal area parallel those that were found when examining the statistics for all cases in the 1984–2003 period. Thus, criminal disputes have not generated greater levels of ideological conflict than those found in all other areas of law. Moreover, when looking at opinion authorship patterns, Justices Lamer and Cory emerged as the task leaders of the post-*Charter* Court in criminal cases, authoring high rates of majority opinions, while Justices Beetz and Chouinard appeared content to follow the lead of others. Justices L'Heureux-Dubé and Deschamps, in turn, were clear outsiders, authoring the largest percentage of dissents despite their location on opposite ends of the ideological spectrum. In the criminal area,

unlike the other two fields studied, there is a clear connection between liberal voting patterns and rates of activism in the post-*Charter* Court, demonstrating a conservative reluctance to invalidate criminal law statutes. The results
also indicate that in the criminal area, the justices exhibited relatively consistent ideological voting patterns over time. The data from the first section of
Chapter 4 provide important evidence of the ideological voting tendencies
of individual justices of the post-*Charter* Court in criminal cases. The results
in the second section illustrate that the full-fledged attitudinal model does a
remarkable job of explaining the voting patterns in prominent post-*Charter*
criminal disputes. Most notably, they indicate that the newspaper ideology
measure presented in Chapter 3, and not the party of the appointing prime
minister, serves as a powerful predictor of attitudinal decision making in
right to counsel and search and seizure cases. Its impact remains significant
even when controlling for a host of rival explanatory variables. The prominence of ideology in these cases is crucial because the attitudes and values of
nominees are often downplayed in the judicial appointment process in
Canada. Our findings also reveal that a myriad of case facts act as cues for
liberal and conservative votes by the justices, and that members of the Court
at different ends of the ideological spectrum respond in distinctive manners
to different case characteristics. This latter finding highlights a degree of attitudinal complexity that has emerged in the Canadian Supreme Court that
distinguishes the justices' voting behaviour at the two ends of the ideological
spectrum. Overall, the results in Chapter 4 indicate that pervasive liberal/
conservative ideological conflicts have dominated the Court in these two
criminal areas in the post-*Charter* period.

Chapter 5 highlights decision making in the civil rights and liberties
area. The initial data suggest that these disputes foster greater rates of conflict
than in criminal cases or collectively across all other categories of law. Chief
Justices Dickson and Lamer stand out as leaders of the Court in these cases,
authoring the largest percentage of majority opinions, while a handful of
justices – Binnie, Estey, Gonthier, and Le Dain – can be considered as opinion followers in this area of law. Justices McLachlin and L'Heureux-Dubé, in
turn, exhibited outsider activity with a large volume of dissenting opinions.
Their distinctive voting behaviour, along with the patterns of the three other
female justices in our study, confirm that women on the post-*Charter* Court
have developed a feminist approach that is distinct from their male counterparts toward equality cases and the bulk of free expression claims in the first
twenty years under the *Charter*. The substantial gender gap on the Canadian

high court in the civil rights and liberties area is remarkable, because it stands in stark contrast to the more mixed results with regard to gender differences in the US public law literature (see Songer and Crews-Meyer 2000). Moreover, these findings have great significance for prime ministers, members of Parliament, and court watchers who may be interested in the legal and political ramifications of naming female justices to the high court. In contrast to the criminal area, the data in Chapter 5 reveal that there is a weak association between judicial ideology and activist voting, which means that conservative justices are just as apt to hand down activist rulings as their liberal counterparts in civil rights and liberties disputes. Moreover, about half of the justices in the civil rights and liberties cases exhibited unstable ideological voting patterns over time, which differs from the relative stability found in the criminal area. Taken together, these data suggest that those who follow and study the Canadian Court, along with comparative law scholars, must be mindful that complex manifestations of ideological behaviour may emerge among the justices in different areas of law.

The second part of Chapter 5 further amplifies the critical role that gender differences play in judicial voting in discrimination and free expression cases. Put simply, the progressive stance taken by the female justices remains prominent even when controlling for a host of factors, including the ideological proclivities of the justices on the high court. Unlike the findings in Chapter 4, the two a priori indicators of ideology are not effective in predicting liberal and conservative votes in these two areas of law. This remarkable finding might shock scholars more familiar with the US Supreme Court, because most would think that civil rights and liberties cases would be the most likely to provoke ideological tensions on the court. Moreover, this result unmasks the flaw in thinking that attitudinal decision making will apply neatly and easily across national boundaries, and demonstrates the need for more systematic cross-cultural studies assessing the applicability of the attitudinal model, even in countries that share many of the same political and institutional features as the US.

The results in Chapter 6 indicate that panel participation rates in economic cases are roughly the same as in the criminal area and those found across most other cases. There were, however, higher rates of unanimity in economic disputes than in all other areas combined. In line with their business law acumen, Justices Iacobucci and Estey acted as the task leaders in economic cases, authoring far more majority opinions than the average, while Justice Stevenson stood out as the sole economic outsider during his brief stay on the Court. Most of the justices serving in the 1984–2003 period appeared to cluster around the moderate middle of the Court when casting votes in economic cases. The connection between activism and liberalism in economic disputes is more mixed, and thus falls somewhere between the strong patterns found in the criminal cases and the virtually non-existent relationship in the civil rights and liberties area.

Our findings in the three areas of law have broad implications for the larger debate about judicial activism that is taking place in the Canadian literature. The disparate results suggest that the charge of liberal activism levelled by leading court critics must be tempered because conservatives are as likely as their liberal counterparts to engage in activist rulings in prominent civil rights and liberties and economic cases. The data charting ideological stability over time in the economic area suggest that while most of the justices are consistent, several have very unstable records over a six-year time period, a pattern similar to that found in the civil rights and liberties area. The instability across two of the three substantive areas suggests that legal practitioners and court observers need to be aware that some justices on the Court may indeed change their ideological stripes over the course of their tenure on the Court, which may have a profound impact on the direction the law takes over time. Moreover, our data suggest that comparative scholars need to be sensitive to the fact that changes in justices' voting behaviour over time may be more systematic on a court than one would expect given the contention by US scholars that political elites supposedly harbour clear and consistent ideological stances (see Campbell et al. 1960).

The second half of Chapter 6 echoes many of the themes set out in Chapter 4. As in the criminal area, the justices exhibited relatively clear patterns of ideological voting in both union and tax cases, and the party of prime minister measure did not perform well in any of the models. Moreover, factual scenarios in economic cases played a prominent role in shaping the disparate votes of the justices at different ends of the ideological spectrum, which parallels our findings in the criminal fields. It should be noted, however, that conservative justices in the economic cases tended to be more animated to follow their ideological proclivities than their liberal counterparts when responding to case facts. In our statistical models of the union cases, experience as a private attorney was highly correlated with the newspaper ideology measure, and thus, not surprisingly, served as a useful surrogate of judicial liberalism. In fact, it performed better as a predictor of liberal voting than our newspaper scores across all union cases as well as in non-unanimous disputes. In the tax area, although the newspaper ideology measure was not statistically significant when examining all tax cases, it proved to be the most powerful predictor of voting behaviour in non-unanimous disputes. This finding matches our results for non-unanimous rulings in the two areas of criminal law discussed in Chapter 4. The disparate finding in the tax area for the impact of the newspaper ideology measure points to the significant role that factual circumstances can play in the minds of justices when assessing all cases, namely, that ideological considerations take a backseat to specific case facts, but when justices disagree, ideological tensions play a much stronger role in shaping their voting behaviour. The dynamic relationship between ideology and facts in the tax area, along with the fact that private practice served as a viable surrogate for liberalism in the union cases, collectively point to the complex impact of ideology on judicial voting in prominent economic cases. Having said this, the findings in Chapter 6 reinforce the conclusions from Chapter 4 that the attitudinal model is a prominent theoretical paradigm for explaining judicial decision making in four of the six areas of law studied in the post-*Charter* Canadian Court.

One important finding to be garnered from Chapters 5 and 6 is that intervenors had mixed success in their effort to influence the votes of Supreme Court justices. While the appearance of the Women's Legal Education Action Fund (LEAF) had a dramatic, positive effect for rights claimants in equality cases, the presence of the Canadian Civil Liberties Association (CCLA) had a negligible impact on the Court in free speech cases. As mentioned in Chapter 5, one reason why the CCLA has had such a negligible impact may be its tendency to intervene in the most difficult free speech cases. In contrast, the appearance of the Canadian Labour Congress (CLC) in union/management disputes did have a significant, pro-union impact on judicial votes across all cases. When blue collar and public safety workers were litigants in union disputes, the justices also cast more votes in their favour. Our mixed findings in this area suggest that Canadian scholars might want to explore in greater detail why certain types of intervenors have a greater influence on judicial votes than others (for exceptions, see Brodie 2002; Manfredi 2004). Comparative scholars might also want to focus more attention on the political success of various interest groups in other high courts to see whether there are any consistent cross-national patterns.

Chapter 7 integrates the results found in the substantive chapters by examining the extent to which individual justices maintain ideologically consistent voting patterns across the three distinct areas of law. This chapter borrows from the ideological framework championed by Janda et al. (2004), which examines the inherent tensions found in all democracies between the competing values of freedom, order, and equality. We present four different scatterplots that assess how Canadian justices have balanced these competing values across economic, criminal, and civil rights and liberties cases (for a similar approach, see Morton et al. 1994). We use this analysis to identify the ideological labels that best fit the justices of the post-*Charter* Court, and to catalog their ideological consistency across different issue areas. Ultimately, eleven justices display ideologically consistent voting records, with Justices Arbour and Wilson falling into the liberal quadrant while Justices Beetz, Gonthier, La Forest, Lamer, and McIntyre are quintessential conservatives. In contrast, Justices Cory, Dickson, and L'Heureux-Dubé earn the communitarian label, while Justice Iacobucci straddles the conservative-communitarian divide. Our findings reveal that the six remaining justices exhibited ideologically inconsistent voting patterns, and five of them happen to be members of the McLachlin Court. Among this group, Justices McLachlin, Bastarache, and Binnie took a pro-government stance in the criminal area and a pro-litigant stance in civil liberties cases, while Justice Sopinka did the exact opposite.[1] Overall, most but not all justices took issue stances, whether from an extreme or moderate position, that validate the contention that most political elites possess ideologically consistent beliefs across different issue domains. Our findings also show remarkable patterns of ideological consistency in the aggregate rulings of the Dickson, Lamer, and McLachlin Courts when various issue areas are examined, with the exception of the McLachlin Court's libertarian swing in civil liberties disputes. Collectively, the consistency found in these two sets of data reinforce the legitimacy of the attitudinal model for explaining decision making in the first twenty years of the post-*Charter* Court.

In the final chapter, we summarize the major findings of the book and discuss their implications for court watchers, political scientists, politicians, journalists, and legal scholars both within and outside of Canada. For instance, we explore the importance of the chief justice's ability to structure panel compositions in the Canadian setting, and the potential for ideological considerations to filter into that institutional process. We discuss the different leadership styles of the post-*Charter* chief justices and examine how legal specialization, opinion leadership, and outsider activity emerge in a court that is largely collegial in its work style. In addition, we link our empirical findings about judicial activism to the broader debate about the Court's proper role in a Canadian system that is rooted in parliamentary supremacy.

We also discuss the implications of our ideological findings for Supreme Court nominations and the possible politicization that could emerge with the institution of different types of parliamentary oversight procedures. We explore the linkages between attitudinal decision making and the rise of interest group activity in the Canadian courts in recent decades. We also discuss the impact that female justices have on rulings in the realm of equality law, and suggest that prime ministers should be aware of the significance of gender when considering future Supreme Court appointments. We speculate on the practical implications that our findings regarding case facts might have for the strategic choices that lawyers, litigants, and intervenors might make on whether to pursue an appeal to the Supreme Court. The discussion of these and other implications demonstrates that this book might have broad appeal to politicians and the general public, as well as public law scholars interested in the architecture of a more global theory of attitudinal decision making for a multitude of democratic high courts.

The data from our study identify some important overarching conclusions that scholars should take away from this work. First, a consistent theme throughout the book is that while ideology has significant prominence in the post-*Charter* Court, its impact is far less definitive than that found in the US Supreme Court, where rote ideological decision making has flourished. Evidence of this complexity is provided by the absence of ideology as an important explanatory variable for the votes of Canadian justices in the free expression and equality results presented in Chapter 5. The fact that ideology plays a more nuanced role in the Canadian context is largely attributable to the fact that the two courts operate in different cultural, institutional, and political environments. One should note that the more subtle impact of ideology is amplified by the different voting and writing patterns that individual justices register in different sets of cases. For instance, our data demonstrate that individual justices may serve as an ideologically moderate opinion leader in one area of law but a more conservative outsider in another, depending on the policy issue that the Court addresses. Thus, one of the significant features of this study is that not only is ideological voting more muted in the Canadian setting but some of the individual justices engage in distinctive patterns of ideological behaviour across different areas of law.

A second important theme to be drawn from this book, especially for Canadians concerned about the political nature of judicial activism, is that outside the criminal area, judicial activism does not fall along liberal/conservative lines. In other words, in most areas of law, the judicial act of nullifying statutes is no more a province of liberal justices than of their conservative counterparts. A third prominent theme is that case characteristics do influence voting behaviour on the Canadian high court, and that critical distinctions emerge regarding the types of facts that are important to the justices at opposite ends of the ideological spectrum. A fourth theme is that gender differences do structure the distinctive voting patterns of male and female justices in a host of equality circumstances and non-unanimous free speech cases.

Overall, we believe that these overarching themes demonstrate that our book makes a significant contribution to the literature. Our research not only stands on the shoulders of previous attitudinal scholars by examining the model in a systematic way across multiple issue areas in a new court setting but also lends credence to the possible development of an overarching paradigm for explaining judicial conflict in democratic high courts around the world. The study also presents an account of judicial behaviour that is distinct from the overt ideological patterns prevailing in the US Supreme Court. At the end of the day, in response to Justice Iacobucci's query regarding what drives conflict on the contemporary Canadian Court, we would have to assert that although ideological differences do help explain divisions that emerge on the bench, the discord is less transparent and more varied than attitudinal theorists might have expected.

2

The Viability of the Attitudinal Model in the Canadian Context

Even though the Supreme Court of Canada obtained an enhanced power of judicial review under the *Canadian Charter of Rights and Freedoms,* it was not a foregone conclusion that members of the high court would radically change their approach to constitutional interpretation in the wake of their new constitutional mandate.[1] One reason for suspecting little change was that the Court had failed to breathe any real life into the statutory bill of rights enacted by Parliament in 1960. In order to better understand how today's court fits into Canada's current political structure, it is necessary to provide a quick overview of the Court's legal development in Canadian society and its operational procedures. This review will also provide a backdrop for understanding the various political, institutional, and legal characteristics in modern Canadian society that might lead one to believe that justices on the Canadian high court may or may not engage in attitudinal decision making in the post-*Charter* era.

History and Operation of the Court

The prominence of the Canadian Supreme Court in the current policy-making process represents a radical departure from the role it played throughout much of its history.[2] Because the founders of the Canadian Confederation created a government based on the British Westminster model of parliamentary supremacy, the Court operated as a subordinate institution throughout much of its history (Jackson and Jackson 1994, 194). Although the Court was given the power of judicial review, this power was limited in scope because the Court was essentially relegated to the meagre role of settling jurisdictional disputes in the Canadian federal system (Manfredi 1993, 28-29). For the first seventy-five years of its existence, the Canadian high court simply functioned as an intermediate court of appeal because its decisions could be reviewed by a higher tribunal in Britain, called the Judicial Committee of the Privy Council of Britain (JCPC). In fact, during this period, provinces often directly appealed to the JCPC in an effort to bypass the Canadian high court altogether because it was perceived to have a pro-national bias for much of its early history, and because many considered it largely an extension of the federal government (Russell 1987, 337-38). These early characteristics led scholars, such as Russell (1987, 336), to conclude that at this time, the court "was supreme in name only" (see also McCormick 2000). Even though the Court became the court of last resort in 1949, at least in constitutional matters, its role remained fairly benign because it continued to largely re-solve jurisdictional disputes in Canada's federal system.

When Parliament passed a statutory bill of rights in 1960, it was a po-tential watershed in the legal history of the Canadian Court. Although the parliamentary bill contained many of the same individual guarantees found in the US Bill of Rights, the Supreme Court did not seem to take such legal protections seriously. According to Morton and colleagues (1991, 61-62), over the course of the next twenty years, the Court decided only thirty-four bill of rights claims, and handed down rulings in favour of the individual in only five of those cases (see also Russell 1987, 343). Some jurists and schol-ars contended that the statutory bill of rights had a negligible impact because the individual rights were not entrenched in the Constitution itself, and thus could be easily repealed by Parliament at any time. Moreover, the bill was not taken seriously by members of the Court because it did not apply to provincial governments (L'Heureux-Dubé 1993, 153; Russell 1987, 343). In summing up the statute's impact, Gibbins (1993, 137) aptly pointed out: "The Bill of Rights [was] analogous to a little stone tossed into the pond of Canadian political life; it produced a small splash and some minor ripples, then sank from sight within a national political culture that was still pre-dominantly parliamentary and governmental in character." Given the statu-tory bill of rights' perceived failure, some scholars argued that the Court would not take civil liberties seriously until they were elevated to constitutional status (MacKay 1983, 59).

Constitutional status for a bill of rights would come in 1982 but not before the Supreme Court experienced changes in its power to review cases. Its procedures for taking cases on appeal are outlined in the *Supreme Court Act* of 1975, which set limits on avenues of appeal in civil cases and gave the Court wide discretion to reject applications for appeal from lower court liti-gants that did not raise issues of "public importance" (see Russell 1987, 344-54; McCormick 2000, 86-88; Flemming 2004, 5-10). In view of these changes,

Flemming (2004, 6-8) suggests that the Canadian Supreme Court hears three distinct types of cases: one set consisting of the appeals that it agrees to hear; a second constituting criminal cases that it must hear under the 1975 law, labelled "as of right" disputes; and a third containing reference questions that are filed with the Court by the federal or provincial government to dispose of constitutional questions pertaining to legislation under review. Currently, the bulk of the cases heard by the post-*Charter* Court are discretionary in nature, since reference questions and "as of right" criminal disputes constitute roughly a quarter of the Court's caseload (see Russell 1987; McCormick 2000, 87; Flemming 2004, 8).

The mechanism that the Court uses for assessing whether to grant review for the larger set of leave to appeal applications takes the form of three-judge panels. Once applications are received by the Court, and brief summaries of the files are written by staff members, a case generally needs two of the three justices to agree to grant review of the case before it is scheduled for oral argument (Flemming 2004, 15). Members of the entire Court have an opportunity to revive discussion of a rejected case if they so desire. Flemming (2004, 15) reports that most of the decisions on applications for leave are unanimous at the panel level, and once these votes are cast, the full group typically ratifies the decision and releases an order communicating the cases for which leave to appeal have been granted or rejected. In light of these procedures, it is clear that the Canadian case selection process is more decentralized than the US system, where the votes of four justices are needed to grant review of a lower court ruling. Despite these differences, the two courts share a remarkably similar power to control the bulk of the cases that get placed on their calendar.

Once cases are accepted for oral argument, the chief justice of the Canadian Court has a unique power that sets her apart from her US counterpart, namely, the power of panel assignment. In other words, the chief justice determines how many justices, and which ones, will be assigned to resolve a given dispute (see Greene et al. 1998, 114-17). Unlike the US situation, where all nine justices usually hear a case, in Canada panels can be composed of five, seven, or nine justices, depending on the significance of the case. Scholars, such as Greene and colleagues (1998, 116) have found that five-member panels are frequently created to hear "as of right" criminal cases and appeals grounded in Quebec civil law; for the latter group, a majority of justices on the panel hail from that province. We discuss the potential strategic ramifications of the chief justice's panel assignment power later in this chapter.

Beyond these differences, much of the Court's internal operating procedures parallel nicely those found in the US Supreme Court.

A clear difference between the two courts is the length of time that they have operated with an expansive power of judicial review under a constitutional bill of rights. While the US Supreme Court has had over 200 years of experience issuing rulings that centre on rights claims, the *Charter* is a truly modern phenomenon in the Canadian political process. After the *Charter's* adoption in 1982, many court watchers questioned the relative impact it would have in Canadian society. While some believed that an American style of judicial review would come to dominate judicial decision making in the post-*Charter* period, others said the Court would remain a passive tribunal, given its historic role as a junior player in a system based on parliamentary supremacy (see Verney 1987; MacKay 1983; Hogg 1987; Slattery 1987; Russell 1982). At the heart of this initial debate was the recognition that there are striking similarities between Canada and the US that would lead one to theorize that an American form of attitudinal decision making might prevail under this new *Charter* mandate. Having said this, there are several important societal differences to suggest otherwise. In the next three sections of this chapter, we highlight the various political, institutional, and constitutional factors that might mitigate or enhance the likelihood of the Canadian justices' engaging in attitudinal decision making.

Political and Historical Factors Fostering or Mitigating Attitudinal Expression

Since the Canadian Supreme Court had played a relatively subordinate role throughout much of its earlier history, there are viable theoretical reasons for believing that members of the high court would have been reluctant to engage in attitudinal decision making in the post-*Charter* era. This muted expression of attitudes on the Canadian Court may stem partly from the fact that despite acquiring an enhanced power of judicial review, the Supreme Court continues to operate in a political system based on a strong Westminster parliamentary model. In such a system, the prime minister has significant power at the national level, which is actualized through strict party discipline in the legislature, virtually complete control over the selection of cabinet members and Senate appointments, and ultimate power over the naming of federal judges. These political features give the prime minister far more authority than the US president has under the separated institutions of shared power found in the United States (see Ostberg 1995, 11-12). In light of the prime minister's dominance, some might argue that providing the Court with the constitutional power to strike down parliamentary statutes undermine the structure of government that was established and is paradoxical in nature. Indeed, the justices themselves have expressed an interest in remaining sensitive to the legacy of parliamentary supremacy and the need for maintaining judicial deference in such a system. Writing in 2001, Chief Justice McLachlin (72) stated:

> Thus far in the Charter's short history, the courts have repeatedly countenanced respect for the choices of Parliament and the legislatures. They have repeatedly affirmed that it is not the Court's role to strike the policy compromises that are essential to effective modern legislation.

The Court's respect for traditional notions of parliamentary supremacy, coupled with the fact that the Canadian Constitution itself allows for legislative override of court rulings, may prompt the justice to be more likely to defer to parliamentary mandates at the expense of engaging in attitudinal decision making. If this line of thinking is correct, then post-*Charter* Canadian justices should be less prone to engage in attitudinal expression than their southern counterparts.

Besides the tradition of parliamentary supremacy, there are historical and cultural differences between the two countries and courts suggesting that Canadian justices should be less likely than their US colleagues to utilize their own attitudes and values when resolving disputes. Comparative scholars, such as Lipset (1990, 1996), have argued that the cultural differences between Canada and the United States can be largely traced to distinct organizing principles that were derived from the separate historical tracks taken by the two countries after the American Revolution. According to this argument, the US was born out of revolution and founded on the Lockean principles of freedom, equality, and limited government, while Canada was born out of counter-revolution, where British loyalists and Francophone elites sought to preserve a more class-aware, law-abiding, statist, and collectively oriented society (Lipset 1990, 2-8). Lipset claimed that the distinct organizing ethos of these two societies are best illustrated in their founding documents. While the *British North America Act* of 1867 emphasized the collectivist values of peace, order, and good government, the Declaration of Independence enshrined individualistic values of life, liberty, and the pursuit of happiness (Lipset 1990, 8; Ostberg 1995, 11; McLachlin 2004). The distinct cultural heritage of these two societies may encourage contemporary justices of the two courts to adopt different approaches to rights claims and the practice of judicial review. Since Canadian justices operate in a culture that has traditionally emphasized collectivist values and deference to governmental authority, they may be more prone than their southern counterparts to curb their attitudinal proclivities when resolving rights disputes. In other words, the cultural legacy of greater deference to majoritarian will that has existed in Canada throughout its history may trump a modern justice's desire to impose his or her own attitudes and values in a given case.

The distinct criminal justice systems that have emerged on each side of the border provide additional theoretical reasons for believing that Canadian justices would be less likely to uphold procedural guarantees for the criminally accused, and thus be less likely to engage in attitudinal decision making than their US colleagues. Throughout most of its history, Canada has abided by a "crime control model," which emphasizes the repression of criminal conduct for the benefit of society as a whole at the expense of safeguarding individual rights throughout the adjudicative process (Packer 1968; Ostberg 1995, 17). According to Packer (1968), this model exemplifies an assembly line system of justice that stresses the need to move the accused toward conviction as quickly as possible (Lipset 1990; Morton 1987; Morton et al. 1991; Manfredi 1993, 2001; Stuart 1987; Ostberg 1995; Wetstein and Ostberg 1999, 2005). In contrast, the modern US criminal justice system adheres to a due process model that rose to prominence in the Warren Court era. This model emphasizes the need to protect the rights of the criminally accused throughout each stage of the criminal process and ensure that procedural fairness is maintained over society's interest in securing speedy convictions (Packer 1968; Wetstein and Ostberg 1999, 760-61). Although the Canadian Court has clearly moved in a due process direction in the wake of the legal guarantees secured under the *Charter*, the Court's historic allegiance to the crime control model may limit the degree of attitudinal support for due process claims in the post-*Charter* era. This line of thinking suggests that the post-*Charter* Canadian justices would be more likely than their US counterparts to suppress their pro-rights attitudinal proclivities in criminal cases.

The fact that Canadians have tolerated greater restrictions on a host of individual rights throughout the twentieth century indicates that they are far more deferential than Americans to governmental authority, and may provide further evidence that attitudinal voting would be less prominent on the modern Canadian Court. A relatively recent and notable example of such societal tolerance is illustrated in the October Crisis of 1970, when the federal government imposed martial law and ordered Canadian troops into Quebec to regain control of that province after two government officials were kidnapped by Front de libération du Québec (FLQ) extremists. According to Came (1990, 19) most of the 465 people imprisoned at the time had not engaged in any criminal act. Although few Canadians would approve of such war measures today, polls at the time indicated that over 80 percent of the public supported the suspension of civil rights by the government (Bain 1990, 24; Chambers 1996, 162-63). Tolerance for restrictions on individual rights can also be seen in the media area, where media bans on publication during criminal trials were readily accepted in Canada before 1994. In the area of gun ownership, Canadians are much more tolerant of federal restrictions on firearms, and are far less likely to use guns while committing crimes (Canadian Centre for Justice Statistics 1999, 166-73). Glendon (1991, 6-13), in turn, argues that the political discourse about individual rights has become increasingly polarized in the two countries since the Second World War and the civil rights period. While the dialogue in Canada remains deferential to authority and encourages a balance between individual rights and one's obligation to the community and collective responsibility, the modern discourse in the US invokes the stark language of individual entitlement and "rights talk" with little regard for responsibility to majoritarian values (Glendon 1991, 14-15). Collectively, these examples illustrate that Canadian citizens are far more deferential to governmental restrictions on individual rights and liberties than their southern counterparts. As such, it makes intuitive theoretical sense to believe that the Canadian justices would be more reluctant to substitute their own attitudinal preferences for policy restrictions on individual rights that emanate from majoritarian institutions. This sentiment was echoed by MacNeil (1991, 418), who suggested that Canadians are willing to accept many limits "as the reasonable cost of a calm and secure society, duller perhaps, but free enough," and this sentiment, in turn, may resonate in the rulings of the contemporary Canadian Court.

Another, more tenuous but important theoretical reason for believing that attitudinal decision making would be less prominent in the post-*Charter* era pertains to increasing levels of criticism that have been levelled at the Court, especially beginning in the late 1980s. Although this increased external criticism indicates that attitudinal decision making was occurring more frequently in the early post-*Charter* period, it may have prompted some of the more recent justices to pull back from attitudinal decision making in response. There is substantial evidence supporting the notion that members of the late Lamer Court were put on the defensive and felt that they had to justify the rulings that they were handing down (Wallace 1999, 14). Indeed, Chief Justice Lamer took aim at critics in 1999 for their "judge-bashing" and suggested the Court was merely heeding the public will "by ensuring all laws comply with the 1982 Charter" (Wallace 1999, 14). The Court's sensitivity to this type of criticism can also be illustrated by its unique formal efforts to clarify and limit the impact of its widely criticized ruling in *R. v. Marshall*, [1999] 3 S.C.R. 456, a case dealing with year-round Aboriginal fishing rights (see Geddes 2000, 32). This type of response by the Court to increased external criticism, along with Chief Justice McLachlin's efforts to make the Court more transparent to the Canadian public, suggests that justices in recent years may have been more reluctant to hand down rulings that appear to go against majoritarian stances. Although court critics could argue that there is a continuing trend of activist rulings in recent years, it is possible to theorize that under Chief Justice McLachlin's tutelage, members of the Court may have tempered the expression of their attitudes and values in an effort to quell criticism of some court watchers. If this argument is valid, then the attitudinal model would have less holistic explanatory power for the entire post-*Charter* period than it has for the modern US Supreme Court.

While the political factors cited above might prevent the same degree of attitudinal expression from appearing in the Canadian and US courts, there are theoretical reasons for believing that other political pressures in Canadian society might promote an American style of attitudinal decision making in the post-*Charter* period. It is important to point out that some of these political factors may have emerged well after the *Charter*'s enactment, thus influencing the justices' decision-making patterns at a later stage of *Charter* jurisprudence. Regardless of when these factors became prominent, the point to be made here is that the analysis of the various political factors over the entire post-*Charter* period may demonstrate a pattern of attitudinal decision making in the Canadian Supreme Court that is as pronounced as in the US Supreme Court.

A principal reason for believing that Canadian justices would engage in the same degree of attitudinal decision making as their US counterparts stems from the political transformation that the Court experienced at the time of the *Charter*'s enactment. Indeed, the *Charter* enhanced the Court's institutional profile in the Canadian political system by giving it an explicit mandate to strike down any acts of Parliament or provincial legislatures that violated provisions of the *Charter* (see McLachlin 2001, 67; Wilson 2001, 75). As Russell (1982) noted at the time of its adoption, the document instigated a major shift in power toward the judicial branch because it gave the judiciary a much more systematic and authoritative role in interpreting individual rights. Under this new mandate, members of the Canadian Court were thrust into an increasingly political environment that enhanced their ability to interpret the Constitution in line with their own attitudes and values. This political transition provides a viable theoretical rationale for maintaining that the justices of the Canadian Court would be as motivated by their policy preferences as their southern counterparts.

The fact that prominent politicians, legal scholars, and journalists have levelled sharp criticism at many of the Court's rulings over the last twenty-five years provides strong evidence that the Court has indeed become an active political player in the policy process, and lends credence to the contention that attitudes and values may be exerting the same degree of influence on the post-*Charter* Canadian Court as on the US Court. Critics, such as Morton and Knopff (2000), have suggested that the justices of the Supreme Court have helped instigate a "*Charter* Revolution" that advances minority liberal rights claims at the expense of majoritarian policy making by the legislative and administrative branches of government. Criticism of recent judicial activism has also been articulated by politicians like federal Minister of Justice and Attorney General Vic Toews, who once excoriated the Lamer Court for engaging in a "frenzy of constitutional experimentation that resulted in the judiciary substituting its legal and societal preferences for those made by elected representatives of the people" (House of Commons Debates, 1 March 2001, as cited in Roach 2001, 86). These and other comments have sparked an intense academic and legal debate over the proper role of the Canadian Court in a parliamentary system (see Hogg and Bushell 1997; Roach 2001; Kelly 2005; Manfredi and Kelly 1999, 2001; Hogg and Thornton 1999; McLachlin 2001; Hiebert 2002; Hirschl 2004; Hennigar 2004a). The criticism that the Court has faced not only suggests that it has become a prominent policy-making forum but also provides theoretical and empirical fodder for the notion that the post-*Charter* Canadian justices would be as capable of infusing their attitudes and values into their rulings as their southern counterparts.

Another political factor that encourages the justices to engage in attitudinal decision making, despite the criticism that has been levelled at some of the Court's rulings, is that the Court continues to garner a high degree of support from the broader Canadian public. This support has been catalogued in a number of public opinion polls and recent political science scholarship. According to national public opinion polls conducted 1987 and 1999, eight out of ten Canadians believed that "the Charter [was] a good thing ... for Canada," and by 2002 fully 92 percent of the public took this position (Fletcher and Howe 2000, 7; Centre for Research and Information on Canada 2002, 8). Moreover, just over 70 percent of Canadians believed that the Court, not the legislature, should have the final say on the constitutionality of laws (Centre for Research and Information on Canada 2002, 22). This same question was posed in another study, which reported that support for the Court's constitutional power remained as strong among legal elites as among the public (Sniderman et al. 1996, 164). A subsequent study by Hausegger and Riddell (2004, 40-41) exploring possible generational differences discovered greater levels of support for the Court's judicial review power among younger Canadians than among their older counterparts. Taken together, these findings suggest not only that popular support for the Court exists among all political classes but that it will be sustained for years to come. From an attitudinal perspective, the fact that the Court enjoys broad public support theoretically enhances the likelihood that justices would feel free to vote according to their own attitudes and values without the fear of causing a widespread popular backlash. In short, high levels of popular support may provide the necessary leeway for Canadian justices to engage in the same kind of attitudinal voting as their US colleagues.

The rise of interest group activity in the judicial system in the late twentieth century may further enhance the likelihood that current Supreme Court justices will engage in attitudinal decision making. According to scholars, such as Epp (1996, 1998, 15-22) and Brodie (2002), changing societal values in the 1960s and 1970s, the growth of rights-based advocacy groups, and government-funded support for rights claims helped establish an institutional support structure in sectors of the legal and academic community that fuelled increasing interest group litigation in both Canada and the US (see also Morton and Knopff 2000; Manfredi 2004). According to Brodie (2002, 16), the *Charter*'s enactment in 1982 further accelerated the role that interest groups played in the judicial process. Although the Court initially clamped down on intervenor activity under the *Charter*, by the end of the 1980s the

Supreme Court was willing to entertain the arguments of most interest group intervenors (Brodie 2002, 47-48). To the extent that disadvantaged groups push the rights envelope in the course of advancing their *Charter* claims, one could theoretically argue that justices would be likely to draw on their attitudinal proclivities in the course of grappling with novel arguments. We believe that rights-based litigation has helped create an environment where there is a greater likelihood that attitudinal disagreement would emerge among the justices. If this contention is correct, then the attitudinal model may provide as viable an explanation for judicial rulings in the Canadian Court as in the US Court.

Institutional Characteristics Fostering or Mitigating Attitudinal Expression

Even though the Fathers of Confederation did not create a system of shared powers across separate institutions that enabled the judiciary to provide a strong check against the other branches, the modern Canadian Supreme Court enjoys a great degree of institutional independence and abides by operational procedures remarkably similar to those found in the US system. These elements provide strong theoretical support for believing that the attitudinal model provides a robust explanation for judicial decision making in the post-*Charter* era. There are, however, some important institutional differences that may deter such behaviour. This section discusses various institutional similarities and differences that may work to foster or impede attitudinal expression in the modern Canadian Supreme Court.

Like their US counterparts, Canadian Supreme Court justices enjoy a great deal of structural independence once they are appointed to the high court. Since they serve on the court of last resort in Canada, and their rulings are not subject to appellate review by a higher authority, attitudinalists would contend that these justices are free to vote according to their attitudes and values without fear of their rulings being overturned by a higher tribunal (Rohde and Spaeth 1976, 72-74; Segal and Spaeth 1993, 2002; Wetstein and Ostberg 1999, 2005; Ostberg et al. 2002; Ostberg, Johnson et al. 2004). Their political independence is further enhanced by the fact that they, like their US counterparts, are not directly accountable once in office (Rohde and Spaeth 1976, 72). Although the justices may experience critical commentary from outsiders regarding specific rulings, they are ultimately secure in the knowledge that they cannot be removed from office in the way that elected officials can. Although they must step down at the age of seventy-five, they essentially enjoy a life-tenure appointment. This sense of freedom is reinforced by the fact that most members of the Court view their appointment as the pinnacle of their professional careers. Since promotion to the bench is held in such high esteem, and justices are appointed late in life, they tend to serve on the Court without any ambition for higher office, and do not hand down rulings with an eye toward the impact they may have on their own political future. Taken together, these elements of judicial independence provide further theoretical justification for believing that attitudinal decision making would be as relevant in the modern Canadian context as in the US high court.

Both the Canadian and US Supreme Courts follow virtually identical procedural steps in the course of resolving legal disputes, creating a similar environmental setting for attitudinal behaviour to take place. As with its US counterpart, most cases come to the Canadian Supreme Court through an appellate process, and (after acceptance by the Court) proceed through the stages of oral argument, conference deliberation, and drafting of opinions before a final judgment is handed down. At each of these stages, the justices have the opportunity to pose questions or take stances that might reflect their attitudinal predispositions, and thus trigger conflict among members of the Court. From a theoretical standpoint, these similar institutional opportunities mean that Canadian justices would be as likely to engage in attitudinal decision making as their southern counterparts. Another critical institutional feature mentioned earlier is that both courts have virtually complete discretionary control over their own dockets. Once the Canadian Court obtained this power in 1975, it was able to select a greater percentage of cases that it wanted to hear (Russell 1987, 344). Although there are important differences in the way that the two courts initially select cases for review (see Russell 1987, 346-49; Flemming 2004, 5-10), the expansion of its docket control and the adoption of the *Charter* have enabled the Canadian justices to take more public law cases dealing with complex problems of national importance. Given the current similarities between the two courts' operating procedures, attitudinal scholars would predict that the similar environments would foster the same kinds of value differences in the two court settings.

Despite the various similarities between the two courts that might promote attitudinal decision making, there are significant structural and institutional features that may reduce the likelihood that attitudes and values will play as strong a role in the Canadian judicial decision-making process as in its southern counterpart. Most notably, the appointment of high court justices in Canada features elements that are far less political in nature than in the US (see Wetstein and Ostberg 1999). Since appointments to the Canadian bench are made by the prime minister and cabinet, and do not require parliamentary confirmation, they are not subject to the same ideological battles that are typically waged among senators, interest groups, and executive officials in the US. Indeed, journalistic accounts of recent judicial nominations in Canada spend as much time discussing a prospective appointee's regional fit on the Court, bilingual skills, gender, and legal expertise as they do the ideological proclivities of the new appointees (see Smith 2000; we discuss this in more detail in Chapter 3). Even though some scholars speculate that future appointments may be more rancorous as the Court becomes increasingly politicized, and there are growing demands for parliamentary oversight in the selection process, commentary by scholars and Canadian journalists alike often refer to the appointment process as "apolitical" in nature (see Schmitz 2000; Wilson-Smith 1999, 17). For example, as Morton and colleagues pointed out (1994, 51), "in Canada ... there has thus far been little evidence that the federal government has consciously relied on ideological criteria to guide its Supreme Court appointments."[3] Given the smaller role that ideology plays in the Canadian appointment process, and the fact that the government continues to focus on finding the best overall fit according to multiple criteria, it makes sense to argue that the Canadian justices would be less likely to be as ideologically driven as their southern counterparts (Wetstein and Ostberg 1999, 762). If this is a valid argument, one would expect that ideological differences will play a much less significant role in the decision-making process of post-*Charter* Canadian justices, which in turn raises questions about the systematic applicability of the attitudinal model in the Canadian setting.

One critical institutional feature of the Canadian Supreme Court that could mitigate the level of attitudinal conflict that appears in a case is the chief justice's power to strike decision panels that typically feature five, seven, or nine justices. As indicated earlier, this power enables the chief justice of the Canadian Court to create smaller panels of like-minded justices that would be more likely to agree on the merits than larger, more ideologically diverse nine-member panels. From a purely mathematical standpoint, smaller panels will tend to generate fewer attitudinal conflicts than larger ones, simply because it is easier to obtain agreement among five individuals than nine, all other things being equal. Data from the Court's post-*Charter* record validate this truism, with five-member panels handing down unanimous rulings 85 percent of the time. The rate of unanimity dropped to 75 percent for seven-member panels, and 66 percent when all nine justices heard a case. The question of whether chief justices pay attention to the ideological pro-clivities of the justices when creating decision panels was recently analyzed in a study by Hausegger and Haynie (2003). Their findings reveal that although the first two post-*Charter* chief justices did not abuse their panel assignment power, they did tend to appoint like-minded justices at dispro-portionately higher rates in *Charter* cases. These scholars concluded that "when panels concern salient [*Charter*] issues ... Canadian Chief justices appoint judges [ideologically] closer to them more often" (Hausegger and Haynie 2003, 655). A similar point was made by Heard (1991, 305), who suggested that the outcomes of early *Charter* claims were influenced by the particular judges assigned to hear the appeal. It should be noted that Canadian justices might bristle at the assertion that ideological considerations influence the chief justice's construction of panels, and Chief Justice Lamer himself has asserted in past interviews that he made a concerted effort to ensure that all nine justices heard salient, contentious cases (Greene et al. 1998, 119). Other members of the Court have reinforced Chief Justice Lamer's statement by indicating that he sought to maintain a balanced workload in terms of hand-ing out panel and opinion assignments (Greene et al. 1998, 119). However, the recent statistical analysis by Hausegger and Haynie (2003) calls these judicial assertions into question. Moreover, from a purely rational choice perspective, it makes intuitive sense that chief justices would utilize this power strategically in order to have some degree of control over the ideological direction of their own court (Wetstein and Ostberg 2005). In short, this Canadian institutional feature provides a further theoretical justification for believing that when smaller panels are created, attitudinal disagreement would be less apt to appear in the Canadian context. This highlights the need to test this theoretical model in settings that employ different panel assignment mechanisms than the US Court.

The presence of a high degree of collegiality in the post-*Charter* Canad-ian Court is another institutional feature that may inhibit the occurrence of attitudinal conflict between the justices. We believe that a pervasive norm of consensus operates within the Court that discourages most justices from readily expressing attitudes and values that conflict with their colleagues. Indeed, between 1984 and 2003, 75 percent of the rulings handed down by the Canadian Court were unanimous. In contrast, the US Court handed down unanimous decisions only 38 percent of the time during a similar twenty-year period (1975–94) (see Epstein et al. 1996, 194).

THE VIABILITY OF THE ATTITUDINAL MODEL IN THE CANADIAN CONTEXT

The norm of consensus in the Canadian Court may be attributed to numerous factors, several of which we discussed earlier. First, since Canada adheres to a system of parliamentary supremacy, there may be an institutional legacy of suppressing attitudinal beliefs in an effort to defer policy making to other institutions of government. Second, since the prime minister selects justices based on a variety of factors besides ideology, it is not surprising that Canadian justices are less ideologically driven, and thus are more likely to behave in a more collegial manner than their southern counterparts. Third, since the chief justice has the power to create smaller panel sizes, there is a greater mathematical probability that consensus will emerge. Fourth, since her promotion to the centre chair, Chief Justice McLachlin has made a concerted effort to foster collegiality on the Court and has stated publicly that she would encourage the justices to carefully consider and reflect upon the views of other members of the Court in an effort to build consensus (Schmitz 1999, paragraphs 9-11). Lastly, workload pressures on the Court have also increased in the wake of the *Charter*'s adoption, providing more incentive for the justices to agree with their colleagues rather than take the time to write yet another dissenting or concurring opinion. Collectively, these findings suggest that the justices of the post-*Charter* Canadian Supreme Court would be far more inclined to abide by a norm of collegiality than their southern counterparts (see Ostberg, Wetstein, and Ducat 2004, 525-26). This pervasive norm of consensus, in turn, not only helps maintain harmony on the Court but also provides further incentive for the justices to check their attitudes and values when they diverge from those of their colleagues.

Provisions of the *Charter* Fostering or Mitigating Attitudinal Expression

The belief that the attitudinal model will have relevance in the post-*Charter* Canadian context also stems from the fact that there are striking similarities between many of the specific provisions found in the constitutional documents of Canada and the US. Although the *Charter* differs from the US Bill of Rights because it safeguards a myriad of group rights, such as Aboriginal and minority language education rights, many of its provisions protecting individual rights and liberties are remarkably similar to those found in the US Constitution. As such, Canadian justices would be as likely as their American colleagues to enjoy the freedom to invoke their attitudes and values in the decision-making process.

The similarities between the two documents are found in a core group of substantive rights that protect fundamental freedoms and legal rights, and ensure that individuals are treated equally under the law. For example, section 2 of the Canadian *Charter*, like the US First Amendment, protects the freedom of speech, religion, press, assembly, and association, although the Canadian provision is more comprehensive since it also ensures the "freedom of thought, belief, opinion, and expression." Moreover, like its US counterpart, the *Charter* contains a host of legal protections for the criminally accused (sections 7-14). For example, the *Charter* affords those who are arrested or detained counsel rights (section 10b), the right to be presumed innocent (section 11d), and the right to a fair and speedy trial within a reasonable time by an impartial tribunal (sections 11b and d). In addition, the *Charter* protects Canadians from unreasonable search and seizure (section 8), self-incrimination and double jeopardy (sections 11c and h), and being subjected to cruel and unusual punishment under the law (section 12). The *Charter* also includes a due process clause that achieves principally the same objective as the US Fifth Amendment, although it is stated as protecting an individual's "right to life, liberty and security of the person" (section 7). In addition, the *Charter* ensures that Canadians obtain equal treatment under the law, although section 15 is more comprehensive than the US Fourteenth Amendment because it explicitly prohibits discrimination based on "race, national or ethnic origin, colour, religion, sex, age or mental or physical disability." Clearly, the specificity of this provision indicates that the framers of a twentieth-century charter of rights realized the need to include equality rights for historically marginalized groups rather than simply relying on the broad-based guarantee of equality for all individuals that is found in the US Constitution. The parallels between these core substantive provisions establish constitutional frameworks that might lead the justices on both courts to engage in the same type of attitudinal decision making when resolving constitutional cases. At the heart of this contention is the belief that all other things being equal, the textual principles enshrined in the two documents enable the justices on both courts to engage in similar patterns of attitudinal decision making.

Since many of the *Charter* provisions are similar to those found in the US Bill of Rights, it makes intuitive sense that members of the Canadian Court would turn to their southern colleagues for guidance on how to interpret these principles. From an attitudinal perspective, Canadian justices might turn to US case law for two reasons: (1) to simply adopt the American attitudinal approach as a sound one, or (2) to use the precedents as a tool for convincing other justices to adopt their approach to resolving the case. Data drawn from the opinions of the Court indicate that the citation of US case law has become more frequent in the post-*Charter* era, with nearly half of the *Charter* rulings handed down in the 1984-95 period making at least one reference to a US case (Ostberg et al. 2001, 392; see also Bushnell 1986; Manfredi 1990).[4] Indeed, in the search and seizure area, the Canadian Supreme Court fully adopted the American warrant requirements established by the Warren Court in *Katz v. United States*, 389 U.S. 347 (1967) even though the text of the *Charter* does not contain a warrant requirement (Ostberg et al. 2001, 392). This wholesale adoption of US principles indicates that the same type of attitudinal decision making is taking place on both high courts in the search and seizure area. Attitudinal scholars, such as Segal and Spaeth (1993, 2002), would contend that the amount of citation of US case law by Canadian justices is irrelevant because reference to any case simply acts as a smoke-screen for legitimizing a justice's own policy preferences. Regardless of the truth of this claim, we believe that when the Canadian justices holistically adopt similar interpretations of constitutional rights from their US brethren, the same degree of attitudinal decision making is arguably at play in both courts. It is also clear from prior research that citation of US case law is much more frequent in post-*Charter* cases that feature dissenting and concurring opinions than in unanimous rulings (see Ostberg et al. 2001, 396). This indicates that reference to US rulings tends to increase when attitudinal conflict emerges within the post-*Charter* Canadian Court. Data from the first eleven years of post-*Charter* decisions show that reference to US case law was uncommon in unanimous cases (appearing in only 15 percent of the opinions). Meanwhile, cases featuring one or two dissenting opinions contained US citations over 37 and 46 percent of the time, respectively. This suggests that when Canadian justices are unable to win a majority coalition through the use of Canadian precedents, they often look abroad in their efforts to persuade their colleagues to join their preferred position. This finding lends credence to Schattschneider's contention (1960, 101) forty-five years ago that "one of the best ways to win a fight is to widen the scope of the conflict." Since the citation of US case law occurs in nearly half of *Charter* cases, it is telling evidence of the prevalence of attitudinal conflict in the post-*Charter* Court, and provides further ammunition for those who contend that the attitudinal model is as relevant for modern Canadian justices as for US Supreme Court justices.

While certain features of the *Charter* might promote patterns of attitudinal expression similar to those found in the US Court, there are several interpretive clauses that may discourage justices from engaging in attitudinal policy making. The most prominent is section 1 of the *Charter*, which allows the Court to sanction legislative limits that have been imposed on some *Charter* rights as long as they can be "demonstrably justified in a free and democratic society." Another important interpretive clause is section 24(2), which enables judges to admit unlawfully obtained evidence in criminal proceedings unless it would "bring the administration of justice into disrepute." These two provisions are clearly aimed at elevating communitarian values at the expense of individual rights in certain circumstances, and thus allow government to infringe individual liberties protected in the Constitution if the breach can be justified in Canadian society. From a practical standpoint, the Court in the post-*Charter* era has frequently ruled in favour of the government and the community even though violations of *Charter* rights and freedoms have occurred. Viewed through the lens of attitudinal theory, these two *Charter* provisions may encourage members of the Court to suppress their own attitudes and values in deference to the legitimate and reasonable policy choices made by legislatures in the name of the community at large. If the justices yield to this pressure to defer, then attitudinal decision making will be less prominent in the Canadian context.

The notwithstanding clause (section 33) of the *Charter* is a third interpretive provision that might discourage post-*Charter* justices from engaging in attitudinal expression (see Ostberg and Wetstein 2005). In a nutshell, this provision allows the federal and provincial governments to pass legislation that overrides *Charter* guarantees found in sections 2 and 7 to 15, subject to renewal every five years. Even though one might argue that this defeats the purpose of enshrining individual rights and liberties in the Constitution in the first place, some scholars have pointed out that section 33 is an important safety valve to ensure that a system of parliamentary supremacy remains intact in Canada (Stephenson 1991, 88; Massey 1990, 1232; Romanow 1986, 103; Manfredi 2001, 184; Ostberg 1995, 42). Theoretically, its inclusion empowers legislative bodies to override Court rulings that are viewed by these elected institutions as seriously flawed (see Russell 1992, 474-85; Hiebert 2002, 45-46). In the wake of the Court's ruling in *Ford v. Quebec (Attorney*

General), [1988] 2 S.C.R. 712, however, politicians have rarely considered invoking the section 33 override clause, leading some scholars to conclude that section 33 has become toothless and to claim that its demise has shifted the locus of institutional supremacy toward the courts and away from the legislatures (Manfredi 2001, 188; Morton and Knopff 2000, 164-66). Regardless of the truth of this claim, we believe that section 33's presence in the text of the Constitution may serve as an important check on the Supreme Court justices, and acts as a reminder that their rulings should not be too out of step with the will of legislative bodies. In other words, its presence may reduce the likelihood of the justices' following the promptings of their attitudes and values as readily as their southern counterparts.

Conclusion

After the Canadian Supreme Court acquired the power to review legislation that infringed *Charter* rights and liberties, some postulated that an American style of judicial review would become the norm during the post-*Charter* era (Bender 1983; Russell 1982). Since the attitudinal model has become the dominant paradigm for explaining judicial decision making in the US, the question remains whether members of the Canadian high court, like their US counterparts, would increasingly rely on their personal attitudes and values when ruling on complex, emotionally charged issues of national significance. This chapter has reviewed a myriad of constitutional, institutional, and political features of Canadian society that collectively lead us to believe that justices of the post-*Charter* Court would indeed be influenced by their attitudes and values, but that their attitudinal expression might be limited in scope, given the various mitigating forces that influence them as well. In short, we believe that the Canadian justices will engage in a unique hybrid of attitudinal decision making that, although prominent, will not be as ideologically driven as that found in the US Supreme Court.

Table 2.1 summarizes the various factors reviewed in this chapter, and provides an explanation of how each element may foster or impede the appearance of attitudinal behaviour in the Canadian justices compared with their US counterparts. Ultimately, Table 2.1 suggests that features such as the Court's judicial independence, the justices' lack of ambition for higher office, their relative support within the Canadian public, similar institutional patterns of decision making, and parallel constitutional structures might promote the same level of attitudinal decision making as that found in the US.

TABLE 2.1

Factors encouraging and discouraging attitudinal decision making in the post-*Charter* Supreme Court of Canada

Factor or characteristic influencing levels of attitudinal decision making	Degree of attitudinal decision making compared with US Supreme Court
POLITICAL FACTORS INFLUENCING ATTITUDINAL DECISION MAKING	
Enhanced power of judicial review and constitutional mandate to protect *Charter* rights	Same
High degree of diffuse support from public	Same
"Rights revolution" and increased litigation by interest groups	Same
System of parliamentary supremacy that encourages judicial deference	Less prominent
Historical and cultural traditions that emphasize judicial deference and collective values (e.g., crime control, tolerance for restrictions)	Less prominent
Criticism of activist rulings that may put justices on the defensive and lead to less attitudinal expression	Less prominent
INSTITUTIONAL FACTORS INFLUENCING ATTITUDINAL DECISION MAKING	
Judicial independence, existence as court of last resort, and justice's lack of ambition for higher office	Same
Similar case processing stages: case selection, oral argument, conference deliberation, opinion circulation, final ruling	Same
Appointment process less animated by ideological considerations; fewer extremist judges	Less prominent
Panel sizes that are smaller and therefore less subject to attitudinal conflict	Less prominent
Chief justice's strategic power to assign like-minded justices to panels	Less prominent
Overriding norm of consensus and greater collegiality on the Court	Less prominent
***CHARTER* CHARACTERISTICS INFLUENCING ATTITUDINAL DECISION MAKING**	
Similarity of core rights provisions that promote similar types of conflicts	Same
Citation of US case law, reflecting either the adoption of attitudinal approaches or evidence of attitudinal disagreement on the Court	Same
Interpretive clauses (sections 1 and 24[2]) that elevate communitarian values and promote judicial deference to other branches	Less prominent
Notwithstanding clause (section 33), which serves as a formal check on judicial decisions that legislative bodies oppose	Less prominent

There are, however, several unique Canadian features, such as a tradition of cultural deference, a political system based on parliamentary dominance, a less politicized appointment process, and the institutional norm of consensus, that might suppress attitudinal decision making in Canada to a greater extent than in the US.

Clearly, the aforementioned similarities and differences between Canada and the US provide ample theoretical justification for assessing the applicability of the attitudinal model in the Canadian setting. Although most US scholars would assume that attitudes and values predominantly govern the decision-making process of high courts in other democracies, the fact that theoretical arguments can be made both for and against its applicability in the Canadian setting indicates the need to test this model before the American assertion can be accepted as valid. Since any sophisticated analysis of the attitudinal model must start with an understanding of the ideological proclivities that the justices bring to the Court, the next chapter examines different ways of constructing the judicial ideology measure that will be utilized in the subsequent regression models. We will present a new ideological indicator for the post-*Charter* justices that will prove vital in the assessment of the attitudinal model in the Canadian context.

3
Measuring Judicial Ideology

Although the political ideology of justices plays a central role in the attitudinal model, scholars have had difficulty measuring this concept because it is a complex phenomenon and justices are unwilling to expose their views to public scrutiny. The most obvious way to determine the ideological proclivities of justices would be to simply ask them at the time of their appointment whether they consider themselves liberal, conservative, moderate, or something else. This explains why, in the US context, senators pepper prospective justices with a slew of questions on how they would vote on issues such as abortion, school prayer, or affirmative action. Of course, judicial nominees are reluctant to answer such questions, and inevitably when they do, they usually sidestep the issue by claiming they cannot respond without knowing the particular case facts or that they are unwilling to prejudge a controversy that might come before the court in the future. Naturally, potential nominees want to portray themselves as fair-minded arbiters who decide controversies on a case-by-case basis, and they resist any attempts to expose ideological tendencies that they might harbour.

A justice's resistance to being pinned down ideologically is prevalent in the Canadian setting as well. At the time of his nomination to the Canadian Supreme Court, Justice Binnie responded to such questions by claiming: "I don't know that I can pigeonhole myself as a conservative or liberal or activist" (*Ottawa Citizen* 1998). When Justice Iacobucci was appointed, a reporter indicated that he "refused to be pinned down about his legal views" (Bindman 1990). Justice Sopinka insisted that "politics very seldom play a role when it comes to the Supreme Court of Canada," and rejected efforts by some commentators to label him a Tory lawyer (Makin and Polanyi 1988). Justice Le Dain said at the time of his appointment that "judges don't come to each case with a predisposition or general tendency or drift," and told reporters that instead they "look at each case and try to do justice" (*Ottawa Citizen*

1984). Even when a justice such as L'Heureux-Dubé provided some hints as to her ideological leanings, she was quick to point out that in deciding cases, "she w[ould] be as open-minded a judge as she c[ould] be" (MacQueen 1987). Collectively, these statements point to the difficulty of getting Supreme Court nominees to openly reveal their ideological leanings to court watchers. At the heart of their reluctance is the realization that justices need to be seen as approaching cases with an objective and open mind in order to be perceived as fair in the resolution of a dispute. Despite efforts to try to live up to this legal ideal, political scientists tend to reject the notion that justices do approach cases in an objective manner. Since justices are not forthright about their ideological tendencies, political scientists have been left to their own devices to try to determine the underlying attitudes and values that particular justices bring to the Court. Consequently, political scientists have developed a number of different surrogate measures to discern the ideological proclivities of individual justices.

Early quantitative research in the US began assessing judicial behaviour by utilizing the actual votes by members of the US Supreme Court to infer the ideological voting patterns of justices on the bench (Pritchett 1941; Schubert 1965, 1974). Specifically, this initial research used Guttman scaling and factor analysis techniques to analyze case votes to determine whether there were consistent patterns of attitudinal decision making among the justices. Although these efforts were groundbreaking for their time, subsequent critics have indicated that such techniques ultimately suffered from circular reasoning problems. Scholars argued that this approach was flawed because it utilized the final vote outcomes by the justices themselves to infer their ideological predispositions, which, in turn, were then said to act as the driving force behind these same vote outcomes. As a result, they argued that new measures needed to be developed to assess a justice's ideology that were distinct and independent from the votes being cast in Supreme Court cases (see Segal and Spaeth 1993, 221-29, 361-62).

One of the most obvious and widely used a priori measures of judicial ideology in the US discipline is the party affiliation of the appointing chief executive (for examples in the US, see Ulmer 1973; Tate and Handberg 1991; Wasby 1993; in Canada, see Tate and Sittiwong 1989; Songer and Johnson 2002; Ostberg and Wetstein 1998; Wetstein and Ostberg 1999). The logic behind this measure is that since presidents and prime ministers seek to appoint justices who are like-minded, the party affiliation of the appointing executive serves as a viable surrogate for the underlying ideology of a judicial nominee. Indeed, most executive appointments have been fairly accurate on this score, although there have been obvious mishaps by chief executives, such as President Eisenhower's appointment of Earl Warren to the helm of the US Supreme Court in 1953. Eisenhower is noted for saying that it was one of the "biggest damn-fooled mistakes" he had made during his presidency (O'Brien 1996, 93). While scholars consider this measure of partisan affiliation to be a reliable and convenient indicator of a justice's ideological tendencies, one must keep in mind it is only a crude indicator at best because chief executives might choose justices who are more ideologically moderate than themselves.

In an effort to fine-tune the party affiliation variable, scholars such as Tate and Handberg (1991) developed a more sophisticated rendering of the party attachment measure by taking into consideration the ideological motivation behind a particular presidential appointment. In short, these scholars claimed that a US president might in fact select an individual who did not share his exact same ideological outlook. As such, they created a trichotomous measure that placed nominees into one of three categories of executive motivation that fell along an ideological continuum: +1 for liberals, 0 for moderates, and –1 for conservatives (Tate and Handberg 1991). Clearly, this is a more nuanced measure of ideology than the president's party identification variable, because some presidents will be more ideologically motivated in the appointment process than others. The value of the Tate and Handberg (1991) measure is that it can identify key differences in the way presidents from the same political party approach the appointment process. One potential problem, however, is that if one studies a sample that lacks ideological variance between chief executives of the same political party, it will ultimately produce scores that are virtually identical to the party affiliation of the nominating president.[1]

In an effort to tap ideology from another angle, Segal and Cover (1989) sought to build an independent ideological indicator of US Supreme Court nominees based on content analysis of editorials in four major newspapers (*New York Times, Washington Post, Chicago Tribune,* and *Los Angeles Times*) at the time of their appointments. Their measure ranked nominees along a liberal/conservative spectrum of civil rights and liberties issues (Segal and Cover 1989; Cameron et al. 1990; Segal and Spaeth 1993, 2002). The beauty of this measure lies not only in its independence from a justice's voting record but also in its ability to predict subsequent civil rights and liberties decisions by the justices once they reach the high court. Some scholars have demonstrated, however, that the measure has limited viability outside the confines of the civil rights and liberties area (Epstein and Mershon 1996, 261-94). Given this limitation, scholars have developed yet another a priori measure that is based on past votes of Supreme Court justices to predict votes sometime in the future (Esptein and Mershon 1996; Segal and Spaeth 2002; Epstein et al. 1989). Although seemingly attractive, this approach, as these scholars have admitted, suffers from the same circular reasoning problems that plagued the scholarship by pioneers in this field (Epstein and Mershon 1996, 281).

A fourth potential measure of judicial ideology that predates a justice's appointment to the high court is one that considers a justice's voting behaviour while serving on a lower court. The rationale behind this approach is that while on the lower appellate court, justices will establish relatively consistent ideological voting patterns that are likely to be replicated once they are elevated to the high court. This measure is attractive because most justices sitting on the modern US and Canadian Supreme Courts have served on lower courts prior to their elevation to the high court, and thus have a track record that can be examined at length. One of the principal flaws of this measure, however, is that there are key institutional constraints that set lower court justices apart from their high court colleagues. As discussed in Chapter 2, justices on lower courts are bound by vertical precedents, and they may have ambition for a higher office, making them less likely to cast votes in accordance with their own attitudes and values. As such, lower court voting patterns may not serve as an accurate surrogate for predicting voting behaviour once judges are elevated to the Supreme Court. Another problem with using this measure in the Canadian context is that several modern justices, such as Justices Sopinka and Binnie, have come to the high court directly from private practice, while others, such as Justices Chouinard and Gonthier, served such short terms on lower courts of appeal that their voting records from published opinions are of limited use.

In an effort to develop the most effective and reliable measure of judicial ideology for each of the modern Canadian Supreme Court justices, we initially created four distinct indicators that are in line with the approaches outlined above. Specifically, we calculated measures based on: (1) party of prime minister, (2) the ideological motivation of the appointing prime minister, (3) ideology scores based on newspaper reports, and (4) lower court patterns of ideological voting behaviour. It was our hope that these measures would assist future scholars who are interested in analyzing the decision-making patterns of the modern Canadian Supreme Court, and that they would be useful in our assessment of the full-fledged attitudinal model in the Canadian context. The rest of this chapter describes the various measures, examines the degree to which each one actually taps the concept of judicial ideology, and offers a cogent explanation for why we think that the newspaper measure is the most accurate predictor of voting patterns in the post-*Charter* period. We conclude by subjecting the newspaper indicator to various tests of external validity in an effort to further substantiate this claim.

Specific Measures of Ideology in Canada

THE PARTY OF THE PRIME MINISTER

The first ideological measure in our dataset – party of the prime minister – is relatively straightforward, with Conservative Party appointees scored as –1 and Liberal Party appointees scored as +1. The data presented in this study feature twenty-three justices who served in the post-*Charter* period from 1984 to 2003, with ten identified as conservative appointees and thirteen categorized as liberals. Liberal appointees included in the analysis were Justices Dickson, Beetz, Estey, McIntyre, Lamer, Wilson, Le Dain, Bastarache, Binnie, Arbour, LeBel, Deschamps, and Fish. Conservative appointees included Justices La Forest, Chouinard, L'Heureux-Dubé, Sopinka, Gonthier, Cory, McLachlin, Stevenson, Iacobucci, and Major. We excluded Justice Ritchie because of the small number of cases he decided during this period.

THE IDEOLOGICAL MOTIVATIONS OF THE APPOINTING PRIME MINISTERS

The second measure follows the logic of Tate and Handberg's prior work (1991) on the ideological motivations of appointing presidents. As in their measure, we coded the nominees as conservative if the prime minister was perceived as making ideological appointments at the conservative end of the spectrum (–1), while appointments at the liberal end were scored +1. If a prime minister was perceived as making moderate or non-political appointments, those justices received a "0" score. Although we acknowledge that the scaling for this measure is somewhat subjective, we believe that an analysis of newspaper accounts, books, and professional commentary will confirm the accuracy of our coding scheme for the post-*Charter* justices. Since both

Prime Ministers Trudeau and Chrétien were perceived to make clear liberal ideological appointments aligned with their own ideological proclivities, all eleven of their appointees received a score of +1 (Justices Dickson, Beetz, Estey, McIntyre, Lamer, Wilson, Le Dain, Bastarache, Binnie, Arbour, LeBel, Deschamps, and Fish). In contrast Brian Mulroney's nine Conservative appointees received moderate scores of "0" because of the seemingly more moderate tenor of his appointments to the bench, and our data in Chapter 5 confirm that such coding was accurate (Justices La Forest, L'Heureux-Dubé, Sopinka, Gonthier, Cory, McLachlin, Stevenson, Iacobucci, and Major). The only appointee who received a score of −1 was Justice Chouinard, whose appointment by Prime Minister Joe Clark was seen as a Conservative partisan selection.

Some critics might contend that since this study features appointments made by only four prime ministers, this indicator lacks sufficient variance across the justices. Given Mulroney's moderate approach toward the appointment process, only Justice Chouinard, a Clark appointee, is found at the conservative extreme, further limiting the range of variance between the twenty-three justices. We acknowledge that this is a valid criticism of the measure, and we believe it explains why this indicator did not perform well in our subsequent checks for external validity.

THE NEWSPAPER IDEOLOGY MEASURE

The newspaper ideology score included in this study expands considerably upon prior work that tabulated a justice's ideology at the time of his or her nomination based on coverage in the Toronto *Globe and Mail* (see Ostberg and Wetstein 1998; Wetstein and Ostberg 1999). Although the measure based on the various articles reported in the *Globe and Mail* was able to help predict 77 percent of post-*Charter* search and seizure votes by the justices (Wetstein and Ostberg 1999, 769), some have questioned its utility because it is based on only one newspaper's account of the appointment process. In response to such criticism, this study presents a more sophisticated newspaper ideology measure based on commentary in news articles and editorials in nine Canadian regional papers that have some of the largest circulations in the country. The papers include the *Globe and Mail, Ottawa Citizen, Halifax Chronicle-Herald, The Gazette* (Montreal), *Toronto Star, Winnipeg Free Press, Calgary Herald, Edmonton Journal,* and *Vancouver Sun.* We believe that this modified measure will be a far more rigorous indicator of judicial ideology because it takes into account the possibility that journalists from different regional newspapers may see appointments to the Supreme Court in different ways. In addition, we believe that it provides a more accurate accounting of the ideological tendencies of the nominees because the journalists base their reports on multiple sources, including academics, litigators, politically connected individuals, and sometimes the justices themselves. Statistically speaking, we believe that our newspaper ideology measure provides a more comprehensive picture of the actual ideological proclivities of the nominees to the Canadian high court when the many news accounts are factored together.

The actual scoring for the newspaper measure is based on content analysis of ideological commentary found in the various articles published at the time of each judicial appointment. The comments were subsequently scored on an ideological continuum ranging from +2 for references that were demonstrably liberal to -2 for very conservative comments; moderate references were scored as 0. Commentary that received the highest liberal score included statements such as: "strong believer in the *Charter*," "champion of the rights of the criminally accused," "noted civil libertarian," "a great democrat," "a liberal judge," and "a liberal feminist." In our view, these comments clearly reflected a belief in the strong liberal leanings of a nominee. Statements that received a more moderate but still liberal score of +1 included more subdued comments such as: "liberal leanings," "moderate liberal," "a small-l Liberal," "willing to invoke the *Charter*," "hinted at a liberal interpretation of the *Charter*," and "quietly activist." Scores found at the other end of the ideological continuum were less frequent but tended to highlight conservative nominees' tendencies toward restraint and their unwillingness to move beyond established canons of law. They included comments such as: "follows the letter of the law," "committed follower of precedents," "will move the court to the right," and "strict constructionist – takes words literally." Scores of -1 were given to more muted comments such as "mildly conservative," "cautious interpreter of the *Charter*," "small-c Conservative," and "shies from legislative interference." The justices who received a score of "0" were often described as "middle of the road," "resisting labels," "can't be categorized as either left or right-wing," "won't bring an agenda to the court," and "straight down the middle." The fact that we found consistent statements across a host of newspapers for each of the justices further strengthens our belief that the resulting scores are reliable assessments of the justices' perceived ideological stances.

It is important to note that our newspaper ideological scoring is different from the Segal and Cover (1989) measure in that it does not focus on newspaper commentary regarding judicial ideology in only civil rights and liberties cases. Rather, the measure we have constructed is based on commentary regarding a given justice's overall approach to the law in general as well as to specific areas of law. For example, if newspaper accounts identified a particular justice as taking different ideological stances in any of the three categories of law included in our study, this was taken into consideration in the coding of that justice. This differentiation allows for the potential to code a justice as liberal in one area of law and conservative in another. Some judgment calls needed to be made when categorizing some of the newspaper comments, especially when debating between giving a particular justice a +1 or +2 score at one end of the spectrum or, alternatively, a –1 or –2 score at the other end. When individual comments were read in the larger context of a paragraph or article, however, a fairly clear ideological picture emerged for each newspaper reference. Moreover, even though a few discrepancies appear in the journalistic accounts for a given justice, once all the news articles and editorials across the nine regional papers were taken into consideration, a consistent overarching ideological vision of the twenty-three justices emerged. In addition, the two researchers involved in the scoring process each categorized the newspaper comments independently of each other, and then resolved any discrepancies in the scoring of a justice only after mutual agreement had been reached. It is also worth noting that any statements referring to an nominee's party ties or service to a particular party in government were not included in the ideological scoring of the justices because a separate indicator of a nominee's party identification was included in the analysis, namely, party of the appointing prime minister.

Table 3.1 provides a detailed example of how we coded newspaper references for Justice Fish based on ideological commentary found in each of the nine newspapers included in the analysis. We present the scores of Justice Fish, the last justice nominated to the Court in the time frame of our study (1984–2003). It is important to understand a few things about our coding scheme before examining his newspaper scores.

We divided the data into four distinct categories of newspaper scores: (1) the *Globe and Mail*, (2) the *Ottawa Citizen*, (3) the average of the seven other regional newspapers, and (4) a cumulative score based on equal treatment of individual comments found in all nine papers. We tabulated separate ideological scores for the first two papers because of the national prominence of the *Globe and Mail* and the fact that the *Ottawa Citizen* is published in the country's capital and therefore the reporters for this paper are likely to be particularly sensitive to the ideological leanings of the nominees. Moreover, both of these papers tended to have far more commentary on appointments made to the Canadian high court than any of the other newspapers examined.

We also created a separate average score across the seven remaining newspapers because they often simply published identical wire service stories, or a slight variation of them; grouping them together avoided the problem of double- or triple-counting the same story that appeared in different newspapers. When reading the stories in the seven regional papers, it was clear that wire service stories tended to appear most frequently for justices who were appointed from outside the region in which the newspaper was located. Not surprisingly, commentary was most in-depth for "hometown" appointments. This pattern is depicted in Table 3.1, where several papers outside Quebec simply printed wire service stories on Justice Fish's appointment to the Court. We also chose to aggregate the ideological comments from the seven regional papers because we often found gaps in the coverage of a particular appointment in one or two of the more remote regional papers. Thus, a synthesis of these more peripheral papers seemed prudent. Lastly, we included a fourth ideological indicator based on an aggregation of all the comments because we were interested in creating a measure that treated each newspaper reference on equal footing. As a result, the cumulative score of a justice reflects the proportional weight of ideological commentary appearing in each newspaper. For example, if the *Globe and Mail* made three ideological references regarding a nominee and the *Vancouver Sun* made one, this proportional disparity is reflected in the fourth newspaper measure for a particular justice.

In Table 3.1, we provide a detailed example of our four scores for Justice Fish in order to demonstrate the scoring methodology. The findings reveal that Justice Fish's average score is 1.2 for the *Globe and Mail*, 1.0 for the *Ottawa Citizen*, 1.1 for the seven other papers, and 1.105 for the cumulative score across all newspaper commentary. As one can see from the data, Justice Fish is found on the liberal side of the ideological spectrum, which ranges from +2 to –2. Moreover, it is important to note that his ideological scores are remarkably consistent, which serves as an internal validity check on the various measures. The relative consistency between the scores helps counteract any possible measurement error problems in our coding of the data. We

TABLE 3.1

Scoring of newspaper commentary for Justice Fish, and tabulation of four distinct measures of newspaper ideology

Newspaper	Comments	Score
Globe and Mail	Strong believer in *Charter*	+2
	Difficult to pigeonhole as either liberal or conservative	0
	Defender of civil liberties	+1
	Not timid to invoke the *Charter*	+2
	Swing in criminal vote toward the defendant	+1
	AVERAGE SCORE	1.200
Ottawa Citizen	Liberal leaning	+1
	Sympathizes with the most vulnerable members of society	+1
	Favours the underdog if treated unfairly	+1
	Antithesis of Gonthier, who sided with government in criminal cases	+1
	AVERAGE SCORE	1.000
Calgary Herald	Same as *Ottawa Citizen* (wire story)	—
Edmonton Journal	Same as *Ottawa Citizen* (wire story)	—
Halifax Herald	Not to be pinned down along ideological spectrum	0
	A great democrat	+2
	More liberal than others	+1
Montreal Gazette	Noted civil libertarian	+2
	Difficult to describe as liberal or conservative	0
	Supporter of civil liberties and defendants	+1
	Described as liberal-leaning	+1
Toronto Star	May swing Court in liberal direction	+1
	Passion for *Charter*	+2
	Defender of free expression	+1
Vancouver Sun	Same as *Ottawa Citizen* (wire story)	—
Winnipeg Free Press	No story published	—
	AVERAGE SCORE	1.100
AVERAGE SCORE ACROSS ALL NEWSPAPER REFERENCES		1.105

SOURCE: LeBlanc and Clark 2003; *Globe and Mail* 2003; Tibbetts 2003a, 2003b, 2003c; *Calgary Herald* 2003; MacDonald 2003; *The Gazette* (Montreal) 2003; DesBarats 2003; Gordon 2003; Ward 2003; Levy 2003; *Vancouver Sun* 2003.

acknowledge at the outset, however, that measurement error is inevitable in our newspaper indicators of ideology because they are based on subjective judgment calls of how to classify a particular comment, some of which are hard calls to make. Granted, some may argue that in Table 3.1 some of the comments that we categorized as +1 for Justice Fish could easily be scored as +2. Although this may be the case, such differences in scoring are the result of inherent measurement error that is found in any effort to quantify a difficult social science concept. Thus, no matter how much we desire measurement precision, some degree of error is bound to exist. Since we were consistent in our coding scheme, we believe that any measurement error occurred in a consistent manner across all of the newspapers and all of the justices, so that any discrepancies are uniform in nature. For example, if a different researcher consistently rescored some of our +1 scores as +2 scores, all the justices would automatically have ideological scores that shift to the left. We are aware that the same dynamic could play out on the other side of the ideological spectrum, but we would expect any shifts in scores in that direction to be consistent as well. Second, we also believe that our coding of the newspaper accounts has a "conservative" bias built into the measure because we were more prone to score a particular comment closer to the middle than at the ideological extreme. As a result, any discrepancies on our part would work against finding statistical significance for the newspaper ideological score in our subsequent tests of the attitudinal model. It is our hope that these various coding efforts helped mitigate the impact of measurement error in our data as much as possible.

Table 3.2 provides a summary listing of each justice's newspaper ideological score taken from the four different perspectives described above. The data in this table illustrate that most of the justices have full information across all three news sources, although three important exceptions are worth mentioning. First, in situations where a news source simply commented on a nominee's party connections without making any ideological reference, we have entered "party" in the table (see, for example, the entry for Justice Deschamps in the *Globe and Mail* column). Second, in circumstances where neither party nor ideological commentary appeared in the newspapers, we have listed "na" (not applicable) in the appropriate column (see, for example, the row highlighting Justice Dickson, near the bottom of Table 3.2). Looking across the data for all the justices, there were eight entries identified as party references and seven others that were labelled not applicable. As a result,

TABLE 3.2

Ideology scores for Canadian Supreme Court justices based on newspaper commentary at the time of appointment, 1984–2003

Justice	Globe and Mail	Ottawa Citizen	Seven other regional newspapers	Cumulative score
Fish	1.200	1.000	1.100	1.105
Deschamps	party	0.000	0.000	0.000
LeBel	−0.300	−0.727	−1.333	−0.704
Arbour	0.467	0.769	1.400	0.727
Binnie	0.000	0.667	0.400	0.211
Bastarache	1.000	1.167	1.556	1.333
Major	−1.167	−1.143	−1.500	−1.320
Iacobucci	−1.000	0.000	0.250	0.000
Stevenson	1.000	0.600	0.333	0.500
McLachlin	1.000	0.000	0.625	0.667
Cory	party	1.250	0.923	0.967
Gonthier	party	−1.000	0.000	−0.182
Sopinka	0.000	0.000	0.273	0.150
L'Heureux-Dubé – Civil liberties	1.125	1.667	1.125	1.320
L'Heureux-Dubé – Criminal	−2.000	n/a	n/a	−2.000
La Forest	1.000	party	1.667	1.500
Le Dain	0.714	0.750	0.737	0.733
Wilson	1.800	1.636	1.556	1.618
Lamer	1.667	party	1.167	1.417
Chouinard	−1.375	party	party	−1.375
McIntyre	0.600	0.000	0.333	0.444
Estey	1.333	0.500	1.500	1.273
Dickson	n/a	n/a	n/a	0.000
Beetz	party	n/a	n/a	0.000

NOTE: Scores entered in the table reflect only ideological commentary from the newspaper articles. All commentary related to party affiliation or ties were removed from the calculation of scores. If one of the three news sources published comments solely based on a nominee's party ties, we omitted a score and entered "party" in the respective column of the table. If the news source did not publish any political or ideological comments, we entered "n/a" in the table. Justices Dickson and Beetz were assigned a middle score of zero because they had no ideological commentary in any of the newspapers. Justice L'Heureux-Dubé's score was divided into separate civil liberties and criminal scores because she was the only justice who received commentary on these two components at the opposite ends of the ideological spectrum. The correlations between the four measures found in Table 3.2 are as follows: *Globe and Mail* and *Ottawa Citizen*, $r = .777$; *Globe and Mail* and seven other regional newspapers, $r = .787$; *Globe and Mail* and cumulative score, $r = .903$; *Ottawa Citizen* and seven other regional newspapers, $r = .871$; *Ottawa Citizen* and cumulative score, $r = .910$; seven other regional newspapers and cumulative score, $r = .957$.

fifteen data cells had missing information out of a total of ninety-six cells. It is important to note that since Justices Dickson and Beetz had no ideological commentary in any of the papers, nearly half of the missing data pertains to these two justices alone (six of fifteen entries). We chose to address the scoring problem for these two justices by labelling them as moderates on the cumulative index measure, and so gave them a zero score in the fourth column. We believe that this is a reasonable way to address this coding problem because it also introduces a "conservative" bias in the subsequent results that makes it more difficult for the ideological independent variable to achieve statistical significance.

There is one other caveat regarding Table 3.2, namely, that the scores for Justice L'Heureux-Dubé are divided into two separate entries, for civil rights and liberties issues and for criminal issues. This differential treatment was necessary because she was the only justice on the post-*Charter* bench that was singled out by commentators as straddling the ideological divide in these two distinct areas of law (conservative in criminal law and liberal in civil rights and liberties issues). Although the comments about her criminal jurisprudence record were drawn exclusively from reports found in the *Globe and Mail*, we believe they reflect a highly accurate assessment of her ideological leanings in this area of law. The differentiation for Justice L'Heureux-Dubé in the two areas of law points to another possible source of measurement error in the newspaper ideology scores. Since we created single scores for the other twenty-two justices, if any of them also voted distinctively, these differences would not be captured well by a single ideological measure. We believe, however, that if consistent distinctive patterns did exist for a given nominee, journalists and court watchers would have commented on them at the time of their appointments, as they did in the case of Justice L'Heureux-Dubé.

Looking at Table 3.2, one should realize that we believe the most important score for each justice's ideological proclivities to be the cumulative score found in the last column of the table, because this score is based on an average of all the distinct references made across all the newspapers included in the study. Based on the scores in this column, the most conservative ratings are reported for Justice L'Heureux-Dubé in the criminal area (–2.000), followed by Justice Chouinard (–1.375) and Justice Major (–1.320). Justices scoring most liberally included Justices Wilson (1.618), La Forest (1.500), and Lamer (1.417). Intriguingly, Justice L'Heureux-Dubé, who scored most conservatively on the basis of media comments about her past rulings in criminal cases, was also considered one of the more liberal nominees in civil rights and liberties cases (1.320). Justices who were found to be the most moderate included Justices Iacobucci and Deschamps (0.000), Sopinka (0.150), and Gonthier (–0.182).

One of the attractive features of Table 3.2 is that by including four separate newspaper snapshots, it is easy to assess the relative internal validity of each of the four measures by comparing the scores against each other. A quick glance at the table suggests that there is substantial correlation across the separate measures; indeed, when justices with full information across all four measures were analyzed, the separate indicators were highly correlated ($r = .77$ and above; see the notes to Table 3.2). The high correlation across the various measures provides a strong endorsement of their validity, or their ability to accurately measure the same concept. In the end, we believe that the cumulative indicator of ideology calculated for each of the justices serves as a useful predictor of attitudinal voting behaviour in the regression analyses conducted in the various areas of law in the next three chapters, because it is based on the greatest aggregation of information obtained across nine regional papers in Canada.

Some scholars might question why we did not cast a wider net in our search for ideological commentary by or about the nominees. For example, why didn't we examine the public speeches or law review articles by or about the justices for further insight into their political attitudes and values? Although we believe that such analysis might prove fruitful for a few of the justices, we excluded these two sources of information for several reasons. First, prior to their nomination, very few nominees had an extensive paper trail of public speeches and law review articles that could serve as a useful source of information; it would have been even rarer to find any ideological commentary in those speeches and writings. Second, we believe that in most cases, any ideological commentary made by a prospective nominee must be viewed with an element of skepticism, simply because they may try to portray themselves as politically impartial and not necessarily articulate their true ideological beliefs. Third, independent commentary by academics about Supreme Court nominees also appears infrequently in the law reviews and is largely devoid of ideological assessments. In light of these problems, we believe that our newspaper ideology scores provide a more accurate, complete, and genuine assessment of the ideological tendencies of the twenty-three post-*Charter* justices analyzed in this study. We believe that any errors in the newspaper scores are more predictable and uniform than those that would be found in scores compiled from other sources. Since no scholar to date has developed a fully satisfactory measure of a priori judicial attitudes, we, like others, have no choice but to work with less than perfect measures.

THE JUSTICES' LOWER COURT LIBERALISM

A fourth indicator of judicial ideology taps the lower court liberalism of twenty-one justices in the study.[2] In most instances, the data for this indicator were drawn from a computer search of forty lower court rulings that immediately preceded a justice's nomination to the high court, and reflected the proportion of liberal votes cast in those cases. The percentage scores for Justices Gonthier and Chouinard were based on only twenty decisions, because of the sparse number of lower court cases that they had heard. Justices Sopinka and Binnie received the mean score for this indicator because they were elevated to the high court directly from private law practice, while Justice Beetz received this same score because English-language translations were unavailable for his rulings on the Quebec Court of Appeal in the early 1970s. In each of these cases, we decided to assign a mean value for the justices rather than omit them from the analysis. Admittedly, this introduces some measurement error into the database, but we believe this decision is prudent because a greater number of mean scores for the justices makes it mathematically more difficult to establish a statistically significant coefficient for this variable in our analyses.

All the data for this indicator were drawn from decision summaries published in the *All Canadian Digests,* available online through Lexis, or in published cases found in *Western Weekly Reports.* The lower court liberalism scores ranged from a high of 0.725 for Justice Estey (the most liberal score) to a low of 0.350 for Justice L'Heureux-Dubé, while those who did not serve on a lower court received a mean score of 0.504. One of the major limitations of this measure is that the cases selected could not be drawn uniformly from a particular issue area, so that the liberalism score for one justice may be based predominantly on criminal rulings while for another justice it may be based on economic or civil rights and liberties cases. Moreover, since first-level appellate judges are more likely to be norm enforcers, they have less leeway to make ideological rulings. Given the data problems inherent in this measure, we have the least confidence in its ability to serve as a viable predictor of judicial liberalism once a justice is promoted to the Canadian high court.

Testing the Validity of the Four Measures of Ideology

There are several ways to assess the validity of the measurement of a concept. The most obvious one is referred to as face validity, which is based on the notion that if the measure makes intuitive sense and seems valid on its face, it must be an accurate way to tap a particular concept (Johnson and Reynolds 2005, 162). Utilizing this approach, most readers would acknowledge that the political leanings of a prime minister and his or her ideological motivation for making appointments would have a logical correlation to the ideological beliefs of justices whom they appoint to the high court. Likewise, it seems valid on its face to argue that newspaper commentary on the ideological leanings of a nominee, as well as the nominee's lower court rulings, will necessarily square with their true ideological voting tendencies once they don the red robe. As a result, the four ideological measures included in the study appear to pass the test of face validity, admittedly the easiest and least rigorous conceptual test to pass.

A second, much more difficult test of validity examines the internal validity of a measure by assessing the inter-item correlation between distinct indicators that are presumed to tap the same latent concept (Johnson and Reynolds 2005, 164). In Table 3.3, we provide a bivariate correlation matrix to assess the internal validity of the four distinct a priori measures of judicial ideology. The results reveal that the prime minister ideological motivation measure has a .94 correlation with that of party of prime minister, indicating that these two measures are necessarily tapping the same latent concept, what we would call party affiliation.[3] The measure of newspaper ideology is only moderately correlated with the two party indicators (.41 for prime minister ideological motivation, and .32 for party of prime minister), and is statistically significant with the prime minister motivation indicator at only the 95 percent confidence level. These findings suggest that the newspaper measure, unlike the other two, is only partially tapping the latent concept of party attachment. Ultimately, we believe that the newspaper ideology score more readily captures a separate and distinct latent dimension more proximate to the underlying concept of judicial ideology because this measure is based on journalistic accounts before a justice's appointment. There is some overlap, however, between this concept and the two party measures, as the correlation between prime minister motivation and newspaper ideology demonstrates. Ironically, the lower court liberalism score is not highly correlated with any of the other three measures, suggesting that this indicator is either tapping something vastly different or is seriously flawed as an indicator of judicial ideology. Both interpretations are plausible, although we believe the latter is more accurate because of the various limitations inherent in the measure.

Looking at the correlation matrix holistically, we believe that the newspaper score, and not the two party-based measures, constitutes the best available independent measure of ideology on the Canadian high court because it is a more nuanced measure and is based on multiple assessments by a myriad of journalists relying on the expert opinions of court watchers. Consequently, we believe that this variable will serve as a stronger predictor of voting behaviour than the party measure in a full test of the attitudinal model. Since the party of the chief executive constitutes one of the most reliable measures in the US context, we decided to include it in the regression models for comparison purposes. The prime minister ideological motivation score was excluded from subsequent analyses because it would have been redundant to include it if the party of prime minister indicator was already included. Finally, in light of the weak correlation between the lower court liberalism scores and the other three measures, this variable was also excluded from subsequent analyses.

In order to further verify whether newspaper ideology represents the best available measure of judicial liberalism in the Canadian setting, one critical external validity check that we conducted compared the newspaper scores

TABLE 3.3

Coefficients of correlation between four measures of ideology for Canadian Supreme Court nominees, 1984–2003

Indicator	Cumulative score of newspaper liberalism	Lower court liberalism	Party of prime minister	Prime minister ideological motivation
Cumulative score of newspaper liberalism	1.000	—	—	—
Lower court liberalism	.109	1.000	—	—
Party of prime minister	.320	.163	1.000	—
Prime minister ideological motivation	.408*	.138	.941***	1.000

NOTE: $N = 22$ for lower court liberalism statistics, $N = 24$ for all other correlations. Justice L'Heureux-Dubé's ideological score for both criminal liberalism and other cases are entered as two different observations in the matrix.

* $p < .05$, ** $p < .01$, *** $p < .001$

for each of the justices with subsequent voting records in the three areas of law included in our study. Specifically, this test employed regression analyses to examine the bivariate relationship between this measure and career voting patterns of the twenty-three justices in three different areas of law: criminal, economic, and civil rights and liberties disputes. If this indicator accurately tapped judicial liberalism, we expected to find statistically significant relationships between the newspaper ideology scores and the voting patterns of the justices over time in the three issue areas, and we anticipated that it would produce stronger correlation coefficients than the party of prime minister measure in the dataset. Although we acknowledge that judicial voting might not be consistent across distinct issue areas and that a few justices might alter their voting behaviour over the course of their career, prior scholarship has demonstrated that most justices exhibit stable ideological voting patterns throughout their tenures on a high court (see Segal and Spaeth 1993, 2002; Epstein et al. 1996). Ultimately, this external validity check in these three areas of law helps lay the groundwork for the usefulness of the newspaper measure in our subsequent tests of the attitudinal model in the Canadian setting (in Chapters 4, 5, and 6). The logic of our test here is to determine if our measures of newspaper ideology correlate well with the subsequent voting behaviour of justices over the arc of their career. Thus, we are arguing that career voting data can help validate the accuracy of our ideological measure, presuming that a strong correlation exists between the two indicators.

Before examining the bivariate analyses, one needs to understand how case votes were coded in the three areas of law. A particular justice's career score within an issue area reflects the percentage of times that he or she cast a liberal vote, with our coding based on previous techniques used by attitudinal scholars in the US (see Schubert 1965, 1974; Segal and Spaeth 1993, 2002; Ducat and Dudley 1987; Dudley and Ducat 1986). While determining what constitutes a liberal vote in the criminal and civil rights and liberties disputes is relatively straightforward, the coding scheme used in the economic area is less so. For example, in criminal cases, judicial votes were categorized as liberal if the justices favoured the liberty interests and due process rights of the criminally accused, while votes were considered conservative if justices supported the state interest in protecting citizens from harm and maintaining order in society. In the civil rights and liberties area, we categorized votes as liberal if they supported an individual's freedom or equality claim, whereas conservative votes rejected such claims. For replication purposes, it is important to note that we identified disputes involving free expression, free press, religious rights and freedoms, civil rights, discrimination, privacy rights, abortion, voting rights, Aboriginal rights, liberty and due process, and language rights as falling into this area of law.[4]

It is more difficult to determine what constitutes a liberal vote in the economic area because there is an ever-shifting set of interests that are pitted against each other. For example, individuals sometimes square off against other individuals, making it hard to define who is the economic underdog in the case. When wealthy corporations are at odds with each other, it poses the same kind of dilemma. Lastly, when the government is a party in economic disputes, it may represent either the have-nots or the elites in society, depending on the litigants and issues involved (see Ostberg, Johnson, et al. 2004). Thus, we were forced to pay careful attention to who constituted the economic underdog in each dispute, and we coded judicial votes favouring these parties as liberal, while those favouring elites were given a conservative score (for similar approaches, see Schubert 1965, 1974; Ducat and Dudley 1987). In tax cases, we coded a vote as liberal if the justices endorsed the government's taxing power over the interests of individual or corporate taxpayers. One should note that we omitted any case from the dataset that could not be readily classified as featuring either a liberal or conservative outcome. Ultimately, cases included in our economic analysis featured a multitude of issues, such as disputes over federal or provincial authority, taxes, property, agency regulatory power, union/management relations, creditor/debtor disputes, antitrust, securities, environmental regulation, patents, copyright, public utilities, insurance, contracts, product liability, torts, benefits, pensions, and estates. Taken together, the coding of cases across all three areas of law allows us to gauge the liberal or conservative tendencies of the twenty-three post-*Charter* justices across their careers.[5]

Since justices served on the Court for varying lengths of time, and the Canadian Supreme Court typically sits in panels of five, seven, or nine justices, any analysis of judicial career scores must take into consideration the different number of cases each justice decided during his or her term of service. Comparing the short stint of Justice Stevenson with the long career of Justice L'Heureux-Dubé highlights a potential problem with judicial career vote scores if this issue is not addressed. While Justice Stevenson heard only 52 criminal cases during his two years on the Court, Justice L'Heureux-Dubé handed down a total of 553 rulings in her fifteen years of service. If both justices' career liberalism patterns are treated equally, then Justice Stevenson's score would have a vastly inflated impact and the data would be unrepresentative of the Court's actual voting activity. To address this concern, we followed the lead of other scholars and utilized weighted least squares regression that controls for the relative number of cases each justice heard in the three distinct issue areas (Tate and Sittiwong 1989; Songer and Johnson 2002).

The results in Table 3.4 indicate that newspaper ideology does indeed constitute a better a priori measure than party of prime minister at predicting patterns of career liberalism in the post-*Charter* Canadian Supreme Court. The top half of Table 3.4 examines the relationship between newspaper ideology and career liberalism for all cases heard in the three areas of law. Where written reasons for judgment were provided, we also examine the bi-variate relationships for non-oral decisions in the three areas, to verify whether ideological decision making is not distinctively different in those types of cases. The bottom half of Table 3.4 examines the same types of bivariate relationships with the party of prime minister serving as the independent variable.[6] Overall, the findings reveal that the newspaper ideology measure is a statistically significant predictor of career liberalism in four out of the six bivariate equations (in both sets of criminal and economic cases, statistically significant at the 95 percent confidence level). Meanwhile, the party of prime minister measure is significant in only two of the six equations in the table (in both sets of criminal cases, statistically significant at or beyond the 95 percent confidence level). These data provide further confirmation that the newspaper ideology measure is a much better predictor of career patterns of ideological voting behaviour than the party of prime minister measure in the dataset.

The statistically significant positive correlation coefficients appearing in the top half of Table 3.4 indicate that the justices with higher newspaper liberalism scores had greater rates of liberal voting across all three areas of law in the post-*Charter* era. The newspaper ideology coefficient in all criminal cases is 3.09, suggesting that the most extreme liberal justice is likely to cast 12.4 percent more liberal votes than his or her most conservative counterpart over the course of their career (this figure is derived by multiplying the coefficient of 3.09 by 4, which represents the distance between the two most extreme judicial positions in the newspaper ideology indicator). When the analysis shifts to non-oral criminal judgments, the disparity between the two extreme justices increases to a 16 percent gap (3.99 × 4). In the economic area, the newspaper coefficient for both equations demonstrates that

TABLE 3.4

Testing for external validity: weighted bivariate regression equations of career liberalism, newspaper ideology, and party of prime minister

Indicator of career liberalism	b	Standard error	Statistical significance	Adjusted R^2
NEWSPAPER IDEOLOGY EQUATIONS				
% liberal votes in all criminal cases	3.09	1.65	.038*	.102
% liberal votes in all economic cases	2.89	1.18	.012*	.186
% liberal votes in all civil rights and liberties cases	1.72	2.20	.222	.019
% liberal votes in criminal cases (no oral judgments)	3.99	1.91	.025*	.133
% liberal votes in economic cases (no oral judgments)	2.90	1.25	.015*	.167
% liberal votes in civil rights and liberties cases (no oral judgments)	2.08	2.24	.183	.007
PARTY OF PRIME MINISTER EQUATIONS				
% liberal votes in all criminal cases	8.49	3.16	.007**	.220
% liberal votes in all economic cases	0.76	2.21	.367	.042
% liberal votes in all civil rights and liberties cases	4.44	3.56	.113	.026
% liberal votes in criminal cases (no oral judgments)	7.10	3.97	.044*	.091
% liberal votes in economic cases (no oral judgments)	−0.03	2.32	.495	.048
% liberal votes in civil rights and liberties cases (no oral judgments)	4.58	3.78	.120	.021

NOTE: $N = 23$. Data are weighted by case participation rates.
* $p < .05$, ** $p < .01$

the most liberal justice will cast almost 12 percent more liberal decisions than his or her most extreme conservative colleague over the course of their career (2.89×4). Overall, the newspaper ideological variable explains between 10 and 19 percent of the variance in career liberalism scores for the twenty-three justices in criminal and economic cases, which means that one out of every ten criminal votes and one out of every five economic votes can be explained by the newspaper ideology measure alone (see the adjusted R^2 values in Table 3.4).

The data in Table 3.4 indicate that neither of the ideology measures produces statistically significant correlations with career liberalism voting patterns in civil rights and liberties disputes.[7] There are several possible explanations for this finding. First, since the number of cases in this issue area is four to five times smaller than the number of cases in each of the other two, it is more difficult to obtain statistically significant relationships between the two ideology variables and liberal voting behaviour. It is also the case that in such a small dataset, there is a greater possibility that measurement error distorts the results and prevents statistical significance from emerging (Manheim and Rich 1991). Second, the failure to find statistical significance might also be explained by the fact that a wide variety of cases are included under the civil rights and liberties umbrella. For example, it might be the case that justices who are liberal in the free expression area are less so when addressing discrimination, religious minorities, or right to privacy issues. Indeed, the initial bivariate results appear to suggest that the Canadian justices possess more consistent ideological attitudes in the criminal and economic areas than they do for the varied issues found under the civil rights and liberties rubric. A third explanation might be that legal factors, such as determining the scope of section 1 analysis, play a much more prominent role than ideology in driving judicial conflict in such cases. Alternatively, gender differences between the justices might constitute the most important explanatory variable for discord in this area of law, and we present strong evidence to validate this in Chapter 5 (see also White 1998; Songer and Johnson 2002).

The only way to truly assess this, however, is to analyze decisions in specific areas of law at the judge-vote level while controlling for ideological factors, case facts, and gender differences to determine the relative explanatory power of each variable in such disputes. For present purposes, the key finding of this chapter is that our initial bivariate analysis suggests that the newspaper ideology measure constitutes a better indicator for assessing attitudinal voting behaviour on the Canadian high court than the party of prime minister measure in these three areas of law. This external validation of the newspaper measure using liberal voting career scores in our database suggests that this new variable holds the most promise for performing well in a full-fledged test of the attitudinal model in various subareas of law.

As a final test of external validity, we assessed the bivariate relationship between the cumulative newspaper measure and Supreme Court voting data published by other scholars in the discipline (Morton et al. 1994; White 1998). Specifically, we examined the bivariate correlations with these authors' independent measures of career voting activity, and conducted a parallel weighted regression analysis that mimics the approach presented in Table 3.4. At the outset, we acknowledge that the external validity checks presented in Table 3.5 are limited in nature because the voting data published by these scholars are confined to *Charter* cases and are derived from a shorter time span than our study. Specifically, the data of Morton and colleagues (1994) covers only the 1984–92 period and presents liberal voting statistics in *Charter* cases exclusively, along with a subset of criminal cases that raise *Charter* claims. The authors do not present data on economic voting trends in the post-*Charter* period. The data published by White (1998), in turn, expands on Morton and colleagues' study by presenting liberal voting patterns spanning the 1984–97 period in *Charter* criminal and fundamental freedoms and equality rights cases. We realize that these external validity checks are less encompassing than the results we present in Table 3.4 because they cover fewer criminal cases and only a subset of civil rights and liberties disputes. Despite these limitations, they offer valuable independent confirmation of the validity and predictive power of our newspaper scores and provide insight into their usefulness for explaining attitudinal decision making in criminal and civil rights and liberties cases.

The data in Table 3.5 indicate that our newspaper measures of judicial ideology coincide well with Morton and colleagues' catalog (1994) of liberal voting in both criminal and *Charter* rulings handed down between 1984 and 1992. The correlation between the newspaper and criminal vote measures is statistically significant at the 99 percent confidence level, and the correlation with the voting patterns in the larger set of *Charter* cases is significant at the 95 percent confidence level ($b = 6.62$ and 6.46, respectively; see Table 3.5). The coefficients suggest that for every one-point increase in the newspaper ideology score, there is a corresponding increase of just over 6 percent in liberal voting by the justices in *Charter* and criminal *Charter* disputes. When considering the four-point spread between the most extreme conservative and liberal justices in our newspaper measure, this translates into a 26 percent gap in the voting records of justices across that ideological divide, at least when using the data of Morton and colleagues (1994).

Similarly, the data of White (1998) on criminal voting patterns during the 1984-97 period provides further confirmation of the validity of the newspaper measure as a predictor of ideological voting behaviour in the field of criminal law ($b = 5.32$, $p < .01$). Interestingly, and in line with our own external validity check conducted earlier, the coefficient assessing the relationship

TABLE 3.5

Independent tests of external validity: weighted regression of newspaper ideology and *Charter* liberalism data compiled by other scholars

Indicator of *Charter* liberalism	b	Standard error	Statistical significance	Adjusted R^2
DATA FROM MORTON ET AL. 1994				
% of votes for *Charter* claimant				
1984–92 (N = 15)	6.46	2.97	.024*	.211
% of votes for criminal rights claimant				
1984–92 (N = 14)	6.62	2.48	.010**	.305
DATA FROM WHITE 1998				
% of votes for criminal rights claimant				
1984–97 (N = 13)	5.32	1.57	.002**	.413
% of votes for fundamental freedoms and				
equality rights claimant 1984–97 (N = 12)	6.22	5.23	.130	.033

NOTE: Data are weighted by case participation rates. Bivariate correlations for the judge vote scores and the newspaper ideology measure were: newspaper ideology with Morton and colleagues' *Charter* measure, $r = .538$; with Morton and colleagues' criminal *Charter* measure, $r = .522$; with White's criminal rights measure, $r = .451$; with White's fundamental freedoms and equality measure, $r = .421$.
* $p < .05$, ** $p < .01$
SOURCES: Morton et al. 1994; White 1998. One modification was made to correct a reporting error for Justice Iacobucci's data in White's publication (1998). Otherwise, the data in the table are exact replications of *Charter* voting scores that were published in these prior studies.

between newspaper ideology and liberal voting in *Charter* cases raising fundamental freedoms and equality claims did not prove to be statistically significant, although the impact is in the expected direction ($b = 6.22$; see Table 3.5). These findings suggest that the newspaper ideology measure might not be as useful a predictor of judicial voting behaviour in post-*Charter* civil rights and liberties disputes, while its predictive power appears likely greater in economic and criminal cases.

The constellation of validity tests derived from our own analysis and the published work of other scholars indicates that our newspaper measure captures a more nuanced dimension of ideological beliefs than any other a priori measure of judicial attitudes constructed for the Canadian Supreme Court to date. It remains to be seen whether the newspaper ideology measure will achieve statistical significance in more sophisticated regression models that include a host of variables relating to particular case circumstances, parties and intervenors, and judicial background characteristics, as well as variables controlling for the three different post-*Charter* courts. In other words, will the newspaper ideology measure perform well in tests of the attitudinal model across distinct issue domains? We turn our attention to this question in the next three chapters.

4

Attitudinal Conflict in Criminal Cases

The first twenty years of *Charter* jurisprudence has marked a new era of constitutional development in the field of criminal law. Court watchers have documented that most of the early post-*Charter* activity occurred in criminal disputes, and suggest that these cases have unleashed some of the most activist rulings by the justices (Morton 1987; Russell 1988; Morton et al. 1991; Morton and Knopff 2000; Manfredi 2001). Indeed, the Supreme Court of Canada has given shape and substance to a host of criminal rights, including the right to counsel, the right to be protected from unreasonable search and seizure, and the right to a timely trial by an impartial jury, to name a few. Despite a large volume of legal research that has emerged in this area of law, no study to date has provided a systematic quantitative analysis of judicial voting, writing, and activist behaviour in all criminal cases decided during the 1984–2003 period. The first part of this chapter is devoted to this type of inquiry, and sheds light on patterns of judicial disagreement, rates of opinion authorship, ideological proclivities, degrees of judicial activism, and ideological stability of judicial voting over time in criminal disputes. The second half of the chapter presents a detailed analysis of the degree to which the attitudinal model explains patterns of judicial behaviour in right to counsel and search and seizure disputes, and addresses the question of whether judicial disagreement is driven by different responses to specific case facts, the ideological predispositions of the justices, the parties and litigants in the cases, intra-court factors, or some combination thereof.

Patterns of Judicial Decision Making in Criminal Cases

We begin our overall analysis of criminal cases by highlighting rates of unanimity, along with data on average panel size in the criminal field (found on the right side of Table 4.1), in relation to all other cases heard by the Court (found on the left side of the table). We focus on these two indicators in Table 4.1 because rates of unanimity are a telltale sign of the degree of social cohesion that exists on the Court in a particular area of law, and because panel size can have a direct impact on the ability to arrive at a unanimous ruling. We also use alternate (bold and italic) typeface to indicate the three post-*Charter* courts – the Dickson and Lamer tenures and the first four years of the McLachlin tenure.

The summary data at the bottom of the "Percent of docket criminal cases" column in Table 4.1 indicate that criminal disputes represent fully 46 percent of the Court's entire docket during the 1984–2003 period. The data also reveal that criminal cases have declined in importance during the early McLachlin tenure, with an average of only 38 percent of the caseload, which represents an 8 percentage-point drop from the average of the prior two courts.[1] One plausible explanation for the McLachlin Court's declining interest in criminal litigation may be that current justices are interested in turning to new constitutional questions that they believe merit greater attention. Indeed, data reported in Chapter 5 suggest that the McLachlin Court has begun to pay more attention to new civil rights and liberties issues, which is illustrated by the fact that the Court's caseload in this area has exceeded the average for the entire post-*Charter* period by 3 percentage points. Despite the slight shift in emphasis away from the criminal field in recent years, this legal area remains a critical component of the Court's caseload in the post-*Charter* era.

The rates of unanimity in criminal cases shown in Table 4.1 are identical to those found across all cases heard by the Court in the post-*Charter* period (24 percent non-unanimous in both areas). This suggests that members of the Court are as likely to disagree in criminal disputes as they are across all other areas of law collectively. Some might expect greater rates of disagreement in the criminal area because an individual's liberty is often at stake, which might lead to greater degrees of conflict among the justices, but the evidence does not support this expectation. One should note, however, that rates of disagreement in criminal cases are slightly higher for the Lamer and McLachlin Courts than their Dickson predecessor. We believe that this is due to two factors: (1) the desire of the early post-*Charter* Court to hand down rulings with a more unified voice, and (2) the presence of Justice L'Heureux-Dubé, who is noted as the "great dissenter" on the latter two courts (see McCormick 2000; Ostberg, Wetstein, and Ducat 2004). Moreover, the average panel size across all criminal cases matches that found across all types of

TABLE 4.1

Annual data on case volume, docket level, unanimity, and panel size in criminal cases, 1984–2003

Year	Total cases argued	Percent non-unanimous all cases heard	Yearly average panel size	Percent of docket criminal cases	Percent non-unanimous criminal cases	Average panel size criminal cases
1984	83	9.6	6.4	43.4	19.4	6.8
1985	86	22.1	7.1	43.0	21.6	7.3
1986	72	15.3	6.1	38.9	14.3	6.6
1987	96	26.0	6.0	56.3	24.1	6.3
1988	109	22.0	5.7	48.6	22.6	5.6
1989	131	23.7	6.5	50.4	18.2	6.6
1990	*113*	*28.3*	*6.7*	*42.5*	*35.4*	*6.4*
1991	*123*	*30.1*	*6.4*	*48.0*	*30.5*	*6.2*
1992	*107*	*16.8*	*6.1*	*46.7*	*12.0*	*6.2*
1993	*127*	*36.2*	*7.0*	*60.6*	*33.8*	*6.9*
1994	*110*	*25.5*	*7.5*	*55.5*	*29.5*	*7.7*
1995	*115*	*30.4*	*7.4*	*51.3*	*32.2*	*7.5*
1996	*111*	*24.3*	*7.2*	*56.8*	*27.0*	*7.0*
1997	*106*	*23.6*	*6.7*	*45.3*	*12.5*	*6.3*
1998	*104*	*26.9*	*7.0*	*46.2*	*25.0*	*7.1*
1999	*78*	*17.9*	*6.8*	*38.5*	*26.7*	*6.9*
2000	**77**	**32.5**	**7.6**	**39.0**	**33.3**	**7.6**
2001	**94**	**22.3**	**7.6**	**35.1**	**27.3**	**7.3**
2002	**68**	**25.0**	**7.9**	**35.3**	**20.8**	**7.3**
2003	**78**	**25.6**	**7.9**	**43.6**	**20.6**	**7.5**
Average	99	24.2	6.9	46.2	24.3	6.9
Std. dev.	19	6.1	0.6	7.3	7.0	0.6

NOTE: Justice Dickson's tenure as chief justice, from 1984 to June 1990, is shown in regular type; Chief Justice Lamer's tenure, from July 1990 to 1999, is shown in italic type; and the initial years of Chief Justice McLachlin's tenure, from 2000 to 2003, are shown in bold type.

cases heard by the Court (6.9 for both criminal cases and all types of disputes). This fact helps explain why the rates of disagreement in both areas are also similar. This finding is a little misleading, however, because the criminal area features a large number of oral decisions (351 oral judgments, compared with 119 in other areas of law between 1984 and 2003). Since these "as of right" judgments typically feature smaller panel sizes, such rulings work to decrease the overall panel rates in criminal cases.[2] Still, there is a great degree of consistency in rates of conflict and panel size between criminal cases and all post-*Charter* litigation.

Since any case coming before the Court provides a justice with an opportunity to give written reasons for his or her judgment, this raises the question of which post-*Charter* justices have emerged as opinion leaders, followers, and outsiders in the criminal field. Pioneering scholarship by Danelski (1989) in this area has suggested that those who emerge as task leaders are the ones who exhibit high rates of majority opinion authorship, while outsider activity is denoted by high rates of dissenting opinions (see also Ducat and Flango 1976; Ostberg, Wetstein, and Ducat 2004; McCormick 1993, 1994a, 2000). This research also indicates that while task leaders are held in high esteem by colleagues and are able to consistently dominate majority coalitions, and thus win the right to pen majority opinions, outsiders tend to exhibit loner activity by staking out a position regardless of its isolated nature (see Danelski 1989; Ducat and Flango 1976). Meanwhile, follower activity is exemplified by high rates of majority "joining" activity combined with low rates of opinion authorship, regardless of whether the opinion is found in the majority or in dissent (see Ducat and Flango 1976; Ostberg, Wetstein, and Ducat 2004).

In line with this thinking, Table 4.2 provides a breakdown of participation rates by twenty-two of the post-*Charter* justices in all criminal disputes that feature written reasons for judgment. The data also feature majority voting rates and patterns of opinion authorship for each of the justices during the 1984–2003 period.[3] The justices are ranked according to their percentage of majority authorship (see the "Percent writing majority opinion" column of Table 4.2). The data show that Justices Lamer and Cory were the clear task leaders in the criminal area, authoring majority opinions 28 and 25 percent of the time, respectively, which is well above the average rate of 12 percent. These findings are not surprising in Justice Lamer's case, given his extensive background as a criminal law litigator prior to his service as a judge. His leadership role also makes sense, given his presence at the helm of the Court for half of the post-*Charter* period, and fits nicely with Danelski's notion (1989) that chief justices are more likely to become task leaders on a court that bears their name and in an institutional setting where they have the power to control opinion assignment (see also McCormick 1993, 1994a). The next tier of justices on this measure were Justices Arbour, Sopinka, and McIntyre, authoring majority opinions roughly 22 to 23 percent of the time.

Justice Arbour's presence in this group fits well with her extensive criminal expertise and her leadership role as chief prosecutor for the International Criminal Tribunals for Rwanda and the former Yugoslavia at The Hague. In the criminal law field, it seems that Justice Le Dain wrote the average number of majority opinions (12 percent), while Justices Dickson and Wilson authored opinions at roughly the same rate (13 and 11 percent, respectively). One might be surprised to find Justice Dickson in the middle of the pack in terms of majority opinion authorship, since he has been portrayed as a task leader in other settings (see McCormick 1993, 1994a). One must keep in mind, however, that the data in Table 4.2 only confirm that he was not a leader in the specialized area of criminal law.

The justices least likely to author majority opinions in criminal cases were Justices Deschamps, Beetz, and Chouinard, who averaged 0, 1, and 2 percent, respectively. The pattern for Justice Deschamps might be artificially low, given her relatively recent arrival on the high court and the fact that her rate is based on only twenty-five decisions through 2003. Clearly, Justices Beetz and Chouinard fit into the category of judicial "followers" described by Ducat and Flango (1976) because they joined majority coalitions over 94 percent of the time yet authored very few majority opinions. Their follower activity is also illustrated in their low rates of authorship of concurrences and dissents (see the last four columns in Table 4.2). We would place Justices Gonthier and Estey in this category also, since they wrote relatively few majority, concurring, and dissenting opinions. Since they are found in the majority coalition at an average rate of only roughly 90 percent, however, they fit the "follower" category less well. The overall patterns of majority author-ship in the criminal area indicate that a core group of justices – Lamer, Cory, Arbour, Sopinka, and McIntyre – shouldered the burden of developing key principles of criminal jurisprudence in the post-*Charter* era.

Other justices on the post-*Charter* Canadian Court have displayed "outsider" traits (see Ducat and Flango 1976, 1985; McCormick 2000; Ostberg, Wetstein, and Ducat 2004). In the criminal law context, Justices Deschamps and L'Heureux-Dubé stand out as clear outsiders on the Court, authoring dissents in 16 and 15 percent of the cases they heard (see the last column of Table 4.2). It is important to note that Justice Deschamps' early behaviour on the McLachlin Court indicates that she is 2 standard deviations beyond the mean rate of judicial dissent, which is a common benchmark for denoting extreme outlier behaviour. If her pattern holds up, her activity on this score will trump even that of Justice L'Heureux-Dubé, who is considered one

TABLE 4.2

Panel participation rates and opinion authorship patterns in criminal cases with written reasons for judgment, 1984–2003

Justice	Number of cases	Percent majority votes	Percent writing majority opinion	Percent writing concurring opinion	Percent writing dissenting opinion
Lamer	398	89.9	27.9	8.3	5.5
Cory	289	94.8	24.6	1.7	2.4
Arbour	87	83.9	23.0	4.6	10.3
Sopinka	283	87.6	21.6	12.7	8.8
McIntyre	135	92.6	21.5	7.4	5.2
Stevenson	31	93.5	19.4	9.7	3.2
Binnie	125	94.4	16.0	1.6	4.0
McLachlin	349	85.7	14.3	9.5	8.6
Dickson	164	92.7	12.8	1.2	5.5
Le Dain	92	95.7	12.0	4.3	3.3
Wilson	191	86.9	11.0	13.1	11.0
LeBel	68	89.7	10.3	1.5	8.8
La Forest	327	90.5	9.8	11.0	4.6
Major	258	87.6	9.7	1.9	6.2
Iacobucci	306	94.1	9.2	1.3	1.6
Bastarache	122	91.8	5.7	3.3	4.9
L'Heureux-Dubé	365	77.8[a]	4.7	12.6	14.8[a]
Estey	64	92.2	4.7	4.7	7.8
Gonthier	361	89.2	3.3	5.3	3.3
Chouinard	54	94.4	1.9	0.0	0.0
Beetz	101	96.0	1.0	4.0	0.0
Deschamps	25	84.0	0.0	4.0	16.0[a]
Average	191	90.2	12.0	5.6	6.2
Std. dev.	—	4.6	8.2	4.2	4.3

NOTE: Justice Fish is omitted from the table because he participated in only five cases, but his data are presented here for comparison purposes: 5 cases, 80.0 percent majority votes, 20 percent majority authorship, and 0 concurring and dissenting opinions authored.
a The justice's value for this indicator is 2 times the standard deviation from the mean value.

of the great dissenters of the modern Court (see Ostberg, Wetstein, and Ducat 2004, 521-23).

One should realize that four of the first five female justices appointed to the bench issued the greatest rates of dissenting opinions in the criminal field (Justices Deschamps, 16 percent; L'Heureux-Dubé, 15 percent; Wilson,

11 percent; and Arbour, 10 percent). Meanwhile, Justice McLachlin is virtually tied with Justices Sopinka and LeBel for the fifth highest rate of dissenting authorship (roughly 9 percent). This finding suggests that female justices on the Canadian Court might be approaching criminal cases in a manner distinct from that of their male colleagues, and thus feel compelled to voice their opinion in dissent at far higher rates. Past scholarship examining patterns of gender-based distinctions in various legal settings in the US and Canada has found some differences between the two sexes in terms of judicial voting and criminal sentencing, although some of the differences are only slight (see, for example, Songer and Crews-Meyer 2000; Gruhl et al. 1981; Steffensmeier and Hebert 1999; McCormick and Job 1993; McCormick 1994b; White 1998). An analysis of the rationale behind the dissenting opinions of the female justices demonstrates that they have not formed a distinct feminist coalition in the criminal area but rather dissent for profoundly different reasons. Indeed, as experienced court watchers would expect, while Justices Wilson, Arbour, and Deschamps' dissents are consistently found at the liberal end of the ideological spectrum, Justice L'Heureux-Dubé's dissenting opinions are at the conservative end, while Justice McLachlin's are found somewhere between the two extremes. Taken together, the female justices do not show a clear pattern of agreement in their criminal dissents; consequently, our evidence fails to support other scholarship suggesting that consistent gender differences exist in the area of criminal law.

Table 4.3 identifies patterns of liberal voting for all the post-*Charter* justices in criminal cases that featured a clear ideological direction and where written reasons for judgment were issued. The findings reveal that while Justice Deschamps occupied the most liberal position in the criminal area, casting votes in favour of the criminally accused 68 percent of the time, Justice L'Heureux-Dubé ranked as the most conservative in this area, siding with the accused in only 19 percent of the cases she heard. The most striking aspect of the behaviour of these two justices is the degree to which they were isolated from other members of the Court, illustrated by the fact that their patterns of liberalism are fully 2 standard deviations above and below the average rate of liberal voting by the rest of the Court (43.5 percent). Additionally, their extreme voting activity matches nicely with the outsider behaviour documented in their opinion authorship patterns in Table 4.2. In short, these two justices are opinion outsiders on the Court because they exhibit behaviour at the two ideological extremes in the criminal area. Meanwhile, the justices labelled as followers in Table 4.2 – Chouinard, Estey, Beetz, and Gonthier – are found

TABLE 4.3

Liberal votes in criminal cases with written reasons for judgment, 1984–2003

Justice	Number of cases where ideological direction can be identified	Percentage of liberal votes cast
Deschamps	25	68.0a
Arbour	86	59.3
Chouinard	51	52.9
Sopinka	277	52.3
Wilson	187	51.9
Major	252	48.8
Stevenson	31	48.4
Lamer	386	48.2
LeBel	67	47.8
Estey	61	47.5
Dickson	160	42.5
Beetz	97	42.3
Le Dain	90	42.2
Binnie	122	41.0
Iacobucci	299	40.1
La Forest	319	38.6
McIntyre	130	38.5
Cory	283	37.5
McLachlin	344	34.9
Bastarache	119	28.6
Gonthier	354	28.0
L'Heureux-Dubé	356	18.5a
Average	186	43.5
Std. dev.	—	10.8

NOTE: Justice Fish is omitted from the table because he participated in only five cases. He cast liberal votes in all five decisions.
a The justice's value for this indicator is 2 times the standard deviation from the mean value.

across the ideological spectrum, and do not display consistent moderate tendencies as one might expect (53, 48, 42, and 28 percent, respectively). Thus, followers do not necessarily have to be found at the ideological centre of the Court to engage in follower activity.

The patterns for Justices Lamer and Cory, two of the task leaders in the criminal area, also merit commentary. These justices occupy positions close to the ideological centre on the roster of post-*Charter* justices, having voted in favour of the criminally accused 48 and 38 percent of the time (see Table 4.3). The fact that the two task leaders of the Court in this area of law also happen to stake out relatively centrist stances betrays an obvious principle about judicial leadership – that it is difficult to lead the Court as an ideological extremist. In other words, justices who frequently stake out a far-reaching position will be less likely to garner support from their colleagues on the bench. Moreover, from the perspective of majoritarian theory, there is something intuitively appealing about ideological moderates leading the Court's opinion output. Some would contend that since justices are unelected and unaccountable to the voters, they should not drive the Court to an ideologically extreme position that is out of touch with mainstream societal values (see, for example, Morton and Knopff 2000).

In Table 4.4, we address the degree to which Canadian justices in the post-*Charter* era have engaged in the practice of judicial activism. There is a critical debate among Canadian scholars over whether the post-*Charter* justices have overstepped their constitutional authority by nullifying too many statutes passed by elected majorities in Parliament and provincial assemblies, or by invalidating government actions (see, for example, Morton and Knopff 2000). Although scholars disagree over the appropriate way to measure judicial activism (see, for example, Hogg and Bushell 1997; Manfredi and Kelly 1999; Kelly 2005; Hennigar 2004a, 2004b; Roach 2001; Morton and Knopff 2000), we have chosen to adopt a relatively narrow definition that assessed the percentage of times the justices voted to nullify a law or portions of a law in criminal disputes under the *British North America Act* or the *Canadian Charter of Rights and Freedoms*. A holistic view of the data presented in Table 4.4 suggests that all the justices are relatively evenly distributed around a mean rate of 23 percent activist votes, although Justices Wilson (37 percent), Estey (36 percent), and Le Dain (35 percent) appear to be the most activist members in the criminal area. Justice L'Heureux-Dubé sits at the other end of the activist spectrum, casting votes to nullify a law only 11 percent of the time, and Justices Major and Bastarache are not far behind at 12 percent. When examining the patterns of activism in relation to the findings in Table 4.2, we find no distinctive and consistent patterns of activist behaviour among the task leaders or the followers of the post-*Charter* Court. In other words, task leaders on the Court are no more likely to be activists than opinion followers.

One intriguing question that might be raised is whether rates of judicial activism among members of the post-*Charter* Court are higher among those found on one side of the ideological spectrum than the other. There is a common tendency among people to think that liberal-leaning justices are

TABLE 4.4

Patterns of judicial activism in criminal cases, 1984–2003

Justice	Number of cases raising possibility of statute nullification	Percent of times (n) a justice voted to nullify a law or portion of law		Percent of activist votes (n) cast in majority	
Wilson	51	37.3	(19)	63.2	(12)
Estey	14	35.7	(5)	60.0	(3)
Le Dain	17	35.3	(6)	100.0	(6)
Lamer	96	31.3	(30)	76.7	(23)
Sopinka	72	29.2	(21)	71.4	(15)
Cory	68	26.5	(18)	77.8	(14)
Arbour	21	23.8	(5)	20.0	(1)
LeBel	17	23.5	(4)	0.0	(0)
Dickson	45	22.2	(10)	90.0	(9)
Binnie	27	22.2	(6)	50.0	(3)
Iacobucci	67	20.9	(14)	85.7	(12)
La Forest	84	20.2	(17)	88.2	(15)
Beetz	20	20.0	(4)	100.0	(4)
McLachlin	82	18.3	(15)	73.3	(11)
McIntyre	25	16.0	(4)	100.0	(4)
Gonthier	89	14.6	(13)	100.0	(13)
Bastarache	25	12.0	(3)	100.0	(3)
Major	51	11.8	(6)	50.0	(3)
L'Heureux-Dubé	80	11.3	(9)	88.9	(8)
Average	50.1	22.7		73.4	
Std. dev.	28.7	8.1		28.0	

NOTE: Justices with ten or fewer cases are omitted from this table, but we provide their data here for those interested in complete information on the justices. We include the number of cases heard, the percentage of activist votes, and the percentage of those votes that were handed down in majority or concurring opinions. The data must be interpreted with caution, given the small number of cases heard. Chouinard, 8, 25.0, 100.0; Deschamps, 7, 42.9, 0.0; Fish, 1, 100.0, 0.0; Stevenson, 6, 66.7, 75.0.

more likely to hand down activist rulings than their conservative counterparts, although it is a mistake to necessarily equate activism with liberal voting behaviour because scholarship has shown that activist rulings can appear on both sides of the ideological continuum (Baum 2001, 301-2; Gewirtz and Golder 2005). In order to assess this relationship, we conducted a bivariate regression analysis that compared rates of criminal law activism with the two a priori judicial ideology measures (our newspaper ideology and party of prime minister scores discussed in Chapter 3) to see whether any statistically significant patterns appeared. Obviously, it is necessary to give greater weight to justices who participated in larger numbers of cases, so the regression runs were weighted accordingly. The analyses were based on the nineteen justices highlighted in Table 4.4. The results indicate that the liberal justices were indeed more activist in the criminal area when either measure of ideology is utilized (r = .665 for newspaper liberalism, significant at the 99.9 percent confidence level; r = .493 for party of prime minister, significant at the 95 percent confidence level).[4] Consequently, it appears that in the first twenty years of post-*Charter* criminal cases, there is a grain of truth to the contention that liberal justices are more activist in their orientation, and thus more likely to side with criminal defendants and declare laws unconstitutional. One must be cautious generalizing from this conclusion, however, because this finding might not be borne out in other areas of law.

Table 4.5 builds on the analysis of attitudinal liberalism by exploring the degree to which individual justices across the ideological spectrum cast consistent votes over time. In order to assess this adequately, we examined the relationship between a justice's voting behaviour at two points in time, and compared it with the set of colleagues who served on the Court during the same time period. As Lawrence Baum (1988, 1992) has pointed out, the comparison of a justice's votes with their contemporary cohort is necessary to control for any changes in court membership and changing levels of case difficulty that might influence the overall voting behaviour of justices. A central tenet of Baum's correction technique (1988, 1992) is that most justices have stable ideological views over time, and so any judicial voting change by a particular justice that is remarkably different from his or her cohort must represent actual ideological change by that individual justice over time (see Ostberg et al. 2003, 716).

In line with this thinking, the second, third, and fourth columns of Table 4.5 identify the percentage of liberal votes cast in the criminal area at years 1 and 2 and years 5 and 6 of a justice's service, in order to calculate whether any changes in ideological voting patterns had occurred for that particular justice.[5] The next three columns provide the same assessment of ideological voting patterns for the various justices who served with the individual during that same time period. The last column calculates the true ideological change by an individual justice in this area of law by subtracting the ideological change for the cohorts ("Change in continuing justices" column) from the ideological change for individual justices ("Change in voting" column). This calculation, in turn, enables one to more accurately differentiate those justices exhibiting true ideological change from those who do not.

An overall assessment of Table 4.5 indicates that the justices of the post-*Charter* era exhibit relatively stable ideological voting patterns over time in criminal disputes. When individual justices are compared with their fellow cohorts, the average rate of change was only 3 percentage points more liberal over a six-year time span (see the bottom of Table 4.5). In fact, ten of the justices clustered within 7 percentage points of the roughly average ideological change demonstrated by Justice Lamer (2.6 percent net change). During their first six years on the Court, however, Justices Sopinka and Cory exhibited the greatest change in support for criminal defendants relative to their cohorts, having shifted over 1 standard deviation beyond the mean value (15 percent and 13 percent liberal change, respectively). In contrast, Justices Dickson and Gonthier exhibited the largest conservative swings, casting 16 and 7 percent more rulings in favour of the government than their peers over a six-year time frame.

Since most of the justices cast stable ideological votes over a six-year time frame, the attitudinal model appears to have particular relevance in the post-*Charter* criminal field. We make this statement because one of the fundamental assumptions put forward by attitudinal scholars is that justices vote according to their personal values, which rarely change over time. Our finding of relatively stable ideological voting activity fits well with this underlying premise, and suggests that fruitful results may emerge from an attitudinal inquiry that controls for other variables that might influence judicial decision making in criminal cases. We address this question in the next section.

Right to Counsel Cases

DATA AND METHODS

Our initial tests of the attitudinal model focus on two pivotal areas of criminal law, namely, right to counsel and search and seizure disputes, because they constitute two of the largest subsets of cases heard in this legal category. The data for these two areas are drawn from published opinions in the *Canada Supreme Court Reports* in the post-*Charter* era (1984–2003). We first assess the influence that ideological attitudes, case facts, and court control variables have on judicial voting behaviour in all right to counsel cases where there were written reasons for judgment, and then conduct a second level of analysis that examines only non-unanimous rulings in this area. We include an assessment of all cases because it represents the most difficult test of the

TABLE 4.5

Changes in ideological voting patterns by Supreme Court justices in criminal cases when years 1 and 2 (T1) are compared with years 5 and 6 (T2)

Judge (votes T1, T2, number of continuing judges)	% liberal (T1)	% liberal (T2)	Change in voting	% liberal continuing justices (T1)	% liberal continuing justices (T2)	Change in continuing justices	Difference in value change
Sopinka (53, 60, 3)	47.2	51.7	4.5	38.9	28.8	-10.1	14.6
Cory (57, 71, 6)	40.4	42.3	1.9	43.9	33.0	-10.9	12.8
McLachlin (51, 65, 6)	35.3	33.8	-1.5	44.6	34.5	-10.1	8.6
Binnie (48, 32, 5)	29.2	56.3	27.1	29.4	48.3	18.9	8.2
McIntyre (50, 25, 3)	50.0	44.0	-6.0	57.8	44.0	-13.8	7.8
Bastarache (50, 32, 5)	20.0	43.8	23.8	31.3	51.0	19.7	4.1
La Forest (36, 57, 3)	47.2	57.9	10.7	41.8	48.6	6.8	3.9
Lamer (53, 69, 3)	56.6	46.4	-10.2	55.6	42.8	-12.8	2.6
Wilson (45, 65, 3)	60.0	49.2	-10.8	54.6	41.5	-13.1	2.3
Iacobucci (53, 51, 7)	39.6	37.3	-2.3	38.8	35.0	-3.8	1.5
L'Heureux-Dubé (42, 44, 2)	19.0	20.5	1.5	40.8	43.0	2.2	-0.7
Major (64, 46, 6)	50.0	37.0	-13.0	33.2	24.6	-8.6	-4.4
Gonthier (62, 67, 6)	38.7	23.9	-14.8	44.3	36.1	-8.2	-6.6
Dickson (49, 48, 3)	57.1	33.3	-23.8	55.4	47.2	-8.2	-15.6
Average	42.2	41.2	-0.9	43.6	39.9	-3.7	2.8
Std. dev.	13.0	11.1	14.3	9.3	8.0	11.4	8.0

NOTE: Justices who appear to display significant ideological shifts from those serving as cohorts on the Court are identified in bold text. A simple rule of thumb was used: if the value difference exceeded 1 standard deviation (8.0) when comparing a justice's ideological change with the change score of other justices on the Court with him or her, that justice was highlighted as exhibiting a significant ideological change. Obviously, changes in ideological scores are more reliable when the comparison groups of justices are larger; thus, we have the most confidence in the change scores for justices McLachlin, Cory, Gonthier, Iacobucci, and Major. For Justice Bastarache, the data for the first two years of service are drawn from the three calendar years he sat on the Court (1997–99) as he heard only one criminal case in his first year because he was appointed on 30 September 1997. As a result, the data for his second time frame are derived from 2002–03.

attitudinal model by examining ideology's influence on judicial behaviour not only in non-unanimous cases but also in circumstances where all the justices were in agreement. This necessarily introduces a conservative bias into the results because the inclusion of non-unanimous cases restricts variation in the dependent variable, making it more difficult for independent variables to achieve statistical significance. We acknowledge that the second level of analysis represents an easier test case of the attitudinal model, simply because ideology is likely to be a fulcrum of conflict between the justices when they disagree. Yet the singular focus on contentious disputes is necessary to understand the relative importance of various independent variables in the equation when justices disagree, and to highlight the degree to which ideology is central to the decision-making process in these contested disputes.

The first equation that we present encompassed a total of forty-one right to counsel cases decided between 1984 and 2003 that featured written reasons for judgment. The second model narrowed the focus to fifteen non-unanimous rulings. Since the attitudinal model theorizes that the votes of the justices will be a product of each justice's ideological leanings along with the attitudinal responses they have toward particular factual circumstances, the unit of analysis for the dependent variable was at the judge-vote level for each case (Segal 1984; Segal and Spaeth 1993, 2002). The dependent variable for each of our equations was a dichotomous indicator identifying whether a justice cast a liberal vote in favour of the criminal defendant in a right to counsel dispute (vote = 1), or a conservative vote in favour of the government (vote = 0). Thus, our initial analysis examined a total of 303 votes cast by the justices in all right to counsel cases, while our subsequent analysis examined the 121 votes cast in contested cases. Ultimately, we were interested in predicting as many of those votes as possible correctly by utilizing ideology and factual circumstances as the key predictors of vote outcomes.

Since advocates of the attitudinal model acknowledge that a judge's predisposition toward facts (in addition to ideology) can influence vote outcomes, we included independent variables that are typically found in Canadian right to counsel cases.[6] The factual indicators in both of our equations were coded from the lower court opinions in an effort to identify reliable, a priori factual indicators and to evade possible distortion of the facts by the Supreme Court justices themselves. Coding the factual circumstances in this manner ensured that the statistical model did not suffer from problems of circular reasoning.

The model examining all right to counsel cases featured eight factual dichotomous variables: (1) whether police failed to provide an adequate right to counsel warning (flawed warning); (2) whether no right to counsel warning was given by police to the defendant (no warning given); (3) whether police provided a warning after detention (after detention); (4) whether police arrested a defendant after normal working hours (after-hours arrest); (5) whether police were provided tips in a drug-related arrest (tips to police); (6) whether a defendant requested a counsel and made an effort to talk to one (ask for counsel/effort); (7) whether police engaged in deceptive questioning practices (police deception); and (8) whether the case involved an impaired driving charge (impaired driving). The coding scheme and hypothesized relationship for these dichotomous variables was straightforward. For example, in cases where police did not appropriately warn the suspect of his or her right to counsel, it was expected that justices would tend to vote in favour of the criminally accused because a clear *Charter* violation had occurred. Obviously, if police provided an adequate warning, justices would be predisposed to favour the government, all other things being equal. Consequently, the "flawed warning" variable was scored as "1" if police failed to provide an adequate warning and "0" in all other cases, and we anticipated a positive coefficient in the regression results for this variable.

Two other independent variables address the nature and timeliness of a police warning. It was expected that justices would be more likely to favour the criminally accused in situations where police failed to provide a warning to defendants at all, or where a warning was given only after the accused had been detained for some time. These two factual scenarios are contrasted with situations where an immediate warning was given at the time of arrest or detention, which is omitted from the regression equation for comparison purposes. As a result, if no warning was given or if a warning was provided only after detention, a case was coded as "1" for these "facts," while a score of "0" was entered for all other situations.[7] We expected that positive coefficients would appear for these variables. In addition, we hypothesized that the justices would be predisposed to rule in favour of the criminally accused if they were arrested after normal working hours, because these cases were more likely to feature questionable police interrogation practices without the defendant having an attorney present. Thus, we expected a positive coefficient in cases featuring late-night arrests.

There are a number of cases in Canada that address both right to counsel and search and seizure claims. In these instances, one salient feature that might draw the attention of the justices is whether police were responding to anonymous tips from citizens or other law enforcement agencies. In these cases, justices might be swayed to favour the prosecution because there exists an element of corroborated suspicion flowing from the "before the fact" observations of someone other than the police. In short, the right to counsel claims of a defendant might be trumped in the minds of the justices by the accumulation of damning evidence gathered from tips and the subsequent police search. In line with this reasoning, when tips were a central part of the case, we scored those disputes with a "1" while all other cases received a "0," and we expected a negative coefficient in our regression results.

A sixth independent variable identified situations where defendants did not consult with an attorney even though they had asked for and made an effort to contact one. We coded such cases as "1" and expected the justices to be more sympathetic to the plight of the defendants, who were, in effect, ultimately denied the benefit of sound legal advice. We expected a positive coefficient for this factual variable compared with all other cases lacking this scenario. Since the Canadian Court has also addressed several cases dealing with some form of police deception or clear intention to ignore the defendant's request for an attorney, a seventh variable was included in the model to capture police deception or trickery. For example, if police ignored a request to speak to a lawyer, or fostered the impression that a lawyer was not available, we coded that case as "1" for the variable "police deception." In contrast, all other cases that did not feature this or a similar scenario were coded as "0." We anticipated that justices would be more sympathetic to the defendant's *Charter* claims if some form of police deception occurred in the case, and thus expected a positive coefficient for this variable.

The last factual variable in the model captured cases involving impaired driving incidents (1 = impaired driving cases, 0 = all other cases). It was expected that justices would be much less sympathetic toward defendants involved in drunk driving cases, given the societal harm presented by such drivers, and a negative coefficient was expected in the equation for this variable.

The ideology measures used in our model analyzing all right to counsel decisions included the cumulative newspaper ideology scores for each justice that were described at length in Chapter 3. The values for this indicator ranged from +2 for the most liberal justices to –2 for the most conservative ones. A second potential measure of ideology pertained to the party of the appointing prime minister, which was coded as +1 for Liberal appointees and –1 for Conservatives. In line with the attitudinal model, it was expected that liberal justices would tend to vote in favour of the defendant more frequently than their conservative counterparts. It was likewise expected that Liberal Party appointees would be more likely than their Conservative colleagues to side with the criminally accused. We anticipated that these two ideological measures would produce positive and statistically significant coefficients even in the face of controlling for the eight factual variables in the equation.

A final variable included in the equation tested whether the Lamer Court treated right to counsel cases differently from the Dickson Court, its predecessor.[8] We did not provide a directional hypothesis for this variable because we could not identify a plausible theoretical justification for why the Lamer Court would rule differently from the Dickson Court in this area of law. Rather, the inclusion of this variable was designed to see whether any statistically significant shift in right to counsel voting occurred among the Lamer Court justices compared with their Dickson Court predecessors, even when controlling for case facts and their ideological predispositions. Since no directional hypothesis was proposed, a substantive shift in the judicial voting behaviour on the Lamer Court could be signified by a statistically significant coefficient in the equation in either the positive or negative direction. A positive coefficient would indicate that the Lamer Court was more liberal than the Dickson Court in right to counsel cases, while a negative coefficient would suggest the opposite. It is our contention that if such a change occurred, it would be due to either the intra-court dynamics between the justices or the Court's response as an institution to value changes taking place in Canadian society.

RESULTS

All Right to Counsel Cases

A logistic regression model was utilized because the right to counsel equation features a dichotomous dependent variable that takes on the value of "1" for a liberal vote or "0" for a conservative vote (Aldrich and Nelson 1984). Table 4.6 provides logistic regression coefficients for the eight factual variables, two ideology indicators, and the Lamer Court control variable. The voting data indicate that the overall frequency of liberal votes in the entire dataset was 56 percent, which means that if one were to simply guess a "liberal" outcome for each justice's decision, one would correctly identify 56 percent of the votes. The full model (featured in Table 4.6) was able to accurately predict the voting behaviour of the justices 70 percent of the time, which indicates that the model is able to predict an additional 32 percent of the remaining variance in voting behaviour beyond that of the simple guessing strategy of always predicting liberal outcomes (see the bottom of Table 4.6).[9] These findings reveal that the combination of the eight factual circumstances, the two ideological measures for the justices, and a Lamer Court control variable help to explain a significant proportion of the voting patterns in all post-*Charter* right to counsel cases.

The results at the judge level in Table 4.6 indicate that ideology measured from newspaper reports of the nominees has a statistically significant impact on the votes of justices in contested right to counsel cases ($b = 0.42$, significant at the 99 percent confidence level). It is important to note that while the coefficient for newspaper ideology has an absolute value that is smaller than most of the factual variables in the model, this is only because it is measured on a different scale, which ranges from -2 to $+2$ (as opposed to from 0 to 1). The relative power of ideology's influence compared with the eight factual variables can be found in the last column in Table 4.6, which compares the probability, or odds, of a liberal outcome when the value of the variable is set low (-2) with the probability of a liberal outcome when the value of the variable is set high ($+2$), while holding all other variables at their mean level. The change between these two conditions, found at the top of the last column, indicates that an extremely liberal justice is 40 percent more likely than an extremely conservative justice to cast a liberal vote in a right to counsel case. A comparison of the change in probability scores in the model demonstrates that this variable proved to be the third most powerful indicator in the equation. In contrast, the party of prime minister coefficient constituted one of the weaker predictors of liberal voting behaviour ($b = -0.21$), and its impact was in the unexpected direction. Since this variable is not statistically significant, it is clear that the party of prime minister indicator is not a useful surrogate for judicial ideology in the realm of right to counsel cases. As mentioned in Chapter 3, one explanation for the weak performance of the party measure may stem from the fact that Prime Minister Mulroney did not appoint justices at the conservative ideological extreme (see Tibbetts 2003c; Fine 1997) but rather named relatively moderate justices to the high court. The findings clearly indicate that the newspaper ideology measure is a much stronger predictor of ideological voting in these criminal disputes.[10]

Five of the eight factual variables in the equation are statistically significant at or beyond the 95 percent confidence level, and the impact of each of

TABLE 4.6

Logistic regression estimates of liberal votes in all right to counsel cases, 1984–2003

Variable	b	Statistical significance	Probability of liberal vote when x is low	Probability of liberal vote when x is high	Change in probability
JUDGE-LEVEL VARIABLES					
Ideology	0.424	.002**	.334	.732	.398
Party of prime minister	−0.206	.135	.613	.512	−.101
CASE CHARACTERISTICS					
Flawed warning	0.312	.209	.553	.629	.076
No warning given	3.788	.000***	.465	.975	.510
After detention	0.028	.469	.576	.582	.006
After-hours arrest	1.102	.003**	.455	.715	.260
Tips to police	−1.119	.013*	.616	.344	−.272
Ask for counsel/effort	0.102	.418	.572	.597	.025
Police deception	1.709	.000***	.401	.787	.386
Impaired driving	−1.846	.000***	.706	.275	−.431
COURT CONTROL VARIABLES					
Lamer Court	0.993	.014*	.439	.679	.240
McLachlin Court[a]	—	—	—	—	—
CONSTANT AND MODEL FIT STATISTICS					
Constant	−1.504				
−2 LLR chi-square		330.889***			
Nagelkerke R^2		.327			
Percent correct		70.0%			
Reduction in error		31.7%			

NOTE: N = 303.

a The McLachlin Court indicator was omitted from this equation because there were no right to counsel cases decided between 2000 and 2003.

* $p < .05$, ** $p < .01$, *** $p < .001$

these variables is in the expected direction. The confidence level suggests that 95 times out of 100 we are certain that these five factors help explain liberal voting patterns among all the justices, and that their impacts are not simply due to chance. The most important factual variable in the equation is whether an individual failed to receive a right to counsel warning (b = 3.79, significant at the 99.9 confidence level). As expected, the results indicate that justices of all ideological stripes are 51 percent more likely to rule in favour of the defendant when no right to counsel warning has been provided by police (see the last column of Table 4.6). The importance of this factor can be seen in one of the early *Charter* landmark rulings of the Court, *R. v. Therens,* [1985] 1 S.C.R. 613, where a drunk driver was asked to go to the police station to provide a breath sample, but was not made aware of his counsel rights at either the roadside or the police station. The Court ruled for the defendant, demonstrating that the justices would be more likely to favour the accused when no right to counsel warning is given at the time a person is initially stopped by police. In contrast to the *R. v. Therens* ruling, impaired driving cases usually cut in the opposite direction for the criminally accused, with the justices casting 43 percent fewer votes in favour of the defendant (b = −1.85, significant at the 99.9 percent confidence level).

As expected, justices do not respond favourably to authorities in situations where the accused has been subject to deceptive questioning tactics by police (b = 1.71, significant at the 99.9 percent confidence level). The results indicate that when this occurs in a case, individuals have a 39 percent greater chance of obtaining a ruling in their favour. One early example of this type of situation is illustrated in *R. v. Manninen,* [1987] 1 S.C.R. 1233, where police acquired inculpatory statements through barbed questioning of an armed robbery suspect even after he had indicated that he did not want to speak until his lawyer was present. The results indicate that most justices on the post-*Charter* Court have not looked favourably on police when they purposely trick suspects into providing inculpatory statements in direct violation of their counsel rights.

The fourth significant factual variable in the equation involved situations where tips were provided to police (b = −1.12, significant at the 95 percent confidence level). As expected, the findings indicate that the justices were 27 percent less likely to rule in favour of the criminally accused when police were tracking down leads from tips. For example, in *R. v. Jacoy,* [1988] 2 S.C.R. 548, the Court upheld the admission of evidence in a case that featured police tips about a suspected drug smuggler entering the country. Even though the Court acknowledged that Jacoy's right to counsel had been infringed, they concluded that excluding evidence in this case would have brought the administration of justice into disrepute.

The final significant factual variable in the equation pertains to arrests that take place after normal working hours (b = 1.10, significant at the 99 percent confidence level). An example of this case fact can be found in *R. v. Ross,* [1989] 1 S.C.R. 3, where police were able to charge Ross with breaking and entering on the basis of a lineup, despite his desire to contact a lawyer in the middle of the night. Indeed, in cases like *R. v. Ross*, the justices were 26 percent more likely to rule in favour of the criminally accused than in situations where arrests took place during regular workday hours.

The last statistically significant variable in the equation was the Lamer Court control variable ($b = 0.99$, significant at the 95 percent confidence level). This finding demonstrates that when controlling for the factual circumstances found in the various cases and for the ideological leanings of particular justices, justices on the Lamer Court were 24 percent more likely to rule in favour of the criminally accused (issuing more liberal rulings) in right to counsel cases than their Dickson Court predecessors. Even though a clear liberal trend appears in the Lamer Court, it is unclear whether this distinction is due to some intra-court dynamics taking place behind the red velour curtain or whether the change reflects a response to some societal shift on the part of Canadians toward right to counsel claims.

The three remaining case-level variables – flawed warning, after detention, and ask for counsel/effort – were not statistically significant in the model featuring all right to counsel disputes. These findings suggest that if police gave a flawed right to counsel warning or provided a warning after detention, or when a suspect asked for an attorney and made an effort to call an attorney, one cannot confidently conclude that the justices will be more or less likely to rule in favour of the criminally accused. In other words, these three variables do not help explain much of the voting behaviour when all right to counsel cases are analyzed.

Collectively, the variables in the model produce a robust account of the variance in all right to counsel claims in the post-*Charter* era. Five of the factual variables are statistically significant, with coefficients in the hypothesized direction, and comprise important dimensions that are likely to remain pivotal variables for explaining judicial conflict in this area of law both within Canada and potentially in other cultural settings. The findings indicate that ideology is also pivotal and was one of the top explanatory variables for judicial voting across all right to counsel cases. This means that even when unanimous cases are taken into consideration, the ideological predisposition of the justices influences their decision patterns. The question remains, however, whether the impact of ideology is as salient in non-unanimous cases, and, if so, whether it is the pivotal feature driving disagreement on the Court, as advocates of the attitudinal model would presume. We now turn to our second level of analysis to address this question.

Non-Unanimous Right to Counsel Cases

The equation for the non-unanimous right to counsel cases parallels the first model but excludes two factual variables because of high collinearity with another variable in the equation. Specifically, the measures of late-night arrests and impaired driving were omitted from the second model because both are highly correlated with cases involving right to counsel warnings that occur after detention.[11] One new variable was added to the analysis because it reflected an important factual element that was more prominently found in the non-unanimous cases. This new indicator captured circumstances where a defendant sought to stretch counsel protections beyond the initial post-custody phase (post-charge application). For example, in *R. v. Jones*, [1994] 2 S.C.R. 229, the defendant tried to invoke this right at a pretrial psychiatric evaluation, and in *Winters v. Legal Services Society*, [1999] 3 S.C.R. 160, a convict sought to expand the right to a prison disciplinary hearing. It was hypothesized that in such circumstances, justices would be less sympathetic to stretching the right to counsel warning to novel situations because they believed that this right should typically be triggered only at the time of arrest and detention. The logic behind this hypothesis was that justices might take timing into consideration, so that defendants who seek the right to counsel at the time of arrest or at the station house would be looked upon more favourably than those who attempt to utilize the right further on in the trial or post-trial process. Our measure of this variable was coded as "1" if this right was sought at the later phase of the criminal process and "0" in all other cases, and we expected a negative coefficient in the equation. Outside of these changes, the model for non-unanimous right to counsel cases was identical to that used to assess all right to counsel disputes. Ultimately, the second equation featured seven factual variables, in addition to the two measures of ideology and the Lamer Court control variable.

The results of the second model enable one to more accurately predict the voting behaviour of the justices when disagreement occurs in right to counsel cases. Indeed, the model accurately predicts three-quarters of the case votes, and represents a 39 percent improvement in forecasting the variance in voting behaviour compared with a simple guessing strategy (see Table 4.7). Moreover, this model increases the accuracy of prediction by 5 percent over the analysis of all right to counsel cases (75 percent in Table 4.7, up from 70 percent in Table 4.6). Collectively, the seven factual variables and the two ideology and court control indicators are able to explain a

TABLE 4.7

Logistic regression estimates of liberal votes in non-unanimous right to counsel cases, 1984–2003

Variable	b	Statistical significance	Probability of liberal vote when x is low	Probability of liberal vote when x is high	Change in probability
JUDGE-LEVEL VARIABLES					
Ideology	0.921	.000***	.177	.896	.719
Party of prime minister	−0.196	.285	.642	.548	−.094
CASE CHARACTERISTICS					
Flawed warning	−0.215	.393	.644	.593	−.051
No warning given	2.911	.008**	.573	.961	.388
After detention	2.147	.001***	.419	.860	.441
Tips to police	−0.276	.357	.628	.562	−.066
Ask for counsel/effort	−0.282	.353	.636	.569	−.067
Police deception	1.880	.007**	.372	.795	.423
Post-charge application	−1.492	.057	.670	.314	−.356
COURT CONTROL VARIABLES					
Lamer Court	0.825	.193	.463	.663	.200
McLachlin Court [a]	—	—	—	—	—
CONSTANT AND MODEL FIT STATISTICS					
Constant	−2.008				
−2 LLR chi-square		120.347***			
Nagelkerke R^2		.404			
Percent correct		75.2%			
Reduction in error		38.8%			

NOTE: $N = 121$.

a The McLachlin Court indicator was omitted from this equation because there were no non-unanimous right to counsel cases decided between 2000 and 2003.

* $p < .05$, ** $p < .01$, *** $p < .001$

substantial degree of judicial voting behaviour in contested post-*Charter* right to counsel disputes.

One of the most interesting findings in Table 4.7 is the fact that the newspaper ideology variable becomes the most powerful predictor of judicial voting in non-unanimous cases ($b = 0.92$, significant at the 99.9 percent confidence level). Indeed, the change in probability score found in the last column suggests that the most liberal justices are 72 percent more likely to rule in favour of the criminally accused in disputed right to counsel cases, which is a 32-point jump in the odds ratio found across all right to counsel cases. One would expect ideology to play a role in contested disputes in this area, because it was significant in the first model and also because ideology is an obvious attribute that tends to divide justices. The magnitude of the swing in the odds is remarkable, however, and demonstrates that ideology plays a central role in determining how justices resolve these cases. It is also note-worthy that the party of prime minister plays a negligible role in the equa-tion in concert with the first model. This suggests that the party of prime minister measure is not effective at explaining ideological vote outcomes in Canadian right to counsel cases.

Another feature worth noting in Table 4.7 is that the Lamer Court indi-cator is no longer statistically significant in the equation. This shows that the Lamer Court's institutional tendency to cast liberal votes is more apparent in unanimous rulings than in non-unanimous cases, with the change in odds decreasing by 4 percentage points in the second model (20 percent in Table 4.7, down from 24 percent in Table 4.6). Put simply, when the justices of the Lamer Court agreed, they tended to be more liberal in their voting orienta-tion than the Dickson Court, and more liberal than in non-unanimous cases.

Three of the seven factual variables are statistically significant at the 99 percent confidence level, and two of them, no right to counsel warning given and police deception, were also significant in the first equation. The coeffi-cients and changes in probability scores for these indicators did not change much across the two models ($b = 2.91$, change in probability = 39 percent for no warning; $b = 1.88$, change in probability = 42 percent for police decep-tion). These findings suggest that two key factual circumstances that justices home in on when resolving both unanimous and non-unanimous right to counsel disputes are whether a warning has been given and whether police have engaged in deceptive interrogation practices.

The only variable to achieve statistical significance in the second model that was not significant is the first is whether a right to counsel warning was given after detention ($b = 2.15$, significant at the 99.9 percent confidence level). In contentious cases that feature this factual scenario, the justices are 44 percent more likely to rule in favour of the criminally accused, all other things being equal. An example of this scenario is found in *R. v. Elshaw*, [1991] 3 S.C.R. 24, where police did not inform the accused of his counsel rights when they first stopped and questioned him at a park and obtained his ID, or when they subsequently questioned him in a police van. It was only after he was formally charged with child molestation at the police station that the defendant was informed of his right to counsel. The majority concluded that Elshaw's counsel rights were violated and went on to stress the importance of providing a timely right to counsel warning to criminal suspects.

The fact that this variable (whether a right to counsel warning was given after detention) attained statistical significance in the second model and not the first, and represented the second strongest explanatory variable in the equation, highlights its importance as a source of division among the justices that is necessarily masked when unanimous cases are added to the mix. This finding raises another critical question, namely, whether the justices found on opposite ends of the ideological spectrum respond differently to the different factual scenarios in right to counsel disputes. In other words, do liberal justices respond to facts differently from their conservative counterparts?

The Impact of Case Facts on Liberal and Consertative Justices
in Non-Unanimous Right to Counsel Cases
The true importance of Segal and Spaeth's (1993, 2002) full attitudinal model becomes more evident if one can clearly identify systematic differences in the way that factual variables influence the justices at opposite ends of the ideological continuum. We know of no scholarship to date that has provided an ideological comparison of this nature, and we address this question in Table 4.8.

In order to determine whether there is differential treatment of case facts, we split the non-unanimous dataset into two ideological camps for separate data analysis: conservatives plus moderates, and liberals plus moderate-liberals. To be more precise, we identified the median ideological position of the nineteen justices in the right to counsel dataset based on their respective newspaper scores, and created two mutually exclusive categories of justices for comparison purposes. One group features moderate and conservative justices, consisting of the ten lowest-scoring justices on this measure (0.444 or less on the ideology scale), while the other includes the nine most liberal-leaning justices (0.500 or greater). For the nine most liberal justices, the only factual variable that has a statistically significant influence on their vote choice is whether police deception was involved in the case ($b = 1.91$, significant at the 95 percent confidence level). In such situations, liberal-leaning justices were 36 percent more likely to favour the defendant than in cases where this

TABLE 4.8

Estimates of liberal votes by liberal-moderates, and conservative-moderates in non-unanimous right to counsel cases, 1984–2003

	Moderate-liberals and liberals		Moderates and conservatives	
	b	Change in probability of a liberal vote ($N = 54$)	b	Change in probability of a liberal vote ($N = 67$)
CASE CHARACTERISTICS				
Flawed warning	−0.901	−.175	0.133	.033
No warning given	0.787	.127	3.811**	.522
After detention	1.223	.216	2.398**	.528
Tips to police	−0.719	−.153	0.172	.043
Ask for counsel/effort	−0.553	−.113	−0.237	−.059
Police deception	1.905*	.363	1.600	.380
Post-charge application	−1.667	−.377	−1.423	−.326
COURT CONTROL VARIABLES				
Lamer Court	0.185	.036	1.130	.270
McLachlin Court [a]	—	—	—	—
CONSTANT AND MODEL FIT STATISTICS				
Constant	0.312		−2.713	
−2 LLR chi-square		54.996		72.326**
Nagelkerke R^2		.254		.352
Percent correct		77.8%		74.6%
Reduction in error		25.0%		48.5%

a The McLachlin Court indicator was omitted from this equation because there were no non-unanimous
   right to counsel cases decided between 2000 and 2003.
* $p < .05$, ** $p < .01$, *** $p < :001$

factual scenario was not present (see the "Change in probability of a liberal vote" column in Table 4.8). It is important to realize that conservative justices are also more likely to rule in favour of defendants in these situations (38 percent), even though this finding is not statistically significant. This lack of statistical significance may be due to the slightly larger number of case votes in the data set ($N = 67$) and the greater importance of other factual variables that appear in that model. In large measure, however, the two sides of the Court responded in roughly the same manner to the presence of police deception.

Two important differences between the ideological camps are evident when the justices are confronted with cases where no warning is given at all, or when a warning is given after detention. In these cases, conservatives were 52 percent more likely to favour the defendant if no right to counsel warning was given (b = 3.81, significant at the 99 percent confidence level), and 53 percent more likely to do so in cases where a warning was given after detention (b = 2.40, significant at the 99 percent confidence level). Liberals on the Court were not likely to significantly favour the defendant in these two situations, however. One explanation for this discrepancy may lie in the fact that liberals and moderate-liberals have a greater propensity to side with the criminally accused in the first place, voting in their favour 70 percent of the time. Thus, while the presence of these particular facts appears to foster a greater number of liberal votes by the conservative justices, it did not for their liberal counterparts. Clearly, the existence of these two factual scenarios triggers starkly different attitudinal responses from justices on different sides of the ideological spectrum. The cumulative importance of these findings is that, at least in the right to counsel area, some facts are more important than others to some justices. In general, this analysis suggests that future comparative studies of the attitudinal model would do well to explore whether similar differential impacts are evident in other high court settings and in other issue areas.

Search and Seizure Cases

DATA AND METHODS

The second test of the attitudinal model in this chapter examines search and seizure disputes, an area of criminal law that has generated a significant number of important rulings by the Court. Prior studies of the Canadian and US Supreme Courts have documented the validity of the full-blown attitudinal model in this area (Segal and Spaeth 1993, 2002; Wetstein and Ostberg 1999). Our research builds on this prior work by providing an updated dataset of decisions and a more complete model for assessing the relevance of the attitudinal framework in the first twenty years of *Charter* jurisprudence. As with the right to counsel area, data for this portion of the chapter are derived from all search and seizure cases published in the *Canadian Supreme Court Reports* during the post-*Charter* era (1984–2003). Cases were included in the study if content analysis demonstrated that a search and seizure issue was a central component of the case and there were written reasons for judgment in the dispute (total number = 85).[12] As with the right to counsel area, we conducted two different mathematical tests of the attitudinal model. The first examined 626 judicial votes drawn from eighty-five search and seizure cases (both unanimous and non-unanimous); the second featured 244 votes drawn from thirty-three non-unanimous cases. In line with our earlier examination, each justice's vote served as the unit of analysis, with the dependent variable reflecting the justice's willingness to rule in favour of the criminally accused (a liberal vote) or in favour of the government (a conservative vote).

The independent variables included in the analysis of all search and seizure cases featured thirteen factual circumstances, along with the same two ideological measures employed in the right to counsel area, and two court control variables. More variables are included in the search and seizure analysis because there is a wider range of factual circumstances that emerge in these types of disputes, and the number of case votes is twice the size of that found in the right to counsel area. The factual scenarios for these models were also coded from the lower court opinions after a close reading of each of the cases to ensure that the facts were scored independently from the justice's own opinions. All thirteen variables were coded as "1" if that particular factual circumstance was evident in the case, and "0" otherwise. The inclusion of these variables enabled us to examine whether case facts trigger attitudinal voting responses among the justices that either favour or work against the interests of criminal defendants.

Four of the independent variables pertain to the location and property interests surrounding a search, namely, whether the case involved a search of a house, car, business, or person (1 = yes, 0 = no for all four places). These variables replicate prior research, and were included because the Canadian Court, like the US Court, has drawn distinctions between searches when the accused has a property interest at stake and other types of searches (Segal 1984, 1986; Segal and Spaeth 1993; Wetstein and Ostberg 1999). In all four of these circumstances, the accused has a property interest, and thus has a more legitimate claim to *Charter* protection than in cases where property rights are not involved. In regard to searches of persons, the Canadian Court has also recognized heightened levels of privacy interest in blood seizure cases. For instance, in *R. v. Pohoretsky*, [1987] 1 S.C.R. 945, the Court indicated that the taking of blood from an individual without authorization was "a violation of the sanctity of a person's body [that] is much more serious than that of his office or his home." In a subsequent blood seizure case, the

Court reiterated that "when the search and seizure relates to the integrity of the body rather than the home ... the standard is even higher than usual" (*R. v. Dyment*, [1988] 2 S.C.R. 417 at 438). The Court has also drawn a distinction between administrative and regulatory searches of businesses, where a lower standard may be applied because of the need for random monitoring of companies by government (see *R. v. McKinlay Transport Ltd.*, [1990] 1 S.C.R. 627; and *Thomson Newspapers Ltd. v. Canada*, [1990] 1 S.C.R. 425). In short, regulatory searches of businesses entail a lower expectation of privacy than criminal searches of the home. Finally, in *R. v. Wise*, [1992] 1 S.C.R. 527, the Court recognized that automobile travel entails an even lower expectation of privacy. The Court indicated that "although there remains an expectation of privacy in automobile travel, it is markedly decreased relative to the expectation of privacy in one's home or office" (*R. v. Wise* at 534). In the end, the Court's opinions appear to have developed a hierarchy of privacy interests in search and seizure cases, with bodily integrity of the person at the top of the privacy continuum, followed by homes, businesses, and automobiles, respectively. Thus, we expected that the justices would be more likely to rule in favour of the accused in cases involving these four property interest variables than when property interests are not at stake. In addition, we hypothesized that the strength of the coefficients would follow that same hierarchy, with seizure of evidence from the person's body having the strongest positive relationship, followed by searches of homes, businesses, and cars in that order.

Two other factual variables in the equation included whether police obtained a valid search warrant and whether the police had probable cause in the absence of a warrant. Since the language in section 8 of the *Charter* is ambiguous and does not mention a warrant requirement, the Court had to fashion one in its early post-*Charter* rulings. In doing so, it relied heavily on Fourth Amendment principles found in US case law, and determined that a reasonable search and seizure could not be conducted without a warrant or probable cause (*Hunter v. Southam*, [1984] 2 S.C.R. 145, and *R. v. Collins*, [1987] 1 S.C.R. 256). Since the Canadian Court has adopted much of the probable cause and warrant requirements developed by the US Court, we expected these variables to have a similar impact on the decision-making process of the Canadian Court. Thus, we believed that when these criteria are present, the justices would be more likely to rule in favour of the prosecution in search and seizure cases, and we anticipated negative coefficients for these two variables.

Another set of case characteristics pertained to circumstances surrounding a search and arrest – whether the search was conducted before an arrest, or whether it occurred incident to or after a lawful arrest. These two circumstances were juxtaposed with cases where no search had transpired and individuals were attacking the validity of a warrant issued by a court. Cases featuring this last set of circumstances were excluded from the equation for comparative purposes. It was hypothesized that justices would be least supportive of the defendant in cases where no search had occurred because police had not engaged in questionable conduct that the justices would deem unreasonable. In contrast, it was expected that justices would be most supportive of the accused when searches occurred before an arrest, because in such situations, it is more likely that police have engaged in unlawful behaviour that may violate the suspects' *Charter* rights. Lastly, we thought that searches conducted during or after a lawful arrest would fall somewhere between the other two categories. As a result, we created a hierarchy of judicial support, anticipating that justices would give the least support to the criminally accused in cases where no search had occurred, followed by searches during or after a lawful arrest, and that they would be most supportive when a search occurred before an arrest. Thus, the two variables in the model were expected to feature positive coefficients that demonstrate this hierarchy of support. Another significant variable along these lines pertained to whether or not an unlawful arrest occurred in the case (1 = yes, 0 = no). Since the *Charter* protects the individual from unlawful detention (section 9), it was hypothesized that when one has occurred, the justices would be predisposed to rule in favour the accused because a *Charter* breach had taken place. Once again, we expected a positive coefficient for this variable.

A fourth set of variables pertained to the kind of evidence seized and the unique context of searches at border crossings or ports of entry. We included border searches as a dichotomous variable because it represents a prominent factual circumstance that has led the Canadian Court to carve out an exception to the probable cause requirement. In *R. v. Simmons*, [1988] 2 S.C.R. 495, the Court indicated that there is a lower expectation of privacy at border crossings, which places a less severe burden on government in defending a warrantless search and seizure. Thus, border searches are not held to the same strict procedural safeguards as other searches, and represent one area where the Canadian Court has created a clear exception that mimics the US Court's treatment of border cases (see *Carroll v. United States*, 267 U.S. 132 [1925]; *U.S. v. Ramsey*, 431 U.S. 606 [1977]; and *U.S. v. Montoya de Hernandez*, 473

U.S. 531 [1985]). In line with this logic, it was hypothesized that in cases dealing with border searches, the justices would tend to favour the government because of the lower expectation of privacy at border crossings, and we anticipated that the border search coefficient would have a negative value.[13]

Another variable included in the equation pertained to whether police obtained evidence through eavesdropping or wiretapping techniques (1 = wiretapping cases, 0 = all other cases). Given the intrusive nature of such searches and seizures, we believed that the justices would be more inclined to side with the privacy interests of defendants, and we expected a positive coefficient in the equation for this variable. In a similar manner, a dichotomous variable was created to identify cases where physical evidence was obtained during a search (1 = yes, 0 = all other cases). We believed that when material goods were seized, this would serve as a powerful cue for the justices regarding the culpability of the defendant, and thus expected that justices would tend to favour the prosecution in these cases.

A final dichotomous factual variable included in the equation was whether tips were provided to police about criminal activity (1 = yes, 0 = all other cases). In line with our hypothesis in the right to counsel area, it was expected that cases involving tips would cause the justices to support the government because such information provides a secondary source of evidence regarding the guilt of the accused. This led us to anticipate a negative coefficient for the "tips" variable. Taken together, these thirteen factual variables identify salient characteristics that were common to these types of disputes in the first twenty years of post-*Charter* jurisprudence, and we believed that they would collectively explain a substantial portion of the variance in the justices' voting behaviour across all search and seizure cases.

In general, the factual variables readily match the variables found in prior studies by Segal and Spaeth (Segal 1984, 1986; Segal and Spaeth 1993, 2002) and Wetstein and Ostberg (1999). We do not, however, replicate some of the exceptions included in prior US studies because they have been addressed in too few Canadian cases to warrant inclusion in the data analysis in this study. As a result, readers will not find a discussion of hot pursuit, plain view circumstances, searches where consent has been given to authorities, or searches where evidence is being used in an administrative hearing or by grand juries. While there are slight differences between the model used in this study and the earlier American research, in most circumstances the indicators are sufficiently identical to justify our test of the full-blown attitudinal model in the Canadian cultural context.

Besides the thirteen factual variables in the equation, four variables were included that assessed the ideology of individual justices and any differences that might be found between the three post-*Charter* courts. As in the right to counsel area, ideology is captured by the newspaper scores created in Chapter 3 and by the party of the appointing prime minister. In line with the earlier analysis, we hypothesized that liberal justices would be more prone to rule in favour of the criminally accused than their conservative counterparts. Since there was a roughly even distribution of search and seizure cases across the three post-*Charter* courts, we were able to include both the Lamer and McLachlin Courts as control variables in the analysis to see how they compared with Dickson Court rulings. One must keep in mind that we posit no directional hypothesis for these variables; instead, we are interested in identifying whether these two courts have taken a distinctively liberal or conservative approach in relation to their predecessor. As mentioned earlier, if a significant positive or negative coefficient appeared for either of the court control variables, it would suggest that a dramatic liberal or conservative shift had taken place on one or both of the later courts in the search and seizure area.

RESULTS

All Search and Seizure Cases

As in the right to counsel area, logistic regression techniques were required because the dependent variable in the search and seizure area is dichotomous (Aldrich and Nelson 1984). Table 4.9 provides maximum likelihood estimates for the independent variables, and the results at the bottom of the table provide model fit statistics indicating that our full-blown attitudinal model is able to accurately predict 78 percent of the case votes correctly, a 37 percent improvement over the modal guessing strategy of 65 percent. One should note that this level of predictive accuracy is even stronger than that found in the right to counsel area, and constitutes the most impressive model across all of the equations in this book. Moreover, the model fit statistics presented for this equation surpass those reported by Segal and Spaeth (2002, 325) in their analysis of US search and seizure votes between 1962 and 1998 (71 percent correct, proportional reduction in error of 34 percent). Collectively, the variables explain a significant portion of variance in the dependent variable and produce a robust model fit statistic (chi-square = 557, significant at the 99.9 percent confidence level). Clearly these variables do an impressive job explaining differences in voting behaviour among the justices across all search and seizure disputes.

TABLE 4.9

Logistic regression estimates of liberal votes in all search and seizure cases, 1984–2003

Variable	b	Statistical significance	Probability of liberal vote when x is low	Probability of liberal vote when x is high	Change in probability
JUDGE-LEVEL VARIABLES					
Ideology	0.331	.002***	.146	.391	.245
Party of prime minister	−0.506	.028*	.306	.210	−.096
CASE CHARACTERISTICS					
Search of house	−0.621	.040*	.302	.189	−.113
Search of car	−2.576	.000***	.347	.039	−.308
Search of business	0.849	.009**	.229	.410	.181
Evidence from person	1.020	.008**	.216	.434	.218
Probable cause	−1.922	.000***	.506	.130	−.376
Obtained valid warrant	−1.380	.000***	.317	.105	−.212
Before arrest	1.694	.000***	.141	.471	.330
During or after arrest	2.381	.000***	.123	.602	.479
Unlawful arrest	2.600	.000***	.205	.776	.571
Border search	−2.524	.002**	.294	.032	−.262
Tip to police	−.721	.017*	.301	.173	−.128
Wiretap/eavesdropping	1.516	.000***	.218	.560	.341
Physical evidence[a]	0.673	.017*	.202	.331	.130
COURT CONTROL VARIABLES					
Lamer Court	0.103	.364	.259	.279	.020
McLachlin Court	0.063	.435	.265	.278	.013
CONSTANT AND MODEL FIT STATISTICS					
Constant	−2.061				
−2 LLR chi-square		556.756***			
Nagelkerke R^2		.457			
Percent correct		78.1%			
Reduction in error		37.1%			

NOTE: $N = 626$.
a Since breathalyzer and physical evidence were highly collinear, we opted to include only one of the variables in the equation.
* $p < .05$, ** $p < .01$, *** $p < .001$

As in the right to counsel area, the coefficient for the newspaper ideology measure in the search and seizure model indicates that justices who are more liberal do vote more frequently in favour of criminal defendants ($b = 0.33$, significant at the 99 percent confidence level). As mentioned earlier, the values in the last column of Table 4.9 help to gauge the true impact of the ideology measure compared with all others in the equation. This measure indicates that liberal justices are 25 percent more likely to side with the accused than their most conservative colleagues, and that the impact of ideology on judicial voting is more muted in the search and seizure setting than in right to counsel cases (eighth out of seventeen variables). Having said this, we believe that the models demonstrate ideology's importance as a driving force behind judicial decision making in these two areas of law. In contrast, the indicator for party of prime minister, although statistically significant, is in the unanticipated direction ($b = -0.51$, significant at the 95 percent confidence level). The results suggest that Conservative Party appointees are 10 percent *more* likely to rule in favour of the criminally accused than their Liberal Party counterparts, all other things being equal. As mentioned in the right to counsel section, this anomaly may be due to the fact that several of Prime Minister Mulroney's appointees came to the Court with relatively moderate to liberal voting tendencies in criminal cases, and this is particularly true in the search and seizure area.

Turning to the privacy interest variables, all four are statistically significant, and the two coefficients for searches of persons and businesses are in the expected direction relative to cases where no property interests are at issue (b for person = 1.02, b for business = 0.85, both statistically significant at the 99 percent confidence level). Meanwhile, the two coefficients for searches of cars and homes are in the unexpected direction (b for car = -2.58, significant at the 99.9 percent confidence level; b for house = -0.62, significant at the 95 percent confidence level). Although the hierarchy is somewhat askew from our original expectations, the results confirm that evidence seized from an individual generates the strongest positive coefficient. Indeed, when evidence is taken from a person, the justices are 22 percent more likely to support the criminal rights claimant than when no property interest is at play (see the last column of Table 4.9). The coefficient for this variable makes intuitive sense given that several of the cases feature intrusive body searches, three of which were conducted without the accused's consent (see *R. v. Dyment*, [1988] 2 S.C.R. 417; *R. v. Greffe*, [1990] 1 S.C.R. 755; *R. v. Stillman*, [1997] 1 S.C.R. 607; and *R. v. Golden*, [2001] 3 S.C.R. 679). Collectively, these cases illustrate that the majority of the Court view these searches as serious breaches of *Charter* principles because they feature egregious violations of personal privacy and human dignity.

Surprisingly, the next most important variable in the hierarchy involves searches of businesses, and not homes. The results reveal that justices are 18 percent more likely to side with the defendant when a business search has occurred than when searches involved no private property interest. Two cases that illustrate this point are *Baron v. Canada*, [1993] 1 S.C.R. 416 and *Kourtessis v. Minister of National Revenue*, [1993] 2 S.C.R. 53, which involved successful challenges to searches conducted under the *Income Tax Act*. In both instances, the Court ruled that the act violated section 8 of the *Charter* because the law restricted a judge's ability to balance a person's privacy interests against law enforcement demands for a warrant. Even though the coefficient for searches of cars is in the unexpected direction, going against the criminally accused, this finding might be explained by the fact that automobiles are mobile, and such searches often involve the confiscation of drugs or material that can be easily whisked away. The fact that the Canadian Court was more likely to favour the government in searches of homes may seem initially perplexing, since justices have long recognized that one's home is one's castle. Since the searches of homes in the first twenty years of *Charter* jurisprudence featured a higher rate of seizure of weapons and drugs than searches of cars and businesses, however, it makes more sense that the coefficient for house searches is negative. The trilogy of *R. v. Grant*, [1993] 3 S.C.R. 223; *R. v. Wiley*, [1993] 3 S.C.R. 263; and *R. v. Plant*, [1993] 3 S.C.R. 281 collectively demonstrates the Court's propensity to be more conservative when drugs were found in homes, even when lawful warrants were not obtained prior to the search. All told, the hierarchy of property interests fits some of our expectations, but there are counterintuitive results in car and home searches.

One should note that our findings regarding the property interest hierarchy vary somewhat from an earlier article that we published assessing the first decade of search and seizure rulings under the *Charter*. In that study, the coefficients for all four variables were positive in relation to cases where no property interests were involved. In addition, the searches of businesses supplanted searches of persons at the top of the hierarchical order (Ostberg and Wetstein 1999, 769). Our current findings suggest that the addition of ten years of data and new factual and court control variables collectively produce a model where the hierarchical relationships are more murky and other factual circumstances are more salient for explaining voting behaviour on the Canadian Court in this area of law.

The estimates highlighting the existence of probable cause and cases where police obtained a valid warrant are statistically significant and in the expected directions ($b = -1.92$ for probable cause, $b = -1.38$ for a valid warrant, both significant at the 99.9 percent confidence level). These findings indicate that when police establish probable cause in the absence of a warrant, or obtain a valid warrant, the justices are 38 and 21 percent less inclined to rule in favour of the criminally accused than in cases where there is neither probable cause nor a warrant obtained by police (see Table 4.9). These findings are not surprising and make intuitive sense, given the Court's mandate to uphold the due process guarantees outlined in the text of the *Charter*. Moreover, the variables pertaining to the timing of a search in relation to an arrest are also statistically significant, albeit in the opposite direction ($b = 1.69$ before arrest, $b = 2.38$ during or after arrest, both significant at the 99.9 percent confidence level). In line with our hypothesis, these two findings suggest that the justices are 33 and 48 percent more likely to rule in favour of the accused when reviewing searches conducted before an arrest or those conducted during or after an arrest, in contrast to cases where no arrest or seizure has occurred. The collective impact of these findings demonstrates two intuitively understandable traits of Canadian search and seizure law: (1) that the establishment of probable cause or the acquisition of a search warrant are important criteria for explaining why justices resolve disputes in favour of the government; and (2) that justices are more likely to side with defendants if a search has occurred in relation to an arrest than if the defendant is merely attacking the legitimacy of a search warrant request made by police.

The factual variable tapping searches after an unlawful arrest or detention is statistically significant and in the hypothesized direction ($b = 2.60$, significant at the 99.9 percent confidence level). Indeed, the presence of this factor had the most important impact on the attitudinal voting behaviour of the justices, and the results indicate that justices are 57 percent more likely to rule in favour of the accused if an unlawful detention has taken place. The power of this scenario is illustrated in one of the earliest ground-breaking *Charter* rulings, *R. v. Therens*, [1985] 1 S.C.R. 613, where the majority determined that breathalyzer evidence must be excluded because a drunk driver had been unlawfully detained without being informed of his counsel rights. This case established the standard that if a defendant is not provided an adequate right to counsel warning at the time of detention, it would be considered an unlawful arrest, and evidence might be excluded if it would "bring the administration of justice into disrepute" (*R. v. Therens* at 616). In short, our findings demonstrate that the unlawful arrest variable is most important in prompting high court justices to rule in favour of the rights claimant.

Three of the remaining four case characteristics – border searches, tips to police, and wiretaps – are significant and have coefficients in the expected direction. While searches conducted at borders and those based on tips to police work to the detriment of a criminal defendant ($b = -2.52$ for border searches, significant at the 99 percent confidence level; $b = -0.72$ for police tips, significant at the 95 confidence level), those based on electronic surveillance work in their favour ($b = 1.52$, significant at the 99.9 percent confidence level). The case of *R. v. Jacoy,* [1988] 2 S.C.R. 548 exemplifies the impact of the first two case scenarios. In this suit, Jacoy was subjected to a frisk search at a border crossing after customs officials had been tipped off by police that he was a suspected drug smuggler. The Court determined that despite a right to counsel violation, the admission of seized evidence would not bring the administration of justice into disrepute because the customs agents had acted in good faith, and thus had reasonable and probable grounds to conduct the search (*R. v. Jacoy* at 549-50). In contrast, the wiretapping cases of *R. v. Garofoli,* [1990] 2 S.C.R. 1421 and *R. v. LaChance,* [1990] 2 S.C.R. 1490 both indicate that members of the Court are far more sympathetic to defendants who are seeking access to sealed packets containing information about wiretap authorizations. For both defendants, access to such information was necessary to present a full defence. Collectively, these three factual scenarios trigger attitudinal responses on the part of the justices and are therefore important predictors of liberal or conservative voting patterns in this area of law.

The factual variable pertaining to whether physical evidence is obtained in the course of a search is statistically significant, although it is in the unexpected direction ($b = 0.67$, significant at the 95 percent confidence level). Contrary to expectations, when physical evidence is obtained, the justices are 13 percent more likely to rule in favour of the criminally accused than in situations where no such evidence is involved. One explanation for this counterintuitive finding is that in the cases where items like drugs, guns, or stolen goods are at issue, police may have a greater tendency to skirt procedural safeguards in an effort to seize evidence quickly. For example, in the notorious murder case of *R. v. Feeney,* [1997] 2 S.C.R. 13, police seized blood-stained clothing in the course of conducting a warrantless search and subsequently coerced a confession from the accused before he was allowed to talk to a lawyer. Likewise, in *R. v. Golden,* [2001] 3 S.C.R. 679, police conducted an unlawful anal cavity search in the course of arresting a cocaine dealer in a sandwich shop. The egregious nature of police activity in these two cases may help explain why the justices favour the criminally accused when physical evidence is at issue in the case.

The last two variables in the equation, which compare the Lamer and McLachlin Court justices with their Dickson Court predecessors, indicate that the justices do not resolve search and seizure cases in a significantly different manner. In fact, there is virtually no change in the probability of a liberal ruling emerging across the justices of the three courts when all other factors are taken into consideration (see the entries of .02 and .01 for the Lamer and McLachlin court variables in the last column of Table 4.9).

Collectively, the seventeen variables in the equation explain over three-quarters of all search and seizure votes in the post-*Charter* era. As in the right to counsel model, newspaper ideology scores, not party of prime minister, prove to be the best judge-level ideological surrogate for predicting liberal votes on the high court. Moreover, the factual scenarios in these cases appear more important to the justices than in right to counsel disputes, with all thirteen variables having a statistically significant impact on the way they vote. Although three of the coefficients are in the unexpected direction (searches of houses, cars, and the seizure of physical evidence), the fact that all the case-level characteristics are statistically significant shows the profound impact that such variables have on the liberal/conservative voting patterns of Canadian justices.

Non-Unanimous Search and Seizure Cases
The second test of the attitudinal model in the search and seizure area narrows the focus to non-unanimous cases to determine whether ideology or case facts have more or less of an impact on the voting patterns of the justices in contentious disputes. It is important to note that while this model mirrors the one analyzing all search and seizure cases, it differs in two respects. First, we omitted the wiretapping indicator and the Lamer Court control variable from the small model because both were highly collinear with cases involving physical evidence ($r = -.537$ for wiretapping, $r = .549$ for the Lamer Court measure). Second, we included breathalyzer disputes as a new variable in the equation, and hypothesized that given the high number of fatalities resulting from drunk driving, the justices would be less supportive of defendants in such cases compared with all other disputes. In line with this thinking, we coded the variable as "1" if a breathalyzer demand was

involved in the case and "0" otherwise, and expected a negative coefficient to appear in the equation.[14]

The results found at the bottom of Table 4.10 indicate that the mathematical model featuring sixteen variables accurately predicts 70 percent of

TABLE 4.10

Logistic regression estimates of liberal votes in non-unanimous search and seizure cases, 1984–2003

Variable	b	Statistical significance	Probability of liberal vote when x is low	Probability of liberal vote when x is high	Change in probability
JUDGE-LEVEL VARIABLES					
Ideology	0.497	.001***	.187	.626	.439
Party of prime minister	−0.579	.057	.471	.333	−.138
CASE CHARACTERISTICS[a]					
Search of house	0.177	.337	.404	.447	.043
Search of car	0.827	.145	.401	.605	.204
Search of business	0.281	.296	.403	.472	.069
Evidence from person	1.550	.011*	.337	.705	.368
Obtained valid warrant	0.058	.455	.415	.429	.014
Probable cause	−1.311	.005**	.545	.244	−.301
Before arrest	1.279	.029*	.282	.585	.303
During or after arrest	1.667	.032*	.256	.646	.390
Unlawful arrest	1.850	.001***	.352	.776	.424
Border search	−0.863	.246	.429	.241	−.188
Breathalyzer case	−1.855	.023*	.446	.112	−.334
Physical evidence	−1.144	.015*	.616	.338	−.278
Tip to police	−0.634	.112	.451	.304	−.147
COURT CONTROL VARIABLES					
Lamer Court[a]	—	—	—	—	—
McLachlin Court	0.963	.041*	.395	.631	.236
CONSTANT AND MODEL FIT STATISTICS					
Constant	−0.953				
−2 LLR chi-square		282.304***			
Nagelkerke R^2		.258			
Percent correct		69.7%			
Reduction in error		31.0%			

NOTE: $N = 244$.

a   The Lamer Court and wiretap indicators were omitted from this equation because they were highly collinear with the physical evidence variable.

* $p < .05$, ** $p < .01$, *** $p < .001$

the votes in non-unanimous search and seizure cases, which represents a 31 percent improvement over the modal guessing strategy. In line with our findings in the right to counsel area, the newspaper ideology measure is the most important variable in the equation (b = 0.50, significant at the 99.9 percent confidence level). The value for this variable in the last column of Table 4.10 suggests that liberal justices are 44 percent more likely to rule in favour of the criminally accused than their most conservative counterparts in contentious cases. Coupled with the right to counsel findings, this illustrates the power that ideology plays in documenting judicial disagreement in two of the most important areas of criminal law. This is impressive evidence that the attitudinal model provides a valid theoretical explanation for judicial behaviour in right to counsel and search and seizure cases.

In contrast to the model analyzing all search and seizure cases, only half of the factual variables significantly influence the justices' voting behaviour in non-unanimous disputes. The two most important factual variables in the non-unanimous equation are identical to those in the previous model: searches after an unlawful arrest (b = 1.85, significant at the 99.9 percent confidence level), and searches incident to or following an arrest (b = 1.67, significant at the 95 percent confidence level). Three other factual variables that play a significant role in both equations include when evidence is taken from a person, searches that are conducted before an arrest, and searches occurring pursuant to probable cause. For all three variables, the swing in the odds of a liberal ruling ranges from 37 percent when evidence is taken from a person to ±30 percent for the other two variables (see the last column of Table 4.10). Incidents involving breathalyzer demands also proved statistically significant in the equation, and the coefficient is in the hypothesized direction (b = −1.86, significant at the 95 percent confidence level). Not surprisingly, the justices are 33 percent less likely to rule in favour of the defendant in such circumstances compared with all other cases. The last factual variable to achieve statistical significance is physical evidence, although its impact runs contrary to the effect found in the larger model (b = −1.14, significant at the 95 percent confidence level). The change in odds measure suggests that in non-unanimous cases, the justices are 28 percent less likely to side with the criminally accused when physical evidence has been seized. This impact fits with our initial expectation that the presence of physical evidence would work against the interests of defendants in the minds of the justices. Unlike in the larger model, the McLachlin Court control variable also proved statistically significant; the justices on this Court were 24 percent more likely than those on the two previous courts to rule in favour of the criminally accused in disputed cases ($b = 0.96$, significant at the 95 percent confidence level).

A survey of the models in the right to counsel and search and seizure area reinforces the conclusion that ideology plays a dominant role in the decision-making process in these two types of criminal disputes. Indeed, the impact of the newspaper ideology score nearly doubles when the focus is only on contentious cases in both areas of law. This finding fits nicely with the contention advanced by attitudinal theorists that when justices disagree, ideology is bound to be the principal factor animating that disagreement. Moreover, most readers would expect that the impact of factual variables would remain relatively stable across the two equations, in which case the model's predictive power would go up when non-unanimous cases are modelled in both areas of law. While this expectation is met in the right to counsel area, it is not borne out in the non-unanimous search and seizure model, where the number of factual variables that are statistically significant declines considerably, from thirteen to seven. This drop suggests that facts are less relevant in explaining the attitudinal voting patterns in contentious search and seizure disputes than in all search and seizure cases. This finding helps explain why the overall predictive accuracy of the non-unanimous model declines by 8 percentage points in the search and seizure area, whereas it increases by 5 percent in the right to counsel area. In the end, the various models point to two fundamental conclusions: (1) that ideology is a prominent predictor of the variance in voting in two key areas of criminal law, and (2) that while a number of facts are relevant for both fields of law, they are substantially less relevant when only non-unanimous search and seizure cases are examined.

The Impact of Case Facts on Liberal and Conservative Justices
in Non-Unanimous Search and Seizure Cases
As in the right to counsel area, we were interested in determining whether some case facts have different impacts on justices at different ends of the ideological spectrum. We examined this question by dividing the justices into the same two ideological categories (ten justices scoring 0.444 or lower for moderates and conservatives, and nine justices scoring 0.500 or higher for moderate-liberals and liberals). The first striking feature of the results in Table 4.11 is that unlike the right to counsel area, both sets of justices are influenced by numerous case characteristics, with the liberal-leaning justices

responding in a statistically significant way to eight factual circumstances, while their conservative counterparts took significant notice of four. Having said this, there are important similarities and differences between the two groups that merit consideration.

For example, in the hierarchy of privacy concerns, the results indicate that both groups were significantly more likely to favour criminal defendants when searches of an individual had taken place than when no privacy interest was in play ($b = 1.83$ for liberal-leaning justices, $b = 2.00$ for conservatives). Ultimately, both sets of justices were between 41 and 46 percent more likely to side with the criminally accused in such circumstances (see the two "Change in probability of a liberal vote" columns in Table 4.11). Aside from this similarity, the two groups appeared to respond to the other three privacy interests in disparate ways, with the liberal side of the Court casting significantly more liberal votes in business search cases ($b = 1.51$), while their conservative counterparts were statistically more prone to respond with a liberal vote in cases involving a search of a car ($b = 2.02$). One might be perplexed as to why neither searches of homes nor searches of cars hit the radar screen of the liberal-leaning justices. One must keep in mind, however, that these insignificant findings simply mean that they are almost as likely to cast a liberal vote where no property interest is at stake as in cases involving searches of homes and cars. One explanation for this counterintuitive finding is that liberal justices are predisposed to side with the defendant at the onset of any search and seizure case; thus, the fact that a search took place at a house or car may have little bearing on their voting tendency.

Since an unlawful arrest was the most important variable for forecasting liberal votes in the regression analysis for all search and seizure cases, it is not surprising that it triggered liberal attitudinal responses on the part of both sets of justices, as shown in Table 4.11. Indeed, liberal-leaning justices are 62 percent more likely to rule in favour of the accused when an unlawful arrest has occurred, while their conservative counterparts are 38 percent more likely to do so ($b = 3.67$ for liberals, $b = 1.61$ for conservatives). The only other significant variable for the conservative-leaning justices is police tips, with conservatives 38 percent *less* likely to rule in favour of the criminally accused in such cases ($b = -2.16$). In contrast, liberals were 26 percent more likely to favour the criminally accused in such situations, although the variable did not have a significant impact on this group ($b = 1.06$). This provides an illustration of how case facts can prompt different attitudinal responses from justices who are ideological opposites. One case that highlights this distinction

TABLE 4.11

Estimates of liberal votes by liberal-moderate and conservative-moderate justices in non-unanimous search and seizure cases, 1984–2003

	Moderates and liberals		Moderates and conservatives	
	b	Change in probability of a liberal vote (N = 116)	*b*	Change in probability of a liberal vote (N = 128)
CASE CHARACTERISTICS				
Search of house	−0.674	−.166	0.953	.224
Search of car	0.144	.036	2.015*	.460
Search of business	1.513*	.354	−0.467	−.103
Evidence from person	1.826*	.406	2.000*	.462
Probable cause	−2.920**	−.599	−0.706	−.159
Obtained valid warrant	−0.397	−.098	0.351	.083
Unlawful arrest	3.673**	.616	1.613*	.383
Border search	−6.600**	−.550	1.257	.304
Tip to police	1.060	.256	−2.155**	−.376
Breathalyzer case	−5.444***	−.556	−0.330	−.072
Before arrest	1.604	.381	1.521	.342
During or after arrest	3.562*	.708	0.745	.171
Physical evidence	−1.750*	−.405	−0.779	−.184
COURT CONTROL VARIABLES				
Lamer Court[a]	—	—	—	—
McLachlin Court	0.043	.011	1.151	.279
CONSTANT AND MODEL FIT STATISTICS				
Constant	−0.674			−1.719
−2 LLR chi-square		124.003***		141.292**
Nagelkerke R^2		.362		.290
Percent correct		75.0%		67.2%
Reduction in error		48.2%		17.6%

a . The Lamer Court indicator is omitted from the equation because it is highly collinear with the physical evidence variable.
* $p < .05$, ** $p < .01$, *** $p < .001$

is *R. v. Kokesch*, [1990] 3 S.C.R. 3, where several of the more liberal-scoring justices invalidated a warrantless marijuana search that was triggered by police tips, while Justices Dickson, L'Heureux-Dubé, and Cory were undisturbed by what they perceived to be a minimal *Charter* intrusion (*R. v. Kokesch* at 25). In this case, the justices at different ends of the ideological spectrum clearly responded remarkably differently to the search and seizure conducted as a result of a police tip.

Intriguingly, in the search and seizure area, five additional factual variables trigger strong significant attitudinal responses on the part of the liberal wing of the Court but fail to have as significant an impact on the conservative bloc. The five circumstances are the existence of probable cause ($b = -2.92$), searches at borders ($b = -6.60$), breathalyzer testing ($b = -5.44$), searches during or after arrests ($b = 3.56$), and the taking of physical evidence ($b = -1.75$); the impact of all five is in the expected direction. The presence of four of the five variables decreases the likelihood that liberal justices will hand down a ruling in favour of the criminally accused, with the reduction in probability ranging from 60 to 41 percent for probable cause and physical evidence respectively (see Table 4.11). The variable generating the strongest change in the odds in the liberal equation involves searches taking place during or after an arrest, with liberal-leaning justices being 71 percent more likely to side with the defendant in such circumstances. Overall, these data not only suggest that justices at different ends of the ideological spectrum respond to some factual scenarios in different ways but also imply that case facts may be more significant for the decision making of liberal justices in the search and seizure area, whereas conservative justices are more animated by their ideological leanings than by case facts. This conclusion is reflected in the model fit statistics at the bottom of Table 4.11, which indicate that there is a 48 percent reduction in forecasting errors when predicting judicial votes with case facts for the liberal justices, compared with only an 18 percent reduction for their conservative counterparts. In short, the two wings of the Court are clearly motivated by different dimensions of the attitudinal model when resolving these types of claims – one being more rooted in ideology and the other more rooted in case facts.

Conclusion

The evidence presented in this chapter provides us with a good overarching understanding of judicial activity that has taken place in the criminal area in the first twenty years of *Charter* jurisprudence. Tables 4.1 to 4.5 indicate that panel sizes and rates of unanimity in the criminal area parallel those found across all other areas of law. The findings demonstrate that criminal cases do not produce greater degrees of conflict than other types of cases. The results also suggest that Justices Lamer and Cory acted as task leaders in the field of criminal law, which is illustrated by their high rates of authorship of majority opinions, while Justices L'Heureux-Dubé and Deschamps were clear outsiders in the criminal law area, willing to march to the beat of their own conservative and liberal drums, respectively. The tables also indicate that all the other justices were relatively evenly distributed in their ideological voting behaviour in the criminal area, and were relatively consistent in their ideological voting patterns over time. While the female justices did dissent more often than their male counterparts, their patterns of dissent cannot be attributed to a cohesive gender split in the area of criminal law. Our analysis of activist voting patterns uncovered evidence that will fuel the debate over judicial power in the Canadian literature, because we found that in the context of criminal cases, there is a connection between liberalism and activism in the Canadian post-*Charter* Court.

The rest of the chapter demonstrates that when justices on the Canadian Court decide cases in the right to counsel and search and seizure areas, judicial ideology is a prominent explanatory variable, even when controlling for a host of case characteristics. One of the most significant findings of this study is the impact of ideology in the regression models; it is the newspaper ideology measure and not the party identification measure that proves to be statistically significant in the expected direction. As indicated earlier, the estimates in the non-unanimous models suggest that the most liberal justices are 72 and 44 percent more likely than the most conservative justices to side with the individual in right to counsel and search and seizure cases, respectively. While this might seem a mundane result to US scholars, the finding that ideology matters so much in the Canadian criminal cases is striking. This result is significant because, as mentioned earlier, ideology is virtually ignored in many studies of the Canadian Court, primarily because many scholars believe that ideology has not played a pivotal role in the judicial appointment process in Canada. The results also indicate that in the search and seizure area, both ideological wings of the Court are influenced by factual variables, although the liberal wing appears far more attuned to the presence of specific case characteristics than their conservative counterparts. In the right to counsel area, both sides of the Court are much less prone to cast attitudinal votes in response to specific factual circumstances, but both criminal areas provide clear evidence that justices from opposite sides of the ideological continuum do indeed respond to different case facts in distinctive ways. Such a finding is of particular importance to public law scholars because it demonstrates for the first time the existence of an element of attitudinal complexity between the two ideological camps that has been missing in prior research on attitudinal voting behaviour. Overall, this chapter demonstrates that the full-fledged attitudinal model does an excellent job of explaining what drives conflict on the Canadian Court in prominent criminal disputes. As a result, the attitudinal framework that dominates accounts of US Supreme Court voting behaviour has considerable validity for explaining judicial activity in the Canadian criminal law context.

Understandably, critics of the attitudinal model might point out that criminal disputes present one of the easiest test cases for the model because the Canadian Court has relied heavily on US concepts in developing criminal due process jurisprudence. Moreover, criminal law disputes fit nicely in a liberal/conservative ideological continuum, which remains a central theoretical component of the attitudinal model. The question remains: Does the attitudinal model provide a useful account of voting disagreements in other areas of law? In subsequent chapters, we examine the applicability of the model in four other issue areas: equality and free speech cases, and economic disputes concerning labour/management conflicts and tax litigation. Only a set of rigorous tests across multiple areas will provide compelling evidence of the viability of attitudinal decision making in the post-*Charter* Canadian Court.

5
Attitudinal Conflict in Civil Rights and Liberties Cases

Not surprisingly, the Supreme Court of Canada experienced a deluge of rights litigation in the wake of the *Canadian Charter of Rights and Freedoms* that forced the justices to develop new legal principles in a host of civil rights and liberties areas. In the course of crafting new standards of rights jurisprudence, the justices were confronted with the possibility that new strains of ideological conflict, opinion leadership, and activist behaviour would emerge on the Court. As in Chapter 4, these themes are assessed in the first portion of this chapter, along with an overall assessment of judicial votes, ideological stability, and concurring and dissenting authorship in civil rights and liberties cases. The second half of the chapter then focuses on testing the attitudinal model in the subfields of discrimination and freedom of expression while controlling for various factual circumstances. These two areas were chosen for analysis because they provided us with a unique opportunity to examine politically salient issues and distinct areas of law that we believed the justices might approach in a different manner.

An initial examination of Table 5.1 reveals that in the first twenty years of post-*Charter* rulings, lawsuits in the civil rights and liberties area constituted an average of 12 percent of the Court's entire docket (see the bottom of Table 5.1). Although this percentage is much higher than that during the Court's twenty years under the 1960 statutory bill of rights, it is much lower than the percentage of the docket devoted to criminal law disputes (46 percent; see Table 4.1). The Court's caseload in this area remained fairly consistent across the first two post-*Charter* courts, although it has increased slightly to 15 percent during the first four years of Chief Justice McLachlin's tenure. As indicated in Chapter 4, the slight rise in these types of disputes has been accompanied by a slight drop in criminal cases during the same four-year period (2000–03).

Table 5.1 indicates that civil rights and liberties cases are more prone to generate conflict among the justices than other areas of law. Roughly a third of the cases in the civil rights and liberties area feature attitudinal disagreement (see the bottom of Table 5.1), compared with only a quarter in the criminal area and across all other cases. No one should be surprised that these cases generate a greater degree of judicial conflict, because they pertain to such salient fundamental human concerns that are central to contested notions of personal identity, human dignity, and individual self-fulfillment.

TABLE 5.1

Annual data on case volume, docket level, unanimity, and panel size in civil rights and liberties cases, 1984-2003

Year	Total cases argued	Percent non-unanimous all cases heard	Yearly average panel size	Percent of docket civil rights and liberties	Percent non-unanimous civil rights and liberties	Average panel size civil rights and liberties
1984	83	9.6	6.4	18.1	0.0	6.2
1985	86	22.1	7.1	9.3	25.0	7.8
1986	72	15.3	6.1	8.3	50.0	7.2
1987	96	26.0	6.0	10.4	40.0	6.1
1988	109	22.0	5.7	13.8	20.0	5.9
1989	131	23.7	6.5	13.7	38.9	7.0
1990	*113*	*28.3*	*6.7*	*8.0*	*22.2*	*7.4*
1991	*123*	*30.1*	*6.4*	*8.9*	*45.5*	*7.4*
1992	*107*	*16.8*	*6.1*	*7.5*	*37.5*	*6.4*
1993	*127*	*36.2*	*7.0*	*7.9*	*50.0*	*8.8*
1994	*110*	*25.5*	*7.5*	*14.5*	*37.5*	*8.3*
1995	*115*	*30.4*	*7.4*	*15.7*	*33.3*	*8.5*
1996	*111*	*24.3*	*7.2*	*13.5*	*20.0*	*8.9*
1997	*106*	*23.6*	*6.7*	*11.3*	*41.7*	*8.2*
1998	*104*	*26.9*	*7.0*	*8.7*	*33.3*	*7.9*
1999	*78*	*17.9*	*6.8*	*11.5*	*11.1*	*7.2*
2000	**77**	**32.5**	**7.6**	**11.7**	**44.4**	**8.1**
2001	**94**	**22.3**	**7.6**	**12.8**	**41.7**	**8.8**
2002	**68**	**25.0**	**7.9**	**14.7**	**30.0**	**9.0**
2003	**78**	**25.6**	**7.9**	**16.7**	**23.1**	**8.4**
Average	99	24.2	6.9	11.9	32.3	7.7
Std. dev.	19	6.1	0.6	3.2	13.2	1.0

NOTE: Justice Dickson's tenure as chief justice, from 1984 to June 1990, is shown in regular type; Chief Justice Lamer's tenure, from July 1990 to 1999, is shown in italic type; and the initial years of Chief Justice McLachlin's tenure, from 2000 to 2003, are shown in bold type.

Even though these cases have fostered greater dispute among the justices, the patterns of conflict have been fairly stable across all three post-*Charter* courts to date.

The data in Table 5.1 suggest that panel sizes for civil rights and liberties cases during the post-*Charter* era averaged 7.7 justices, which is slightly higher than the 6.9 average found across all post-*Charter* cases (see the bottoms of the "Average panel size, civil rights and liberties" and "Yearly average panel size" columns in Table 5.1). The finding that civil rights cases feature larger panels is in keeping with Justice Lamer's contention that he made a concerted effort to strike nine-member panels in cases of "general national importance" (Greene et al. 1998, 115). Since civil rights and liberties cases fit that description more frequently, it makes sense that the average panel size was almost one justice greater for this category of cases. Moreover, this statistic may help explain why greater disagreement emerged in these kinds of cases, because the more justices that hear a case, the greater the likelihood of conflict between them. This phenomenon, in turn, suggests that in high courts where the chief justice has discretionary control over panel size, he or she could have an important impact on the degree of attitudinal conflict among the justices. Even though how a chief justice goes about striking panels is vulnerable to the timing of court retirements and the failing health of individual justices (McCormick 2000, 126), it is worth noting that in the early years of her court, Chief Justice McLachlin has almost always struck nine member panels in civil rights and liberties disputes (8.1, 8.8, 9.0, and 8.4 for the years 2000 to 2003, respectively). She may be trying to ensure that such cases are heard by a full slate of justices in response to the recent criticism of the Court's activist rulings. Regardless of the motivation, it is fair to say that when chief justices tend to strike full panels in a given legal area, the odds that conflict will appear on the Court are increased.

Table 5.2 presents data on individual participation rates in civil rights and liberties cases, along with majority voting and opinion authorship patterns, for all justices during the 1984–2003 period.[1] These data help identify justices who are leaders, followers, and outsiders in the realm of civil rights and liberties. As in Table 4.2, the justices are ranked according to their frequency of writing majority opinions. Justice Dickson has the highest ranking at 29 percent, while Justices L'Heureux-Dubé and Le Dain produced the lowest rates, at 2 and 0 percent, respectively. The data in the "Percent writing majority opinion" column indicate that, unlike in the criminal law area, Chief Justice Dickson was a clear task leader on his own court when it came to authoring majority opinions in the civil rights and liberties area. His authorship rate is over 2 standard deviations beyond the average output for the other justices, and he is the only justice to pass this benchmark on the post-*Charter* Court. Justice Lamer, who was a task leader in criminal disputes, also exhibited task leadership qualities here, authoring majority opinions in over 20 percent of the 149 civil rights and liberties cases he heard. Although Justice Chouinard had the second highest majority authorship rate, his data are suspect because he participated in only 19 civil rights and liberties suits. The fact that Justices Lamer and Dickson emerged as task leaders in the civil rights and liberties area amplifies the point made in Chapter 4, namely, that a chief justice is more likely to take on a task leadership role on a court bearing his or her name (see Danelski 1989; McCormick 1993, 1994a). Furthermore, the prominence of these two justices as opinion leaders in the civil rights and liberties area is logical, given the high profile of such disputes in a democratic society that recently added a *Charter of Rights and Freedoms* to its Constitution. Justices Binnie, Estey, Gonthier, Major, and Le Dain can be categorized as followers in this area, since they joined the majority coalition over 88 percent of the time but authored majority opinions less than 9 percent of the time. Justices Wilson and L'Heureux-Dubé, on the other hand, were excluded from this category because both engaged in unique voting and opinion authorship patterns that set them apart from justices who simply "followed" the lead of others. Overall, the data in Table 5.2 reveal that some of the same justices who emerged as opinion leaders and followers in the criminal area – Lamer, Estey, and Gonthier – also played similar roles in the civil rights and liberties domain.

One should note that several of the female justices who engaged in distinctive judicial decision-making patterns in the criminal area did so here as well. For example, Justice Wilson's propensity to articulate her own legal approach is illustrated by her vigorous concurrence activity in civil rights and liberties disputes. Indeed, she wrote concurring opinions in 16 percent of the cases she heard, which is 2 standard deviations above the average for her colleagues (see the "Percent writing concurring opinion" column in Table 5.2). She also exhibited a rate of dissent that was twice the average of all the other justices (12 percent versus 5 percent). Only two other female justices on the Court matched or surpassed her rate of authoring dissenting opinions: Justices McLachlin and L'Heureux-Dubé (15 and 12 percent, respectively). One would not classify Justice Wilson as an outsider in the civil rights and liberties area because of her high concurrence rates, but Justices McLachlin

TABLE 5.2

Panel participation rates and opinion authorship patterns in civil rights and liberties cases with written reasons for judgment, 1984–2003

Justice	Number of cases	Percent majority votes	Percent writing majority opinion	Percent writing concurring opinion	Percent writing dissenting opinion
Dickson	73	94.5	28.8[a]	5.5	2.7
Chouinard	19	100.0	21.1	0.0	0.0
Lamer	149	94.6	20.1	8.7	2.0
LeBel	39	87.2	17.9	7.7	7.7
Cory	117	90.6	16.2	6.0	7.7
Bastarache	62	87.1	16.1	4.8	6.5
Sopinka	108	94.4	15.7	10.2	1.9
McIntyre	46	91.3	15.2	4.3	6.5
La Forest	136	91.2	14.7	11.8	5.9
Beetz	41	97.6	14.6	7.3	0.0
Deschamps	15	86.7	13.3	0.0	0.0
Iacobucci	141	92.2	12.8	2.1	2.8
McLachlin	157	82.8	12.7	8.3	14.6[a]
Arbour	48	91.7	10.4	2.1	2.1
Estey	24	95.8	8.3	4.2	4.2
Binnie	57	91.2	7.0	3.5	0.0
Gonthier	162	93.8	6.8	1.9	3.1
Major	124	87.9	5.6	2.4	4.0
Wilson	74	86.5	5.4	16.2[a]	12.2
L'Heureux-Dubé	165	77.6[a]	1.8	14.5	12.1
Le Dain	21	100.0	0.0	9.5	0.0
Average	84.7	91.2	12.6	6.2	4.6
Std. dev.	—	5.5	6.8	4.5	4.3

NOTE: Justices Fish and Stevenson are omitted from the table because they participated in ten or fewer cases, but their data are included here for comparative purposes: Stevenson, 10 cases, 100 percent majority votes, 10 percent majority opinions, no concurrences or dissents; Fish, 4 cases, 100 percent majority votes, no opinions authored.

a The justice's value on this indicator is 2 times the standard deviation from the mean value.

and L'Heureux-Dubé clearly fit the role of outsiders on the Lamer Court when it came to these cases (Ostberg, Wetstein, and Ducat 2004; Ducat and Flango 1976, 1985). Compared with other post-*Charter* justices, they were the least likely to vote in the majority and two of the most likely to author dissenting opinions. Justice McLachlin's pattern of dissent is no fluke, for it is 2 standard deviations beyond the mean for the rest of the justices. Collectively, these data indicate that most of the women on the post-*Charter* Court were comfortable blazing their own legal trail in civil rights and liberties disputes, suggesting that female justices on the Canadian Supreme Court may approach fundamental freedoms and equality issues from a different perspective than their male colleagues (see Gilligan 1982, 1987).

The percentage of liberal votes cast by the post-*Charter* justices provides another indication that the female justices take a different stance from their male counterparts in civil rights and liberties disputes (see Table 5.3). As in Chapter 4, the table categorizes the cases where a clear ideological vote can be defined, with liberal votes indicating support for a civil rights or liberties claim and conservative votes rejecting such a stance. Remarkably, all five female justices serving on the Court in the period studied can be found at the liberal end of the civil rights and liberties spectrum, with five of the six most liberal voting patterns on the Court (see Table 5.3). This suggests that the female justices as a group are more protective of underdogs and rights claimants than their male counterparts. This result is quite different from that found in the criminal area, where no distinctive, coherent feminist pattern emerged. Indeed, a reading of the cases in the civil rights and liberties field provides powerful evidence that the female justices have staked out a distinctive "ethic of care" approach to rights claimants and vulnerable interests in Canadian society (for examples, see *Egan v. Canada*, [1995] 2 S.C.R. 513; *Symes v. Canada*, [1993] 4 S.C.R. 695; *Hy and Zels Inc. v. Ontario (Attorney General)*, [1993] 3 S.C.R. 675; and *Rodriguez v. British Columbia (Attorney General)*, [1993] 3 S.C.R. 519). The language used in the opinions authored by these justices is in stark contrast to the "ethic of justice" position frequently advocated by their male counterparts. Whereas the "ethic of care" stance stresses the need to protect individuals and marginalized groups in society from discriminatory treatment, the "ethic of justice" position tends to frame legal issues in this area in the context of due process and an assessment of whether the procedures used by government seem reasonable (see Ostberg et al. 2002, 242-45). The approach taken by Justices Wilson, L'Heureux-Dubé, and McLachlin parallels nicely with the themes articulated in feminist literature – that women seek to foster meaningful relationships between individuals and groups, and are more interested than men in promoting community bonds and commitments to others (see Ostberg et al. 2002; Gilligan 1982, 1987; Lyons 1988; West 1991; MacKinnon 1993).

A perusal of Table 5.3 reveals that the average member of the post-*Charter* Court supported the rights claimant 50 percent of the time in this

TABLE 5.3

Liberal votes in civil rights and liberties cases with written reasons for judgment, 1984–2003

Justice	Number of cases where ideological direction can be identified	Percentage of liberal votes cast
Binnie	56	64.3
McLachlin	147	62.6
Wilson	65	61.5
Deschamps	15	60.0
L'Heureux-Dubé	153	57.5
Arbour	47	57.4
Bastarache	60	55.0
LeBel	38	52.6
Dickson	65	52.3
Cory	108	50.9
Iacobucci	135	48.9
Beetz	36	47.2
Major	116	46.6
Lamer	138	45.7
Estey	22	45.5
Gonthier	152	41.4
Sopinka	101	40.6
Le Dain	20	40.0
McIntyre	42	38.1
La Forest	124	37.1
Chouinard	18	33.3
Average	79.0	49.5
Std. dev.	49.3	9.1

area of law. Justices Cory and Iacobucci most readily occupied this centrist position, whereas Justice Binnie was the most likely to cast a liberal vote (64 percent) and Justice Chouinard the least likely to do so (33 percent). Chief Justices Lamer and Dickson, who emerged as task leaders in this area of law, tended to only moderately support the rights claimant, which parallels nicely the finding in the criminal context, where Justices Lamer and Cory served as task leaders from the ideological middle as well. With the exception of Justice Binnie, those labelled as opinion followers in Table 5.2 tended to cast moderate to conservative votes in the civil rights and liberties area (see the data for Justices Major, Estey, Gonthier, and Le Dain in Table 5.3). While the overall findings from Table 5.3 demonstrate that the female justices on the post-*Charter* Court are more liberal in the civil rights and liberties area, the question remains whether their liberal tendencies stand up when controlling for rival hypotheses. We address this question later in this chapter.

Table 5.4 provides data on rates of judicial activism in the civil rights and liberties area. Following the narrow interpretation of activism set out in Chapter 4, we focus only on the degree to which justices strike down statutes as unconstitutional in this area. The data show that Justices LeBel and McLachlin are the most activist members of the post-*Charter* Court in this issue area, voting to strike down laws half the time (see the "Percent of times a justice voted to nullify a law or portion of a law" column in Table 5.4).[2] Their rates of activism are just shy of 2 standard deviations beyond the average for all the post-*Charter* justices. Interestingly, Justices LeBel and McLachlin were much more deferential in the area of criminal law, where they voted to strike down laws only 24 and 18 percent of the time, respectively. In contrast, Justices Gonthier and Major, two of the most readily identifiable opinion followers in civil rights and liberties cases, were least likely to nullify statutes, and voted to do so less than 35 percent of the time (28 and 35 percent activist votes). Justice Gonthier's low rate of nullification is 2 standard deviations below the average, suggesting an extreme level of deference on his part. Having said this, most of the justices are clustered around the mean, casting activist votes between 35 and 44 percent of the time. The last column of Table 5.4 shows the percentage of activist votes cast when a justice was in the majority. It is interesting to note that the same two followers, Justices Gonthier and Major, almost always cast activist votes while in the majority (100 and 95 percent of the time, respectively). In contrast, Justices McLachlin and L'Heureux-Dubé were much less likely to cast activist votes while in the majority (69 and 62 percent of the time). These data further confirm their outsider status on the Lamer Court in the civil rights and liberties area.

The liberal justices on the post-*Charter* Court tended to be the activist justices in the realm of criminal law, and we were interested in whether this same trend would appear in civil rights and liberties cases. An examination of the weighted correlation between the two judicial ideology measures – newspaper liberalism and party of prime minister – and activism in the civil rights and liberties area reveals no significant connection between the two.[3] In other words, neither ideology measure proved to be significantly correlated with the percentage of activist votes handed down by the thirteen justices identified in Table 5.4 ($r = .320$ for newspaper liberalism, $p = .143$; $r = .317$ for party of prime minister, $p = .146$).[4] Thus, the findings in civil

TABLE 5.4

Patterns of judicial activism in civil rights and liberties cases, 1984–2003

Justice	Number of cases raising possibility of statute nullification	Percent of times (n) a justice voted to nullify a law or portion of law		Percent of activist votes (n) cast in majority	
LeBel	22	50.0	(11)	81.8	(9)
McLachlin	70	50.0	(35)	68.6	(24)
Binnie	27	44.4	(12)	83.3	(10)
L'Heureux-Dubé	63	41.3	(26)	61.5ª	(16)
Lamer	46	41.3	(19)	84.2	(16)
Arbour	27	40.7	(11)	81.8	(9)
Bastarache	28	39.3	(11)	81.8	(9)
La Forest	46	39.1	(18)	83.3	(15)
Sopinka	44	38.6	(17)	82.4	(14)
Iacobucci	65	36.9	(24)	87.5	(21)
Cory	42	35.7	(15)	86.7	(13)
Major	60	35.0	(21)	95.2	(20)
Gonthier	71	28.2ª	(20)	100.0	(20)
Average	47.0	40.0		82.9	
Std. dev.	17.5	5.9		9.8	

NOTE: Justices with ten or fewer cases are omitted from this table, but we provide their data here for those interested in complete information on the justices. We include the number of cases heard, the percentage of activist votes, and the percentage of those votes that were handed down in majority or concurring opinions. The data must be interpreted with caution, given the small number of cases heard. Dickson, 10, 40.0, 75.0; Wilson, 9, 44.4, 25.0; McIntyre and Beetz, 5, 80.0, 75.0; Chouinard and Le Dain, 4, 75.0, 66.7; Deschamps, 8, 62.5, 100.0; Estey, 2, 50.0, 0.0; Stevenson and Fish, 1, 0.0, and 0.0.
a The justice's value for this indicator is 2 times the standard deviation from the mean value.

rights and liberties cases suggest that justices at the conservative end of the ideological spectrum are nearly as likely as their liberal counterparts to hand down activist rulings. The fact that activism in this area of law does not run in lockstep with liberal ideological beliefs lends credence to scholarship indicating that activist and restraintist behaviour does not necessarily follow liberal/conservative lines.

In Table 5.5, we replicate the analysis of ideological stability that was explained in detail in Chapter 4, focusing, obviously, on patterns of voting in civil rights and liberties cases. Using the same techniques to control for changing Court membership, we present evidence of ideological stability and change for each justice over a six-year time period. The results in Table 5.5

indicate that six of the justices do exhibit substantial ideological change in the civil rights and liberties area in the time periods analyzed. For example, the results for Justice La Forest indicate that he increased his liberal voting behaviour by almost 21 percent in his first six years on the bench (see the "Change in voting" column), whereas his three-judge comparative cohort decreased their liberal support by 2 percentage points (see the "Change in continuing justices" column). Thus, the "Baum correction" (Baum 1988, 1992) reported in the last column demonstrates that Justice La Forest in-creased his support for the rights claimant by 23 percent over his first six years on the Court, which constitutes the largest net change in the liberal direction of all the justices in the table.

The overall findings also reveal that Justice Wilson experienced a 17 per-cent shift in the liberal direction, while Justices Binnie, Lamer, and Sopinka experienced similar transitions but in the opposite direction ideologically. The latter three justices became 24, 23, and 20 percent more conservative, respectively, when controlling for membership change and issue evolution on the Court. Justice McLachlin demonstrated the single largest ideological shift of any justice, becoming almost 27 percent more conservative in civil rights and liberties disputes in her first six years on the bench. This figure should be interpreted with caution, however, since she ruled in favour of the rights claimant in all the cases she heard in her first two years on the Court, and there was only one ideological direction that she could take in subse-quent years. Having said this, the fact that she handed down 27 percent more conservative rulings in civil rights and liberties cases is significant and indi-cates a clear ideological movement toward the centre in these cases as she matured on the Court.

The substantial ideological changes made by six justices in civil rights and liberties disputes stand in marked contrast to the relative attitudinal stability exhibited in the criminal area. These data are also quite different from the ideological patterns that have appeared in the postwar US Supreme Court in civil rights and liberties cases. For example, we conducted weighted bivariate regression tests on the career vote scores of US justices collected by Epstein et al. (1996, 451-55) and the newspaper ideology scores gathered by Segal and Cover (1989) to see how they would stack up against our post-*Charter* Canadian data. Our US tests essentially replicate what we presented in Chapter 3 for the Canadian justices (see Table 3.4). We found that the newspaper ideology score in the US accounted for over 50 percent of the variance in career liberalism scores in civil rights and liberties cases between

TABLE 5.5

Changes in ideological voting patterns by Supreme Court justices in civil rights and liberties cases when years 1 and 2 (T1) are compared with years 5 and 6 (T2)

Judge (votes T1, T2, number of continuing judges)	% liberal (T1)	% liberal (T2)	Change in voting	% liberal continuing justices (T1)	% liberal continuing justices (T2)	Change in continuing justices	Difference in value change
La Forest (11, 21, 3)	36.4	57.1	20.7	60.5	58.2	-2.3	23.0
Wilson (18, 28, 2)	66.7	57.1	-9.6	61.5	34.8	-26.7	17.1
Iacobucci (12, 29, 7)	41.7	31.0	-10.7	51.8	36.2	-15.6	4.9
Bastarache (12, 21, 5)	58.3	61.9	3.6	57.3	56.6	-0.7	4.3
Cory (18, 24, 6)	61.1	37.5	-23.6	61.1	36.2	-24.9	1.3
Dickson (22, 28, 2)	59.1	39.3	-19.8	65.7	45.7	-20.0	0.2
Gonthier (19, 24, 6)	47.4	20.8	-26.6	63.6	39.0	-24.6	-2.0
Major (22, 17, 6)	36.4	52.9	16.5	40.4	60.6	20.2	-3.7
L'Heureux-Dubé (15, 18, 2)	60.0	66.7	6.7	26.5	41.4	14.9	-8.2
Sopinka (19, 16, 3)	52.6	37.5	-15.1	45.7	51.0	5.3	-20.4
Lamer (17, 18, 2)	64.7	27.8	-36.9	62.5	48.2	-14.3	-22.6
Binnie (13, 22, 5)	84.6	63.6	-21.0	62.5	65.7	3.2	-24.2
McLachlin (11, 24, 6)	100.0	50.0	-50.0	57.4	34.0	-23.4	-26.6
Average	59.2	46.4	-12.8	55.1	46.7	-8.4	-4.4
Std. dev.	18.1	14.9	20.5	11.3	10.9	16.1	15.6

NOTE: Justices who appear to display significant ideological shifts from those serving as cohorts on the Court are identified in bold text. A simple rule of thumb was used: if the value difference exceeded 1 standard deviation (15.6) when comparing a justice's ideological change with the change score of other justices on the Court with him or her, that justice was highlighted as exhibiting a significant ideological change. Obviously, changes in ideological scores are more reliable when the comparison groups of justices are larger; thus, we have the most confidence in the change scores for justices McLachlin, Cory, Gonthier, Iacobucci, and Major. These change scores must be interpreted with caution, given the small number of civil rights and liberties cases decided during the years of interest.

1948 and 1994 (adjusted R^2 = .517), while our Canadian measure accounted for only 2 percent of the variance (adjusted R^2 = .019). Put simply, while ideology appears to have a powerful impact on US Supreme Court voting behaviour in civil rights and liberties cases, our results for Canada suggest that it has very little impact on the post-*Charter* Court. In light of these findings, and the meagre relationship between career activism and newspaper ideology in the Canadian context, it was doubtful that a full-fledged test of the attitudinal model would have the same relevance for the post-*Charter* justices in the civil rights and liberties area. Since the model assumes that attitudes are stable over time and are animated by a justice's ideological predispositions, the lack of strong evidence to support either of these propositions casts doubt on the model's relevance in such cases. Only a full-blown test of the attitudinal model, which controls for several rival variables at the same time, can resolve this question definitively, however.

Equality Cases

DATA AND METHODS

As with criminal law disputes, we tested the attitudinal model in two distinct types of civil rights and liberties disputes: discrimination claims and cases involving free speech issues. We chose these two sets of cases because they represent some of the most pivotal issues in the civil rights and liberties field. Moreover, classifying cases in this way enabled us to test the impact of specific case facts on the justices' voting behaviour. Cases were included in the equality area if individuals alleged that they had experienced discrimination by government or private interests on the basis of age, sex, disability, sexual orientation, religion, non-citizenship, and common law marital status; the suits frequently pertained to allegations of workplace discrimination, the denial of government benefits, or the lack of recognition of certain status rights under Canadian law.[5] Assuming that the attitudinal model is applicable in the equality realm, we expected ideology to be an important predictor of disagreement between members of the Canadian Supreme Court. The model also assessed the extent to which fact patterns explain disagreement between the justices, and whether justices were prone to favour the arguments advanced by the Women's Legal Education Action Fund (LEAF), a common civil rights intervenor. In addition, the model examined whether gender played a pivotal role in explaining Court conflict in discrimination cases, and controlled for whether a government was a party to the suit and for arguments heard by the McLachlin Court.[6]

As in Chapter 4, the data were taken from all equality decisions published in the *Canadian Supreme Court Reports* between 1984 and 2003 that contained written reasons for judgment. The analysis highlights 557 judicial votes drawn from a total of seventy-one equality rulings handed down during this period. Our second level of analysis, focusing on non-unanimous cases, highlighted 244 votes across thirty-one disputes.[7] In line with Chapter 4, the dependent variable was a dichotomous indicator identifying whether a justice cast a liberal or conservative vote. If a justice supported an individual's equality claim, we coded that vote as "1"; a rejection of the equality argument was coded as "0."

Three independent variables that were included in the model related to the characteristics of the justices: newspaper ideology, political party of the prime minister, and gender. The newspaper liberalism measure was derived from our analysis in Chapter 3, and we anticipated that justices who scored most positively on the liberalism scale (closest to +2) would be more likely to favour individuals who brought forth discrimination claims, while their conservative counterparts would tend to vote the opposite way. In keeping with Chapter 4 and earlier studies, it was expected that justices appointed by Liberal prime ministers (+1) would be more prone than their Conservative party cohorts (–1) to favour the equality claims brought by individuals.

The third judge-level variable, which we introduce for the first time, pertains to gender, with female justices coded as "1" and male justices receiving a score of "0."[8] This variable was included in the analysis because scholarship has suggested that men and women often perceive equality claims from starkly different perspectives. Feminist scholars, such as Carol Gilligan (1982), have argued that men and women approach moral and ethical dilemmas from different vantage points, with women much more interested in trying to strengthen social relationships between individuals (see Gilligan 1982, 1987; Lyons 1988; West 1991; MacKinnon 1993). As such, Gilligan (1987, 24) suggested that women remain committed to a more nurturing, "ethic of care" position that is "grounded in the assumption that [the] self and others are interdependent," and that there is a need to respect others on their own terms (see also Lyons 1988, 4). At the heart of this thesis is the belief that women are more interested than men in promoting the welfare of fellow citizens, and more committed to relieving the physical or psychological suffering of others (Lyons 1988, 35; Ostberg et al. 2002). Interestingly, Canadian Justice Bertha Wilson (1990, as cited in Morton 1992, 96) has argued that "there is merit in Gilligan's analysis," and the liberal voting patterns of female justices found in Table 5.3 support the notion that female justices on the Canadian Court speak "in a different voice." Given this contention, we think it was critical to include gender as an important variable in attitudinal models of decision making whenever the issues suggest that a gender gap might be relevant. Although some Canadian scholarship at the appellate court level has failed to find any differences in decision-making patterns between male and female judges (McCormick 1994b, 114), recent scholarship on the high court has indicated there are significant gender differences in civil rights and liberties disputes (White 1998; Songer and Johnson 2002). In line with such findings and feminist theory, we believed that gender would have particular relevance in the equality area, and that female justices on the post-*Charter* Court would be more likely than their male counterparts to rule in favour of individuals who have endured unequal treatment under the law. In light of our coding scheme for the gender of justices, we anticipated a positive coefficient for this variable in the regression equation.

We included ten case characteristics from the lower court record in our regression analysis because they typically appeared in the post-*Charter* equality disputes. These variables related to the kinds of discrimination suffered, whether multiple *Charter* issues appeared in the case, and whether a human rights commission had ruled on the issues as a first-level tribunal. The seven different forms of discrimination were coded as dichotomous variables ("1" if they appeared in a case, "0" otherwise), and these variables tap whether an individual alleged unfair treatment on the basis of age, sex, religion, disability, non-citizenship, sexual orientation, or marital status. Since the first five types of discrimination were outlawed in section 15 of the *Charter*, we believed that the justices would treat these forms of discrimination in a similar manner.[9] We anticipated that the coefficients for these five variables would not be radically different in size, but that they would be statistically significant in relation to marital status, which was omitted from the equation for comparative purposes. Marital status was singled out from the first five types of discrimination because it was not recognized as a protected classification under section 15 of the *Charter* and therefore lacked a constitutional profile. We also believed that justices would treat marital law cases differently because it is not typically seen as a hallmark of discriminatory treatment under the law. Ultimately, we expected the logistic model to generate positive coefficients of roughly equal magnitude for five of the discrimination variables in the equation.

Although sexual orientation is also not a protected class under section 15, we thought that the justices would treat this last form of discrimination differently from those based on marital status because gay rights disputes have come to represent a new frontier of equality litigation in contemporary Canadian society. This is borne out by the fact that an increasing number of gay rights disputes are on court dockets in Canada, and there has been a greater degree of media attention and political discourse devoted to the topic over the last two decades. Gays and lesbians have been turning to political institutions in record numbers seeking equal treatment in areas such as marriage, child custody and adoption, unfettered participation in the military, and retirement benefits. The federal government's formal recognition of the right of gays and lesbians to marry in 2005 may represent the crowning achievement of this movement to date. Given the elevated profile of gay rights issues in modern Canadian society, and a growing level of intolerance toward this kind of discrimination, we expected justices to have a heightened sensitivity to these types of struggles, and that the justices would treat these claims in a "quasi-constitutional" manner. In fact, the Court's decision to "read" sexual orientation into the *Charter* in *Egan v. Canada*, [1995] 2 S.C.R. 513 is a manifestation of this position. In light of these arguments, we expected the gay rights variable to produce a positive coefficient in the regression model (i.e., more favourable treatment than marital status claims).

Two case characteristic variables used in the analysis measured the type of economic harm suffered by the individual claimant. One type of injury pertained to whether an individual was denied various benefits; this was classified into a three-tiered hierarchy featuring the denial of government benefits at the top (scored as 2), followed by the denial of private benefits, such as insurance (scored as 1), and cases featuring no benefits at all (0). We expected that justices would be most supportive of individuals seeking equal access to governmental benefits, followed by individual claims against private entities, and least supportive in cases where no denial of benefits occurred. The rationale behind this contention is that justices would be more tolerant in situations where benefits were denied in the private marketplace rather than in the governmental sphere because governmental discrimination is anathema to the fundamental values of a democratic society. Given

Canada's traditional emphasis on the collective good and the promise of economic equality, however, we also expected the justices to be more inclined to protect individuals from harms caused by private entities than to find in their favour when there was no economic harm.

A second dichotomous variable in this category measured discrimination that resulted in a job loss or early retirement (1 = job loss cases or early retirement; 0 = all other cases). It was expected that justices would be more likely to support individuals in cases where they faced discrimination that resulted in a loss of employment than in all other types of cases because of the need to maintain a job to ensure one's economic survival and human dignity. Thus, when a lost job appeared as a case characteristic, we anticipated that the justices would hand down more favourable rulings for the individual being harmed, resulting in a positive coefficient for this variable.

Since many equality claims potentially feature other types of *Charter* infringements, another variable was created to assess whether justices would treat cases featuring multiple *Charter* breaches differently from cases involving just a section 15 violation. These two sets of cases, in turn, were set apart from cases that did not raise a *Charter* issue but rather were brought to court under federal or provincial statutes. This case characteristic was coded as a trichotomous variable (2 = cases featuring multiple *Charter* issues; 1 = cases featuring only a section 15 claim; 0 = all other non-*Charter* equality disputes). Given the expectation that justices would view a *Charter* breach with a more critical eye, it was expected that they would most likely rule in favour of an individual in cases raising multiple *Charter* issues, followed by those involving a section 15 infringement, and that they would be least supportive of equality claims grounded only in parliamentary or provincial statutory law. In line with this hierarchy, we anticipated a positive coefficient for the *Charter* variable in our model.

The last case characteristic variable in the regression model assessed whether the Supreme Court justices tended to defer to rulings handed down by human rights commissions (HRCs), which are often the first point of deliberation for Canadian equality disputes at the provincial or federal level. We anticipated that justices on the Court would be more likely to defer to such rulings, given the expertise such commissions have acquired in investigating the facts surrounding specialized discrimination complaints. We expected that the justices would be more inclined to vote liberally if a commission issued a ruling in favour of the individual and conservatively if the commission rejected the discrimination complaint. Although one might argue that justices on the highest court in the country may not be willing to defer to the rulings of a quasi-judicial agency, we believed that since such agencies were established as unique fact-finding bodies to investigate these particular kinds of disputes, justices would be more prone to follow their rulings than to follow the rulings of trial court judges in other areas of law. Consequently, the coding for this variable was +1 for liberal HRC rulings, 0 if there was no HRC decision, and −1 for conservative HRC rulings, and we expected a positive coefficient in the equation for this variable.

A third set of independent variables in the model pertained to various parties involved in the litigation. The first variable measured whether a government entity was a party in the dispute (1 = yes, 0 = no). It was hypothesized that the Canadian justices would be more likely to rule in favour of individuals who alleged discrimination at the hands of government than individuals who brought claims against a private entity, because societal norms dictate that in a democratic system, all individuals should be treated fairly by government agencies. Since notions of equality lie at the crux of all non-discrimination statutes, this principle remains central to the constitutional foundations of a democratic society like Canada. In contrast, since democracies place a high value on individual freedom and liberty in the *private* sector, we believed that citizens would be more tolerant of discriminatory treatment by private entities than by government agencies. Thus, we anticipated that justices would be more supportive of individual claims against governmental unfairness than claims against private acts of discrimination; we believed that a positive coefficient for the government variable would appear in the regression model.

A related but distinct party variable included in the equation identified whether a prominent feminist civil rights group (LEAF) intervened in the dispute. We included this variable because LEAF often intervened in equality cases, and we believed that when such intervention occurred, the justices would be more likely to rule in favour of the individual for several reasons. First, intervenors often provide justices with well-researched information that can offer additional justification for ruling in a party's favour. Second, since LEAF tends to intervene strategically, it has a remarkable success rate in obtaining support for its stances (see Manfredi 2004, Chapter 1). Third, since LEAF attorneys are "repeat players" in the judicial system, they have honed their skills and legal arguments to such an extent that they have consistently obtained rulings in their favour (see Galanter 1974, 2003; Manfredi 2004; Flemming and Kurtz 2002a, 2002b; Flemming 2004). Given the advantages that intervenors like LEAF possess, we anticipated a positive coefficient for this variable.

The last variable in the regression model tested for possible differences in the equality rulings handed down by the McLachlin Court. We included a dichotomous indicator for this court to assess whether the contemporary justices treat equality cases differently from their Dickson and Lamer Court predecessors. If the coefficient for this variable was positive and statistically significant it would suggest that the McLachlin Court as a whole had moved in a more liberal direction over time when resolving equality claims. Taken together, these sixteen variables were included in the model to explain as many of the ideological vote outcomes as possible, and to explore the relative importance of different types of indicators in an attitudinal model of decision making in the equality area.

RESULTS

All Equality Cases

As in our prior analyses, the test of the attitudinal model in the equality area utilized logistic regression based on a dichotomous measure of judicial voting behaviour (a value of "1" for a liberal vote or "0" for a conservative vote; see Aldrich and Nelson 1984). The model fit statistics at the bottom of Table 5.6 suggest that the equation provides a substantial explanation of judicial voting behaviour in equality cases on the Canadian Supreme Court. If one were to employ a guessing strategy expecting justices to always vote liberally across all equality cases, one would predict 53 percent of the votes accurately. When the sixteen independent variables are included in the equation, one is able to predict the voting decisions of the justices correctly 73 percent of the time, which represents a 42 percent improvement over the modal guessing strategy. Overall, the results suggest that the judicial ideology and background variables, along with case-level characteristics, the parties involved, and court control measures help explain a substantial degree of variance in equality cases decided by the Canadian Supreme Court in the post-*Charter* era.

Turning to the measures of judicial ideology in the equation, one should realize that the newspaper ideology measure is not a statistically significant predictor of vote outcomes in equality cases. The coefficient for this variable is 0.10, and the probability calculations on the right side of Table 5.6 indicate that justices with the most liberal ideology scores are only 10 percent more likely than their conservative counterparts to rule in favour of the rights

TABLE 5.6

Logistic regression estimates of liberal votes in all equality cases, 1984–2003

Variable	b	Statistical significance	Probability of liberal vote when x is low	Probability of liberal vote when x is high	Change in probability
JUDGE-LEVEL VARIABLES					
Ideology	0.102	.226	.476	.577	.101
Party of prime minister	0.094	.207	.524	.570	.046
Female justice	1.142	.000***	.466	.732	.266
CASE CHARACTERISTICS[a]					
Age discrimination	−0.548	.063	.571	.435	−.136
Sex discrimination	−0.426	.067	.568	.462	−.106
Religious discrimination	0.885	.020*	.519	.723	.204
Disability discrimination	0.417	.087	.514	.616	.102
Citizenship discrimination	0.636	.081	.531	.681	.150
Gay discrimination	0.713	.047*	.527	.694	.167
Benefits	−0.195	.099	.559	.462	−.097
Job loss	0.081	.398	.534	.554	.020
Charter issues	−0.947	.000***	.700	.260	−.440
HR commission ruling	−0.373	.025*	.644	.462	−.182
PARTIES AND INTERVENORS					
Govt. is a party	−0.632	.010**	.658	.505	−.153
LEAF intervenor	1.012	.001***	.501	.734	.233
COURT CONTROL VARIABLES					
Lamer Court[b]	—	—	—	—	—
McLachlin Court	1.155	.000***	.483	.748	.265
CONSTANT AND MODEL FIT STATISTICS					
Constant	0.718				
−2 LLR chi-square		628.042***			
Nagelkerke R^2		.301			
Percent correct		72.7%			
Reduction in error		42.1%			

NOTE: $N = 557$.

a Family law is omitted from the equation because it appeared infrequently in the dataset.

b The Lamer Court indicator is omitted from the equation because of high collinearity with the McLachlin Court.

* $p < .05$, ** $p < .01$, *** $p < .001$

claimant. The coefficient for the party of prime minister variable, although in the expected direction, has even less of an impact on judicial voting patterns (b = 0.09, probability change of 5 percent). These results suggest that neither of the ideology measures is able to capture significant elements of the voting variance in discrimination cases; they provide a stark contrast to the impact of the newspaper ideology indicator in both areas of criminal law reported in Chapter 4.

One of the most remarkable findings in Table 5.6 is the powerful impact that the gender of the justice has on voting behaviour across all equality cases. Indeed, when controlling for all other variables in the equation, gender is the second most powerful predictor of judicial decisions in these cases, with a coefficient of 1.14 (significant at the 99.9 percent confidence level). Ultimately, the female justices serving on the post-*Charter* Court are 27 percent more likely than their male brethren to rule in favour of discrimination claimants. This demonstrates that in cases involving various types of discrimination, the gender of the justice matters in a profound way, and women on the Canadian Court, regardless of their ideological proclivities, do indeed speak "in a different voice" from their male colleagues. This is a remarkable finding because it emphasizes the sensitivity that female justices have toward discrimination claims in the post-*Charter* Canadian context, and suggests that if there is an increase in the number of women appointed to the high court, it could have a significant impact on the outcome of these kinds of cases (see White 1998 and Songer and Johnson 2002 for a parallel argument).

Turning to the seven different areas of discrimination, religious and gay rights cases were the only types of litigation treated by the justices in a statistically different manner from marital status claims. The positive coefficients for these variables were anticipated, and indicate that religious and gay rights claims were treated more favourably by the justices than any other type of discrimination suit (b = 0.89 for religion, b = 0.71 for gay rights, both significant at the 95 percent confidence level). The results show that the justices are 20 and 17 percent more likely to side with religious and gay rights claimants facing unfair treatment than with those alleging marital status bias. Two unanimous cases pertaining to religious rights demonstrate the Court's proclivity in this area (*Ontario Human Rights Commission v. Simpsons-Sears*, [1985] 2 S.C.R. 536, and *Commission Scolaire Regionale de Chambly v. Bergevin*, [1994] 2 S.C.R. 525). In these cases, the Court ruled that the employers had unlawfully discriminated against the appellants by requiring one to work on the Sabbath (in *Simpsons-Sears*) and the other on a religious holiday (in *Bergevin*), in violation of provincial human rights codes. The Supreme Court's favourable disposition toward gay rights claimants, in turn, may be best illustrated by *Vriend v. Alberta,* [1998] 1 S.C.R. 493, where the Court struck down an Alberta law because the legislation had failed to prohibit job discrimination on the basis of sexual orientation. The Court's ruling in this latter case sparked much criticism from scholars, journalists, and court watchers because it reflected naked judicial activism at the expense of provincial sovereignty (see Morton and Knopff 2000). The results presented here indicate, however, that *Vriend* exemplifies a larger trend by the Court to extend equal protections to homo-sexuals in the post-*Charter* era, and both gay and religious discrimination claims have attained a higher degree of protection than other forms of bias recognized in the *Charter.*[10]

Two of the remaining four factual variables in the model for all equality cases are significant, although both coefficients are in the unexpected direction ($b = -0.95$ for *Charter* issues, significant at the 99.9 percent confidence level; $b = -0.37$ for human rights commission rulings, significant at the 95 percent confidence level). The change in probability score for the *Charter* variable suggests that when two or more *Charter* issues are present in a dispute, justices are 44 percent *less* likely to rule in favour of the rights claimant than in cases where no *Charter* provision is involved. Although this finding is surprising initially, it becomes more understandable if one recognizes that cases featuring multiple *Charter* claims may push the constitutional envelope beyond the justices' comfort level. A prominent example of this *Charter* impact might be found in *Rodriguez v. British Columbia (Attorney General),* [1993] 3 S.C.R. 519, where the majority of the Court rejected the argument that several provisions of the *Charter* could be utilized by terminally ill patients to justify a legal right to assisted suicide. The change in probability score for the human rights commission indicator is also in the negative direction, demonstrating that the justices are 18 percent *less* likely to hand down a liberal decision when an HRC has issued such a ruling. Although this coefficient runs contrary to expectations, it may simply reflect the fact that the justices feel eminently qualified to rule on prominent equality disputes and do not feel the need to defer to these specialized human rights tribunals. The other two factual variables in the model, benefits and job loss, are not statistically significant, and only job loss has a coefficient in the anticipated direction. As such, neither the loss of a job nor the reduction or loss of benefits triggers strong attitudinal responses on the part of the justices in equality cases, all other things being equal.

The three remaining variables tapping government participation, LEAF intervention, and the McLachlin Court are all statistically significant at or beyond the 99 percent confidence level. When a government entity is involved in the suit, the justices are 15 percent less likely to rule in favour the rights claimant ($b = -0.63$). Although this result is contrary to our hypothesis, it bolsters the claim made by some scholars that since government attorneys are repeat players in the legal system, they are more successful than one-shot litigants at winning cases (see Galanter 1974; Kritzer 2003). In contrast, the LEAF coefficient is in the expected direction, suggesting that the justices are 23 percent more likely to rule in favour of the rights litigant when LEAF intervenes in the dispute. Clearly, the arguments presented by LEAF attorneys have a profound impact on the minds of the justices, and their success is evident in cases like *Andrews v. Law Society of British Columbia*, [1989] 1 S.C.R. 143; *Thibaudeau v. Canada*, [1995] 2 S.C.R. 627; *Vriend v. Alberta*, [1998] 1 S.C.R. 493; *M. v. H.*, [1999] 2 S.C.R. 3; and *Little Sisters Book and Art Emporium v. Canada (Minister of Justice)*, [2000] 2 S.C.R. 1120. Our finding across all equality cases parallels recent scholarship by Manfredi (2004, 33), who has maintained that LEAF has been an important catalyst for feminist activism by the modern Canadian Supreme Court. The control variable for the McLachlin Court shows that the contemporary justices are 27 percent more likely to rule in favour of equality interests than their predecessors on the Dickson and Lamer Courts ($b = 1.16$). One of the best examples of this libertarian trend of the McLachlin Court is the majority ruling in the *Little Sisters* case. Although the Court acknowledged that customs officials had the authority to deny the importation of obscene pornographic material, it struck down the reverse onus provision in the *Customs Act*, which required the importer to prove that the material was not obscene. In short, the majority ruled that the bookstore owner had a *Charter* right to receive literary erotica unless the state could justify its denial. In reaching this conclusion, the majority was quick to criticize customs officials for unfairly targeting a gay and lesbian shop that trafficked in erotic material. This ruling, and other empirical data in our study, squares nicely with recent scholarship suggesting that the contemporary Canadian Court is moving in a decisively activist direction (see Morton and Knopff 2000).

The findings across all equality cases indicate that our sixteen-variable model is able to predict 73 percent of the votes, which falls between the predictive power found across all search and seizure and right to counsel cases (78 and 70 percent, respectively). The model for equality cases had the most reduction of error of the three large models presented so far (42 percent improvement), which suggests that the critical factors driving the voting patterns of the justices are easier to identify in this area of law. What is remarkable is that ideology plays a negligible role in explaining the votes of the justices, which does not inspire confidence that attitudinal decision making plays a salient role in the civil rights and liberties area within this cultural context. Instead, other variables such as *Charter* issues, parties, litigants, and the McLachlin Court control provided greater explanatory power in the model. Beyond these factors, the gender of a justice plays a dramatic role in forecasting liberal or conservative votes on the Canadian Court in equality cases. Put simply, female justices speak to the victims of discrimination in a profoundly different, and more liberal, voice than their male brethren. Given the substantial explanatory power of this model, one wonders whether any additional variance in the voting behaviour can be explained when focusing on equality disputes where the justices disagree. Moreover, do the same critical variables emerge as prominent predictors of ideological voting in non-unanimous cases? The results in Table 5.7 address these questions.

Non-Unanimous Equality Cases

The model for non-unanimous equality cases features the same sixteen variables, with the addition of one new indicator for family law cases because of the theoretical importance that this variable might provide to the model.[11] We believed the justices would be far less sensitive to claims of bias in the family law area because they are not typically perceived as a hallmark form of discrimination, at least compared with those relating to job loss, retirement income, or the denial of government benefits to an individual. Thus, it was hypothesized that the justices would be less likely to favour individuals in such cases than in cases involving other types of discrimination, and we anticipated a negative coefficient for this variable in the regression model.

The results in Table 5.7 indicate that there is a substantial boost in the ability to predict the justices' votes when they disagree in equality disputes. Indeed, our second level of analysis accurately forecast 81 percent of the votes, with a 54 percent reduction in error over the modal guessing strategy (see the bottom of Table 5.7). The non-unanimous model increases the accuracy of prediction by 8 percentage points, a pattern of improvement that parallels that found in the right to counsel area. Although this makes intuitive sense because one would expect unanimous rulings to water down the overall predictive accuracy across all cases, it is interesting to note these are the only two

TABLE 5.7

Logistic regression estimates of liberal votes in non-unanimous equality cases, 1984–2003

Variable	b	Statistical significance	Probability of liberal vote when x is low	Probability of liberal vote when x is high	Change in probability
JUDGE-LEVEL VARIABLES					
Ideology	0.366	.061	.212	.538	.326
Party of prime minister	−0.188	.186	.428	.339	−.089
Female justice	2.429	.000***	.256	.796	.540
CASE CHARACTERISTICS					
Age discrimination	0.416	.257	.374	.476	.102
Sex discrimination	0.138	.389	.390	.423	.033
Religious discrimination	0.148	.441	.399	.435	.036
Disability discrimination	1.122	.049*	.365	.638	.273
Citizenship discrimination	0.692	.166	.387	.557	.170
Gay discrimination	1.526	.009**	.340	.704	.364
Benefits	0.041	.446	.398	.418	.020
Job loss	0.494	.206	.373	.494	.121
Family law case	−0.980	.091	.426	.218	−.208
Charter issues	−0.052	.447	.413	.388	−.025
HR commission ruling	−0.294	.273	.488	.346	−.142
PARTIES AND INTERVENORS					
Govt. is a party	−.989	.019*	.591	.349	−.242
LEAF intervenor	1.653	.007**	.340	.729	.389
COURT CONTROL VARIABLES					
Lamer Court [a]	—	—	—	—	—
McLachlin Court	0.891	.032*	.344	.561	.217
CONSTANT AND MODEL FIT STATISTICS					
Constant	−1.659				
−2 LLR chi-square		236.896***			
Nagelkerke R^2		.431			
Percent correct		81.1%			
Reduction in error		54.3%			

NOTE: N = 244.

a   The Lamer Court indicator is omitted from this equation because of high collinearity with the McLachlin Court.

* $p < .05$, ** $p < .01$, *** $p < .001$

areas of law where such a rate of improvement emerges across all the models in the study.

The results in Table 5.7 show that five of the eight variables that are statistically significant across all equality cases are also significant when there is disagreement on the Court. The magnitude of some of the critical variables has increased substantially, however. For example, the impact of the gender of the justice doubled, with female justices 54 percent more likely than their male counterparts to hand down a liberal ruling when they disagree (b = 2.43, significant at the 99.9 percent confidence level). The change in odds value is twice the size of the 27 percent value found in the larger model. A similar pattern emerges in gay discrimination cases, with the justices 36 percent more likely to hand down a liberal ruling compared with non-unanimous marital status claims (b = 1.53, significant at the 99 percent confidence level). Likewise, the impacts for the government and LEAF indicators also increase, with justices 9 percent more likely to side with the government in contested cases, and 16 percent more likely to vote with rights claimants when LEAF intervenes (see the values in the last column of Tables 5.6 and 5.7). While the justices are also more likely to treat disability claims more liberally in non-unanimous disputes (b = 1.12, significant the 95 percent confidence level), the impact of this variable replaces that of religious discrimination from the larger model. This suggests that when members of the Court are at odds with each other, they are significantly more likely to hand down a liberal ruling in cases highlighting disability claims than in those dealing with religious prejudice. This change in variables can be attributed to the different makeup of the cases found in the set of non-unanimous disputes. The coefficient highlighting the distinctive impact of the McLachlin Court justices remains fairly constant, suggesting that they are 22 percent more likely to vote liberally in equality cases than their Dickson and Lamer Court predecessors.

Although the ideology coefficient remains insignificant when the justices are at odds in equality suits, the gap in liberal voting between the two ideological extremes of the Court has increased by 23 percentage points (from 10 to 33 percent; see the last column of Tables 5.6 and 5.7). In fact, the variable's prominence as a predictor of voting patterns has jumped from thirteenth place in the larger model to fourth, indicating that ideology does matter more when the justices are at odds in equality disputes. Since attitudinal theorists contend that ideology is the primary force that drives judicial

voting, it is remarkable that this variable plays such a muted role in contentious discrimination cases, taking a backseat to variables such as gender, interest group participation, and suits where gay rights are at issue. Scholars
familiar with the US Supreme Court would expect ideology to play the most
critical role in the civil rights and liberties area because such cases tend to
strike such an emotional chord in the minds of the justices. The fact that
ideology plays a much less prominent role in Canadian equality claims than
in right to counsel and search and seizure disputes suggests that this variable
may have a much more nuanced and distinctive impact in the Canadian
setting. This raises questions about the attitudinal model's utility as a global
theory for explaining judicial behaviour in different cultural contexts.

Even though the remaining case facts in our model did not prove to be
statistically significant, this finding in and of itself is important, because it
demonstrates that in contested equality disputes, case facts are frequently
trumped by the gender of the justices. Moreover, since ideology is not statistically significant in this model, we did not see a need to assess whether
justices at the two ends of the ideological spectrum treat case facts differently.
It remains to be seen, however, whether ideology plays a more salient or
dominant role in free speech cases.

Free Speech Cases

DATA AND METHODS

In this section, we turn to an analysis of forty-four free speech cases decided
between 1984 and 2003.[12] The cases featured a total of 329 judge votes that
highlight possible attitudinal differences in the Court. The second level of
analysis then focuses on seventeen non-unanimous cases featuring 116 judicial votes. As in previous tests of the attitudinal model, the dependent variable is a dichotomous indicator denoting whether a justice cast a liberal vote
in favour of the litigant's free expression rights (1 = liberal vote) or a conservative vote restricting such a right (0 = conservative vote). We chose to focus
on free speech claims because they comprise the largest subset of fundamental freedoms rulings, representing more than half of the votes cast in this area
of law.

The model analyzing all free speech cases included a total of fourteen
independent variables. Twelve pertained to ideology and judge-level traits,
case facts, such as the type of speech involved, and parties and intervenors;
the other two were court control variables. As in our prior models, the two

ideology variables in the equation consisted of the newspaper ideology score and the party of prime minister variable; it was expected that justices who had the highest score on both indicators would cast the most liberal votes. A third judge-level variable pertained to whether a justice had had significant experience as a law professor. In line with earlier research by Tate and Sittiwong (1989), we anticipated that justices who came from an academic setting could be expected to take a more liberal approach to free expression claims than their colleagues who came from corporate private practice. This hypothesis is based on the belief that justices who served as law professors earlier in their careers would be more prone to champion a litigant's right to free expression, given their greater openness to the argument that a free-flowing exchange of ideas is needed in both the classroom and society to aid in the search for truth and the advancement of knowledge. This variable was operationalized as a trichotomous indicator because several justices had served as part-time faculty only, and so we believed that their socializing experience would be less pronounced. Justices who had served as full-time professors were coded as "2," those who had served as part-time faculty were coded as "1," and all others were coded as "0." We also believed that female justices on the Canadian Court (+1) would be more supportive of free expression claims than their male counterparts (0) because they were likely to be more sympathetic to the pleas of various disadvantaged and marginalized groups who seek a voice in the marketplace of ideas and the political arena. Moreover, we expected female justices to be more supportive of corporate speech claims, because the feminist literature suggests that women are more likely than their brethren to foster an open dialogue in an effort to resolve conflicts, which may translate into a greater preference for free speech claims by all groups, including business and media interests (Lyons 1988; MacKinnon 1993; West 1991). For the law professor and female justice indicators, we expected positive coefficients in the regression results.

Three of the five factual variables in the model dealt with the type of speech involved: political speech, commercial advertising, and obscenity. Each variable was dichotomous and had a value of "1" if it appeared in the dispute and "0" otherwise. We excluded libel/slander and hate speech cases from the equation for comparison purposes, and anticipated a rank-ordered set of coefficients, with political speech expected to receive the most protection from the justices, followed closely by commercial advertising, and then obscenity. Our hypothesis borrows from the theoretical work of Emerson (1970), which stipulates that political speech is the most sacred form of expression because of its importance to maintaining a free and democratic society. We also believed that commercial advertising would be seen as important, although less so, by the justices because it is necessary for promoting good decision making by consumers and producers in a free market economy. Lastly, we expected the justices to be least protective of obscenity because of its remoteness from core democratic values. Since some would contend that it is not as harmful to individuals in the community as libel, slander, and hate speech, we expected a positive coefficient in the equation.

The two other case characteristics in the model pertain to whether a criminal charge was filed in the free speech case and whether the majority of the Court engaged in section 1 analysis to determine whether the infringement is "demonstrably justified in a free and democratic society." We hypothesized that when police brought criminal charges against an individual for expressive activities, such as the solicitation of prostitution, the justices would extend less protection to individuals than in cases not featuring criminal charges (1 = cases with criminal charges, 0 = all other cases). In line with this hypothesis, we expected a negative coefficient for this variable. In contrast, we expected that in cases where the justices found a fundamental freedoms violation and moved to the second stage of *Charter* analysis under section 1, they would be more likely to rule in favour of the *Charter* claimant, given the fundamental nature and salience of such rights in securing and maintaining a democratic society. We expected this indicator to produce a positive coefficient in the equation.

A third set of independent dichotomous variables examined the parties and intervenors involved in the suit, and they assess the relative power of repeat players and one-shot litigants in the legal system. The first variable examined whether an individual bringing a free speech claim received favourable treatment under the *Charter* compared with corporations, unions, or media agencies bringing claims (1 = individuals, 0 = all other types of litigants). Although one might expect the justices to hand down rulings in favour of individuals, as Galanter (1974, 2003) has demonstrated, individuals are bound to be at a distinct disadvantage when litigating complex disputes in the adversarial system, since they frequently do not have the resources or expertise of repeat players (see also McCormick 1993; Songer et al. 2003; Baum 1997; Brodie 2002; Flemming 2004; Kritzer 2003; Flemming and Kurtz 2002a, 2002b). Thus, we hypothesized that justices would be less likely to favour individual rights claimants, and that the coefficient for this variable would be negative. In contrast, since the Canadian Civil Liberties Association

(CCLA) is a frequent intervenor in free speech cases and is likely to gain the attention of the justices, we hypothesized a positive coefficient for this variable (1 = cases where the CCLA intervened, 0 = all other cases). The last party variable examined whether provincial government lawyers are treated differently from federal government lawyers.[13] Since federal government lawyers are the most frequent litigators appearing before the Court, we expected them to have higher success rates as repeat players than their provincial counterparts. Taking all cases into consideration, we expected the province variable to have a positive coefficient because we believed that rights claimants would have better odds of winning against a province than against the federal government and other repeat litigators.

The last two variables in the equation assessed possible differences between the Dickson, Lamer, and McLachlin Courts in the free speech area. These dichotomous variables were coded as "1" if a case was argued before a particular court and "0" otherwise; in line with our prior models, we omitted the Dickson Court measure for comparison purposes. These control variables were included to determine whether the Lamer and McLachlin Courts tended to be more liberal than the Dickson Court in this area of law. If either of these variables produced statistically significant positive coefficients, it would confirm that the entire set of justices has become more liberal over time, even when controlling for the ideological leanings of the individual justices and specific case circumstances. One might speculate that if this liberal shift were to occur on the Lamer and McLachlin Courts among both liberal and conservative justices, it might reflect larger value changes taking place in Canadian society and provide evidence that the voting patterns of the justices are in step with that change.

RESULTS

All Free Speech Cases

The logistic regression results for all free speech cases presented in Table 5.8 provide a robust model that accurately accounts for 71 percent of the justices' voting behaviour. This is a 36 percent improvement over the modal guessing strategy, which would correctly predict a liberal vote 54 percent of the time. Five of the fourteen variables in the equation are statistically significant at or beyond the 95 percent confidence level. Taken together, the results suggest that the model provides a healthy explanation of liberal/conservative voting patterns in this area of law, and the model's overall explanatory power is only slightly less than that found in the equality equation (71 percent in free speech and 73 percent in equality cases).

One of the most intriguing findings from the model is that neither newspaper ideology nor the party of prime minister is a statistically significant predictor of judicial voting behaviour in the free expression cases. Indeed, the coefficients for both variables are in the unexpected direction, and suggest that while controlling for all other factors, liberal justices on the post-*Charter* Canadian Court are slightly more likely than their conservative counterparts to rule *against* the rights claimant ($b = -0.07$ for newspaper ideology, -0.19 for party of prime minister). What makes this all the more remarkable is that judicial scholars in the US context would expect these types of cases to be among the first to generate sizable and stable ideological divisions in the Court. Indeed, US scholars have found that First Amendment jurisprudence remains a prominent area of ideological contention between different blocs of the US Supreme Court, particularly since the Warren era, when civil rights and liberties disputes became one of the most salient issues on the docket (for data, see Epstein et al. 1996, 88-92). Our findings here indicate that although ideology is a reliable predictor of US Supreme Court voting behaviour in the free speech area, this ideological schism is not found in the modern Canadian context. This result parallels our findings in the equality area; collectively, these two areas do not exhibit the ideological division that is so prominent in the field of criminal law.[14]

In contrast to the findings in the equality area, female justices on the Canadian Court are not significantly more likely than their male colleagues to side with the rights claimant in free speech cases ($b = 0.47$). The results in the last column of Table 5.8 indicate that female justices are only 12 percent more likely than their male counterparts to cast a liberal vote in such cases, which is substantially less than the 27-point gap found in discrimination disputes. Thus, when all other things are held constant, female justices approach free speech cases from a perspective remarkably similar to that of their male colleagues. The last judge-level variable – whether the justices had academic experience – also failed to achieve statistical significance ($b = 0.09$), and the change in probability score indicates only a 5 percent difference between justices with full-time academic experience in their background and those with none.

Three of the five case characteristics in the model are statistically significant at or beyond the 95 percent confidence level, with two of the three pertaining to the type of speech involved in the case. As expected, the justices

TABLE 5.8

Logistic regression estimates of liberal votes in all free speech cases, 1984–2003

Variable	b	Statistical significance	Probability of liberal vote when x is low	Probability of liberal vote when x is high	Change in probability
JUDGE-LEVEL VARIABLES					
Ideology	−0.071	.351	.597	.527	−.070
Party of prime minister	−0.190	.104	.587	.493	−.094
Female justice	0.473	.071	.521	.636	.115
Law professor	0.092	.259	.530	.575	.045
CASE CHARACTERISTICS					
Criminal charge	−0.239	.292	.575	.516	−.059
Advertising case	1.407	.003**	.506	.807	.301
Obscenity case	0.670	.049*	.512	.673	.161
Political speech case	0.631	.085	.535	.684	.149
Section 1 analysis	1.199	.000***	.365	.656	.291
PARTIES AND INTERVENORS					
Individual rights claim	−0.930	.004**	.693	.471	−.222
CCLA intervenor	−0.196	.269	.569	.521	−.048
Provincial government	−0.757	.013*	.592	.405	−.187
COURT CONTROL VARIABLES					
Lamer Court	0.523	.078	.498	.626	.128
McLachlin Court	0.318	.233	.534	.612	.078
CONSTANT AND MODEL FIT STATISTICS					
Constant	−0.588				
−2 LLR chi-square		400.166***			
Nagelkerke R^2		.202			
Percent correct		70.5%			
Reduction in error		36.1%			

NOTE: $N = 329$.
* $p < .05$, ** $p < .01$, *** $p < .001$

treat political speech, commercial advertising, and obscenity cases more favourably than hate speech or libel/slander claims, although only advertising and obscenity cases feature significant coefficients (b = 1.41 and 0.67, respectively). When commercial advertising was at issue, the justices were 30 percent more likely to endorse free speech values than when the cases involved libel or hate speech claims. Two salient cases that illustrate the Court's general endorsement of the right of companies to advertise are *Ford v. Quebec (Attorney General)*, [1988] 2 S.C.R. 712 and *RJR-MacDonald Inc. v. Canada (Attorney General)*, [1995] 3 S.C.R. 199. In *Ford*, the Court overturned a Quebec law that required public signs and ads to be printed only in French because it violated an individual's right to use the language of one's choice. Similarly, in *RJR-MacDonald*, the majority ruled that a total prohibition against cigarette advertising violated the company's right to free expression. Taken together, these cases reflect the Court's commitment to promoting free expression in the marketplace of ideas.

The Court also showed a greater willingness to safeguard free speech in the obscenity area than in situations involving hate speech and slander, perhaps because the latter forms of expression are more clearly linked to a purposeful intent to harm others. As expected, however, obscenity received a lower rate of protection than commercial advertising. The odds that the justices would favour free speech arguments in obscenity cases were 16 percent higher than in hate speech and slander cases. The majority ruling in *Little Sisters Book and Art Emporium v. Canada (Minister of Justice)*, [2000] 2 S.C.R. 1120 provides an example of this more favourable treatment of obscene materials. Another example is found in the case of *Saint-Romuald v. Olivier* [2001] 2 S.C.R. 898, where the Court ruled that a nightclub owner could substitute nude dancers for western singers because the switch was not an extreme departure from the nightclub's prior activities and did not constitute a wholly different type of entertainment that would justify governmental restriction. These results indicate that when all things are held constant, the justices do not consider obscenity and nudity as distasteful and harmful to society as the pernicious effects of libel and hate speech.

While advertising and obscenity fit the ranking set out in our hypothesis, political speech cases place an unexpected third in the hierarchy, although the coefficient is in the expected direction ($b = 0.63$). The results indicate that justices are only 15 percent more likely to side with the rights claimant in political speech cases (compared with hate speech and libel), and the value is exactly half the magnitude found in the advertising area. Although the Court does not appear to treat political speech much differently from obscenity cases, most scholars would acknowledge that the smaller coefficient for this variable is surprising in a country where political expression is critical to maintaining a free and democratic society. While these findings are a bit confounding, the rulings by the Court in two salient cases in this area help explain this anomaly. In *Native Women's Association of Canada v. Canada*, [1994] 3 S.C.R. 627, the Court unanimously determined that a denial of federal funding to a Native women's organization that was seeking to participate in constitutional reform discussions did not violate their right to free expression under the *Charter*. Clearly, this case exemplifies an effort by a minority group to try to force government to finance a group's supposed right to participate in the political process. Similarly, in *OPSEU v. Ontario (Attorney General)*, [1987] 2 S.C.R. 2, the entire Court upheld a ban preventing government workers from running for office and engaging in political activities without taking a leave of absence, because the government seeks to maintain an impartial civil service that is free of the perception of political bias and patronage. The Court's rejection of the novel *Charter* arguments in these cases help explain why the political speech variable did not achieve a stronger coefficient and a better rank in the speech hierarchy.

The last case-level variable that is statistically significant pertains to whether or not the Court engaged in section 1 analysis, and indicates that the justices were 29 percent more likely to rule in favour of the rights claimant when the Court engages in "the *Charter* two-step" analysis ($b = 1.20$). Indeed, in over half of the cases (62 percent) where the Court invoked section 1 of the *Charter*, the justices handed down rulings in favour of an individual's fundamental right to free expression.

Turning to the parties and intervenor variables, the findings indicate that, as expected, individual litigants have a statistically significant lower success rate when bringing free speech claims to the Court than other parties that typically have more resources and legal experience at their disposal, such as unions, corporations, and media agencies ($b = -0.93$, significant at the 99 percent confidence level). Thus, in line with the arguments advanced by Galanter (1974, 2003) and McCormick (1993), repeat players have a 22 percent greater chance of winning free speech cases than their one-shot, individual counterparts (see the last column in Table 5.8). The findings reveal, however, that provincial governments fare 19 percent better than other repeat litigants in the system, with the federal government comprising the bulk of that comparative group ($b = -0.76$, significant at the 95 percent confidence level). This counterintuitive result suggests that provincial government lawyers are perhaps slightly better than their federal counterparts at preparing arguments against free speech claimants. Finally, the indicator for CCLA intervention in lawsuits is in the unexpected direction but has only a minimal impact on the Supreme Court justices. Indeed, the justices are 5 percent more likely to cast a conservative vote when the CCLA participates in a dispute (b = -0.2). We believe that this counterintuitive finding appears in the regression model because the CCLA intervenes in some of the most difficult free speech cases, involving assertions in the hate speech and obscenity areas (for examples, see *R. v. Keegstra*, [1990] 3 S.C.R. 697; *R. v. Andrews*, [1990] 3 S.C.R. 870; and *Canada (Human Rights Commission) v. Taylor*, [1990] 3 S.C.R. 892).

Neither of the control variables for the Lamer or McLachlin Courts proves to be significant in the free speech model, indicating no real difference in liberal voting patterns across the three post-*Charter* courts (b = 0.52 and 0.32, respectively). This result contrasts with the decisive liberal trend that the McLachlin Court has shown in equality cases, suggesting that the liberalizing trend that some attribute to the contemporary Court is not equally distributed across all civil rights and liberties disputes. Altogether, the fourteen-variable model is able to predict 71 percent of the justices' votes accurately, which is in step with the predictive power of the search and seizure, right to counsel, and equality models. The model's factual variables perform well as predictors of judicial voting patterns, with section 1 analysis and commercial advertising standing out as the two most important case characteristics fostering liberal votes. Meanwhile, judge-level variables, particularly ideology, played a negligible role in the free speech area. The findings across all equality and free speech cases paint a larger portrait of a Court that is not particularly motivated by ideology in two of the most prominent civil rights and liberties areas, where ideological rancour would be readily expected. These findings suggest that the ideological expectations of attitudinal theorists may not be appropriate for explaining judicial decision making across all cases in the post-*Charter* era.

Non-Unanimous Free Speech Cases
The second model of free speech cases focuses solely on non-unanimous disputes and is identical to the first, except that two variables are omitted for reasons of collinearity. We excluded the individual rights claimant and the McLachlin Court control indicators because they were highly correlated with other variables in the model.[15] Intriguingly, the results in Table 5.9 indicate that the five variables that are statistically significant across all free speech cases do not reprise their role as prominent variables in the small model. Moreover, unlike in the equality and right to counsel areas, the predictive accuracy of the non-unanimous model of free speech cases declines by 4 percentage points, to 67 percent (see the bottom of Table 5.9). In other words,

TABLE 5.9

Logistic regression estimates of liberal votes in non-unanimous free speech cases, 1984-2003

Variable	b	Statistical significance	Probability of liberal vote when x is low	Probability of liberal vote when x is high	Change in probability
JUDGE-LEVEL VARIABLES					
Ideology	−0.503	.066	.805	.355	−.450
Party of prime minister	−0.458	.039*	.588	.363	−.225
Female justice	1.440	.006**	.398	.736	.338
Law professor	0.371	.073	.428	.611	.183
CASE CHARACTERISTICS[a]					
Criminal charge	−1.420	.032*	.689	.348	−.341
Advertising case	−0.664	.266	.538	.375	−.163
Obscenity case	−0.402	.342	.532	.431	−.101
Political speech case	0.957	.254	.503	.725	.222
Section 1 analysis	0.387	.338	.443	.539	.096
PARTIES AND INTERVENORS					
CCLA intervenor	−0.005	.497	.518	.517	−.001
Provincial government	−0.052	.474	.520	.507	−.013
COURT CONTROL VARIABLES					
Lamer Court	−0.212	.379	.540	.488	−.052
McLachlin Court[b]	—	—	—	—	—
CONSTANT AND MODEL FIT STATISTICS					
Constant	−0.008				
−2 LLR chi-square		138.515*			
Nagelkerke R^2		.233			
Percent correct		67.2%			
Reduction in error		33.2%			

NOTE: $N = 116$.

a The indicator for individual litigants was omitted because it was highly collinear with multiple variables in the equation.

b The McLachlin Court indicator was omitted from this equation because it is perfectly correlated with the obscenity variable.

* $p < .05$, ** $p < .01$, *** $p < .001$

we are able to better predict the judicial vote outcomes when both unanimous and non-unanimous cases are combined in the model than when free speech cases with divided rulings are analyzed alone. One explanation for this unexpected decline in predictive power when justices disagree is that case characteristics appear to take a backseat to judge-level differences, and the loss in explained variance from cases facts is not surpassed by the rise in importance of the judge-level variables in the equation.

Several interesting results in the model of non-unanimous free speech disputes deserve comment. First, two of the judge-level variables prove to be statistically significant in the model, although the party of prime minister measure is in the unexpected direction ($b = -0.46$, significant at the 95 percent confidence level). Thus, when justices disagree, Liberal Party appointees are 23 percent less likely than their Conservative Party counterparts to rule in favour of free speech claims, all other things being equal. As mentioned earlier, one plausible explanation for this anomaly is that the nine appointments made by Prime Minister Mulroney were less politically driven than one would expect, and some of them came to the bench harbouring a prominent libertarian bent, particularly with regard to free speech claims. The voting patterns exhibited by Justices McLachlin and Major in divided free speech cases support this contention, with both casting over 90 percent of their votes in favour of the rights claimant (McLachlin, 92 percent in twelve cases; Major, 100 percent in all five of his cases), while they tended to be far more conservative in other issue areas, such as criminal disputes. Overall, it would seem that the appointees of Prime Ministers Mulroney and Chrétien have run counter to traditional ideological expectations in this prominent area of civil liberties jurisprudence.

Second, further evidence of liberal/conservative role switching is provided by the remarkable findings for the newspaper ideology measure, with the most liberal justices on our ideological indicator being 45 percent *less* likely than their most conservative colleagues to rule for the rights claimant in contentious free speech cases ($b = -0.50$). The strength of this measure jumps from a relatively weak position in the model of all free speech cases to the top position for generating a change in the odds of a liberal vote in non-unanimous cases (change in probability is $-.07$ and $-.45$ in Tables 5.8 and 5.9, respectively), although, as in the equality area, it is in the unexpected direction and not statistically significant in the equation. These findings further illustrate the distinctive role that ideology plays in the Canadian setting, because they reflect a pattern of ideological voting completely at odds with the expectation of attitudinal theorists that liberals would vote far more liberally than their conservative counterparts in such cases. Such results suggest that perhaps gaps across the ideological divide are easier to bridge in cultural settings outside the US, and that differences in the judicial appointment process may play a critical role in promoting or inhibiting ideological decision making on a court.

Third, the gender variable, which was most prominent in the equality area, is also a significant force in contentious free speech cases, indicating that women are 34 percent more likely than their male counterparts to cast a liberal vote in the post-*Charter* era ($b = 1.44$, significant at the 99 percent confidence level). One should note that the disparity between the sexes is almost three times the magnitude of that found across all free speech cases (see Tables 5.8 and 5.9). These findings provide additional support for the feminist claim that men and women have fundamentally different approaches to how they communicate with others, and this difference is highlighted in the justices' voting behaviour in the civil rights and liberties area, especially in contested free speech cases.

The only other statistically significant variable in the equation is whether a criminal charge is present in the free speech dispute ($b = -1.42$, significant at the 95 percent confidence level). The findings reveal that when the justices are at odds, they are 34 percent less likely to support the rights claimant if a criminal charge has been filed than in all other cases. This pattern is exemplified in the trio of hate speech rulings handed down by the Court in 1990 (*R. v. Keegstra, R. v. Andrews,* and *Canada v. Taylor*). Although the majority in these cases acknowledged that communication promoting hatred is protected under the *Charter* because it contains expressive content, its criminalization was nevertheless justified under section 1 because of the extensive harm that hate speech causes various targeted groups and society as a whole. Clearly, it is the criminal element of such expression that drives some of the justices to issue conservative votes, for it is one thing to extend liberty interests to individuals who want to be heard in the public forum, but quite another to allow such individuals to engage in unlawful activity that harms their fellow citizens.

None of the other variables achieves statistical significance in the model, suggesting that when the justices are at odds in the free speech area, case characteristics and parties and intervenors in the suit do not significantly influence their voting behaviour. Instead, it is the gender of the justice in tandem with party attachment and ideological proclivities that drive the justices to disagree, albeit in unexpected partisan directions. Thus, in two of the most important areas of civil rights and liberties litigation, the justices on the Canadian Supreme Court exhibit behaviour that is counterintuitive to the dominant theory of attitudinal decision making but that is principally motivated by their gender differences.

Conclusion

This chapter provides a comprehensive analysis of judicial behaviour in post-*Charter* civil rights and liberties disputes. The tables in the first part of the chapter indicate that these disputes foster greater rates of attitudinal conflict than criminal cases. This can be explained in part because average panel sizes are almost one justice larger in civil rights and liberties disputes than in all other cases. The findings also demonstrate that Justices Dickson and Lamer exhibited opinion leadership traits, writing the largest percentage of majority opinions in these cases, while Justices Binnie, Estey, Gonthier, and Le Dain can be categorized as followers. Although three of the female justices (Wilson, McLachlin, and L'Heureux-Dubé) engaged in distinctive patterns of opinion authorship in concurrence and dissent, only the latter two can be labelled outsiders in this arena. The fact that all the post-*Charter* female justices can be found on the liberal end of the civil rights and liberties spectrum confirms that the women on the Court have developed a unique feminist approach toward these types of rights claims. The findings from the first section of the chapter also reveal that conservative justices are nearly as likely as their liberal colleagues to hand down activist rulings. Thus, in this area, unlike the criminal field, we find no significant association between rates of activism and judicial liberalism on the post-*Charter* Canadian Court. The general statistics also indicate that a handful of justices do not exhibit strong patterns of ideological stability over time in civil rights and liberties cases. Collectively, the findings reveal that important distinctive patterns of judicial behaviour have emerged in the post-*Charter* Court in these two high-profile legal areas.

The second part of the chapter documents that gender differences play a major role in influencing liberal/conservative voting patterns in post-*Charter* equality cases and divided free speech cases. Put simply, gender differences do provoke justices on the Canadian Court to speak in distinctively different voices in pivotal civil rights and liberties disputes. From a broader perspective, these findings suggest that the appointment of female justices to high courts around the world may indeed be critical to the development of a more progressive body of law that may transcend national boundaries.

Unlike the right to counsel and search and seizure areas of law, case facts played a much weaker role in the minds of the justices when resolving equality and free speech cases. This is particularly true in non-unanimous disputes, where judge-level variables obviously play a more central role. It is also worth noting that while the McLachlin Court has been decisively more liberal toward equality claims than its Dickson and Lamer Court predecessors, the same cannot be said of the free speech area when controlling for all other factors in the equations. Thus, critics must be more cautious when claiming that a liberal trend across all civil rights and liberties disputes is evident on the McLachlin Court.

Surprisingly, the regression results in this chapter provide mixed evidence regarding the impact of ideology as an important predictor of judicial voting in equality and free speech cases. While the newspaper ideology measure has a negligible impact across all such cases, it has a far greater impact in the non-unanimous cases, as one would expect. It is remarkable, however, that the effect of this variable is in the opposite direction in these two areas of law. This unique finding reveals a distinctive wrinkle in the ideological voting patterns of some justices of the Canadian high court. It suggests that while some justices cast liberal equality votes that meet conventional ideological expectations, they also cast conservative and anti-libertarian votes in free speech cases and possibly other civil rights and liberties suits. In short, the results demonstrate that ideological voting patterns are not always consistent on the Canadian Court in the civil rights and liberties area (we have more to say about this matter in Chapter 7). Even though justices exhibit ideological consistency across a bulk of criminal cases, the fact that mixed results are found in two of the most important civil rights and liberties areas calls into question the universal applicability of the attitudinal model and suggests that a more nuanced interpretation of judicial decision making is necessary in the Canadian context, and perhaps for other high courts around the world.

6
Attitudinal Conflict in Economic Cases

When the Supreme Court decides cases in the realm of economic affairs, the outcomes have a definitive measurable impact on the financial standing of the litigants. The finality of the justices' rulings can mean, for example, the difference between a person obtaining pension benefits or not, between receiving compensation for a harm suffered or not, or between the awarding of an insurance payout or not. The decisions can also have a tremendous effect on government powers to raise revenues and to regulate the activities of corporations and individuals in the marketplace. Given the stakes involved in these disputes, it is natural that the justices will frequently be at odds over the correct resolution of such issues, and often those divisions fall squarely along liberal/conservative lines. Moreover, because these cases make up almost a quarter of the Canadian Supreme Court's caseload in a given year, the conflicts that arise in them are bound to draw the attention of court watchers and scholars.

Our discussion of attitudinal conflict in the economic area parallels the discussions in our earlier chapters, with the first half of the chapter devoted to a discussion of docket size, unanimity, and average panel size, along with statistics on case participation; majority, concurring, and dissenting opinion authorship; and patterns of ideological voting and judicial activism. The second portion of the chapter revisits the theme of assessing the viability of the attitudinal model across all as well as contested economic cases, paying particular attention to labour/management disputes and tax litigation. As in Chapters 4 and 5, we examine the degree to which judicial votes are driven by specific case facts, the ideological predisposition of the justices, the litigants involved in the disputes, and the changing tenor of the three post-*Charter* courts.

Following the pattern set out in earlier chapters, Table 6.1 provides annual data on the percentage of the Court's docket constituting economic cases, rates of non-unanimous decisions, and average panel size. The values at the bottom of the "Percent of docket economic cases" column indicate that economic cases represent a quarter of the Court's docket in the first twenty years of *Charter* jurisprudence, which lies roughly halfway between the percentage found in the criminal and the civil rights and liberties areas of law (46 and 12 percent, respectively). Moreover, there has been a greater degree of fluctuation in the percentage of economic cases across the three post-*Charter* courts than in the other two areas of law. Although there was a marked dip in the percentage of economic cases heard during the 1993-96 period of the Lamer Court (16.7 percent of the docket), economic disputes comprised a more substantial portion of the Court docket in the Dickson Court and the first four years of the McLachlin Court (27 and 31 percent, respectively). The latest increase in the share of economic cases heard by the McLachlin Court has occurred in tandem with a slight increase in civil rights and liberties cases, and was counterbalanced by an 8 percent reduction in criminal cases.

Data found at the bottom of the "Percent non-unanimous economic cases" column of Table 6.1 demonstrate that justices have failed to reach a unanimous ruling an average of 23 percent of the time in the economic area, although the rate of disagreement has increased over time in the three post-*Charter* courts. While the average rate of conflict on the Dickson Court was only 18 percent, it rose to 25 percent during Justice Lamer's leadership and 26 percent in the first four years of the McLachlin Court. Despite this increase, one should note that, overall, the rate of disagreement in this area is comparable to that found in the criminal area, but much lower than the rate found in civil rights and liberties disputes (32 percent). This finding is not surprising since economic issues tend to draw less attention from journalists and the public at large, and are less likely to touch on core constitutional values that foster greater division within the Court. Another explanation for the lower average rates of disagreement in economic cases is that these cases feature a smaller average panel size than civil rights and liberties disputes, which means that it is mathematically easier for justices to reach a unanimous ruling (see the bottom of the last column in Table 6.1).

Like its predecessors, Tables 6.2 sketches out patterns of task leadership, follower activity, and outsider behaviour in the resolution of economic cases. Not surprisingly, the justices who emerge as task leaders in the economic area, Justices Iacobucci and Estey, came to the Court with expertise in these types of cases. Both justices wrote majority opinions in at least 28 percent of

TABLE 6.1

Annual data on case volume, docket level, unanimity, and panel size in economic cases, 1984–2003

Year	Total cases argued	Percent non-unanimous all cases heard	Yearly average panel size	Percent of docket economic cases	Percent non-unanimous economic cases	Average panel size economic cases
1984	83	9.6	6.4	24.1	5.0	6.2
1985	86	22.1	7.1	33.7	20.7	6.3
1986	72	15.3	6.1	37.5	7.4	5.6
1987	96	26.0	6.0	21.9	28.6	5.1
1988	109	22.0	5.7	29.4	21.9	5.8
1989	131	23.7	6.5	17.6	21.7	6.2
1990	*113*	*28.3*	*6.7*	*25.7*	*24.1*	*6.7*
1991	*123*	*30.1*	*6.4*	*23.6*	*27.6*	*6.7*
1992	*107*	*16.8*	*6.1*	*22.4*	*16.7*	*5.6*
1993	*127*	*36.2*	*7.0*	*15.0*	*42.1*	*7.2*
1994	*110*	*25.5*	*7.5*	*16.4*	*11.1*	*7.0*
1995	*115*	*30.4*	*7.4*	*15.7*	*27.8*	*6.3*
1996	*111*	*24.3*	*7.2*	*19.8*	*27.3*	*7.1*
1997	*106*	*23.6*	*6.7*	*23.6*	*36.0*	*6.6*
1998	*104*	*26.9*	*7.0*	*23.1*	*25.0*	*6.7*
1999	*78*	*17.9*	*6.8*	*25.6*	*10.0*	*7.2*
2000	**77**	**32.5**	**7.6**	**24.7**	**26.3**	**7.4**
2001	**94**	**22.3**	**7.6**	**31.9**	**16.7**	**7.7**
2002	**68**	**25.0**	**7.9**	**36.8**	**28.0**	**7.9**
2003	**78**	**25.6**	**7.9**	**30.8**	**33.3**	**8.0**
Average	99	24.3	6.9	25.0	22.9	6.7
Std. dev.	19	6.1	0.6	6.7	9.6	0.8

NOTE: Justice Dickson's tenure as chief justice, from 1984 to June 1990, is shown in regular type; Chief Justice Lamer's tenure, from July 1990 to 1999, is shown in italic type; and the initial years of Chief Justice McLachlin's tenure, from 2000 to 2003, are shown in bold type.

the economic cases they heard, which was at a pace 2 standard deviations above the average (see the top of the "Percent writing majority opinion" column in Table 6.2), while Justices Chouinard and Le Dain exhibited a second tier of leadership activity, authoring majority opinions 23 and 22 percent of the time, respectively. These data, in tandem with the earlier findings, appear to confirm that the Canadian justices are taking leadership roles in areas that play to their legal strengths, which makes intuitive sense and ensures that the workload is appropriately divided in the Canadian Court. This is further illustrated by the fact that Justice Estey, who was a task leader here, was a clear follower in the other two areas of law, while Justice Iacobucci, another economic leader, exhibited a relatively moderate leadership role in the other two areas as well. It is worth noting that, unlike in the other two areas of law, none of the chief justices emerges as a significant task leader in economic cases, although Justices Dickson and McLachlin did write larger than average shares of majority opinions and are found just below the second cut of majority opinion leaders (see Table 6.2). Two explanations for this might be that economic cases do not generate the same degree of public attention and scrutiny as other cases, and that, since none of the chief justices specialized in business law, they may not have felt the urge to lead the Court in such cases.

Justices McIntyre, Arbour, and, to a lesser extent, Lamer exhibit follower behaviour in the economic cases because they join majority coalitions at average or a little above average rates, write few majority opinions, and rarely dissent (see Table 6.2). Justices Gonthier and Cory represent the median justices, writing majority opinions in 14 and 13 percent of the economic cases they heard, respectively. Their patterns of majority opinion authorship in the economic area can be contrasted with their output in the other two areas of law, where Justice Cory demonstrated leadership activity and Justice Gonthier exhibited follower activity. This provides additional evidence that the Canadian justices are more likely to act as leaders in their fields of specialization and are willing to defer to their colleagues outside their areas of expertise.

The quintessential outsider in business cases is Justice Stevenson, who penned dissenting opinions in 18 percent of the cases he heard and joined majority coalitions only 82 percent of the time. Both levels of activity place him 2 standard deviations beyond the mean (see the "Percent majority votes" and "Percent writing dissenting opinions" columns in Table 6.2). The maverick qualities that Justice Stevenson displayed in his brief stay on the Court suggest that he might have emerged as the true outsider in economic cases if he had donned the robe for a longer period. Justice Deschamps exhibited the next highest rate of dissenting activity in the economic area (9 percent), perhaps providing a hint of the outsider position she may stake out in this area of law in the future. Unlike their behaviour in the other two fields, the five women on the Court do not exhibit consistently high rates of dissenting activity in economic disputes, ranging from a high of 9 percent to a low of 2 percent (for Justice Arbour). These data indicate that there is no distinctive pattern of behaviour by the female members of the Court in post-*Charter* economic cases.

TABLE 6.2

Panel participation rates and opinion authorship patterns in economic cases with written reasons for judgment, 1984–2003

Justice	Number of cases	Percent majority votes	Percent writing majority opinion	Percent writing concurring opinion	Percent writing dissenting opinion
Iacobucci	253	94.1	29.2ᵃ	1.6	4.3
Estey	43	95.3	27.9ᵃ	2.3	4.7
Chouinard	48	95.8	22.9	2.1	2.1
Le Dain	68	100.0	22.1	1.5	0.0
Dickson	89	95.5	18.0	2.2	2.2
McLachlin	270	91.9	17.4	6.3	4.1
Binnie	120	93.3	15.8	0.8	4.2
Beetz	91	94.5	15.4	5.5	2.2
La Forest	256	92.6	14.8	3.9	3.5
Major	206	93.2	14.6	1.0	3.4
Gonthier	291	95.2	14.4	1.4	1.4
Cory	198	94.9	13.1	2.5	3.0
Wilson	137	90.5	12.4	8.0	6.6
L'Heureux-Dubé	273	90.8	10.3	5.1	4.0
Sopinka	167	86.8	9.6	7.8	6.0
Lamer	200	92.0	8.5	2.0	4.0
LeBel	86	87.2	8.1	4.7	5.8
Arbour	85	95.3	7.1	2.4	2.4
Deschamps	33	84.8	6.1	3.0	9.1
Stevenson	17	82.4ᵃ	5.9	11.8ᵃ	17.6ᵃ
McIntyre	95	92.6	5.3	7.4	0.0
Bastarache	138	89.1	4.3	1.4	7.2
Average	143.8	92.2	13.8	3.8	4.4
Std. dev.	—	4.1	7.1	2.9	3.7

NOTE: Justices Fish and Ritchie are omitted from the table because they participated in ten or fewer cases. Their data are included here for comparative purposes: Fish, 9 cases, 77.8 percent majority votes, 0 majority opinions and concurrences, and 1 dissent; Ritchie, 4 cases, 100 percent majority votes, 1 majority opinion, and 0 concurrences or dissents.
a The justice's value on this indicator is 2 times the standard deviation from the mean value.

Following the pattern set in Chapters 4 and 5, Table 6.3 identifies liberal voting behaviour where clear ideological patterns emerged. Readers must keep in mind that some of the economic decisions of the Court are not included in these tabulations because of the difficulty of clearly identifying the underdog or elite interests. The findings show that Justices Wilson and Stevenson occupy the two ends of the ideological continuum in business cases, and their isolated activity is 2 standard deviations from the mean (62 and 40 percent liberal respectively). While the number of cases heard by Justice Stevenson is small, his extreme conservative behaviour accords well with his status as an opinion outsider documented in Table 6.2. In general, the data across all three areas of law indicate a fairly logical connection between extreme ideological voting behaviour and an increased likelihood of dissent. The data also indicate that Justices Iacobucci and Estey, who were opinion leaders in the business area, remained relatively centrist in their ideological orientation (50 and 46 percent liberal, respectively). This finding confirms what was found in the other two areas of law, namely, that opinion leaders of the Court tend to lead from the ideological centre. Similarly, Justices Arbour, McIntyre, and Lamer, who appeared as opinion followers in Table 6.2, occupy fairly consistent moderate positions. This finding deviates somewhat from the dispersed ideological pattern that appeared in the criminal area, but parallels nicely the follower and centrist activity that emerged in the civil rights area. Overall, there appears to be a general tendency for opinion leaders to be typically found in majority coalitions at the ideological centre of the Court, whereas justices who exhibit extreme ideological behaviour write more frequently from an isolated position of dissent.

Although we examine the prevalence of judicial activism in economic cases in Table 6.4, readers must keep in mind that there are far fewer opportunities for nullification of statutes in the economic realm. Indeed, the data included in the table show that each justice had an average of only 19 opportunities to invalidate statutes in economic cases, 28 and 31 cases less than in the fields of civil rights and liberties and criminal law, respectively. Justice Wilson was the most determined to strike down legislation in economic cases, doing so 47 percent of the time, and her behaviour is fully 2 standard deviations beyond the average rate. Her patterns in the economic area are consistent with her activist tendencies in criminal disputes; she participated in too few civil rights and liberties cases to establish a clear record in that area of law. Justice Major, who lies at the other end of the economic spectrum, did not cast a single activist vote despite having more than a dozen chances to do so. Since his restrained behaviour is consistent across all three areas of law, we believe that Justice Major stands as the quintessential practitioner of judicial restraint on the post-*Charter* Canadian Court, with Justice Gonthier not far behind in his deferential activity in these three legal areas. Justice McLachlin, on the other hand, occupies the median position in economic

TABLE 6.3

Liberal votes in economic cases with written reasons for judgment, 1984–2003

Justice	Number of cases where ideological direction can be identified	Percentage of liberal votes cast
Wilson	102	61.8[a]
L'Heureux-Dubé	198	61.1
Dickson	72	58.3
La Forest	175	58.3
Cory	130	56.2
Deschamps	30	53.3
Le Dain	46	52.2
McLachlin	187	51.9
Chouinard	37	51.4
Arbour	65	50.8
Gonthier	205	50.7
Iacobucci	176	50.0
Sopinka	109	49.5
McIntyre	73	49.3
Lamer	145	48.3
Bastarache	108	48.1
LeBel	69	47.8
Beetz	66	47.0
Estey	26	46.2
Binnie	89	46.1
Major	141	45.4
Stevenson	10	40.0[a]
Average	102.7	51.1
Std. dev.	59.6	5.4

NOTE: Justices Fish and Ritchie are omitted from the table because they participated in fewer than ten cases. While Justice Fish cast 77.8 percent liberal votes in the nine cases that could be coded, Justice Ritchie cast no liberal votes in his two cases.
a The justice's value on this indicator is 2 times the standard deviation from the mean value.

cases, casting votes to strike down laws only 20 percent of the time (see Table 6.4). This contrasts markedly with her ranking in the civil rights and liberties area, where she was a leading activist justice on the post-*Charter* Court.

When we compare activist voting in economic cases with the findings in Table 6.2, we find that neither the opinion leaders nor the court followers distinguish themselves as strong activists, a pattern also seen in the criminal area. There is, however, a noticeable pattern of activist behaviour coinciding with dissenting votes (see the patterns for Justices Wilson, Beetz, and Dickson

TABLE 6.4

Patterns of judicial activism in economic cases, 1984–2003

Justice	Number of cases raising possibility of statute nullification	Percent of times (n) a justice voted to nullify a law or portion of law		Percent of activist votes (n) cast in majority	
Wilson	19	47.4ᵃ	(9)	44.4	(4)
Beetz	19	36.8	(7)	57.1	(4)
Dickson	18	27.8	(5)	60.0	(3)
La Forest	29	27.6	(8)	75.0	(6)
Le Dain	11	27.3	(3)	100.0	(3)
Lamer	28	25.0	(7)	71.4	(5)
McLachlin	20	20.0	(4)	75.0	(3)
Sopinka	12	16.7	(2)	50.0	(1)
McIntyre	16	12.5	(2)	50.0	(1)
Iacobucci	18	11.1	(2)	100.0	(2)
L'Heureux-Dubé	29	10.3	(3)	100.0	(3)
Gonthier	21	9.5	(2)	50.0	(1)
Cory	13	7.7	(1)	100.0	(1)
Major	13	0.0	(0)	0.0ᵃ	(0)
Average	19.0	20.0		66.6	
Std. dev.	6.1	12.8		28.4	

NOTE: (1) The data in this table must be interpreted with caution, given the small number of cases addressing the possible nullification of a statute in the economic area. We include this analysis in order to present data that can be compared with those in other chapters. (2) Justices with ten or fewer cases are omitted from this table, but we provide their data here for those interested in complete information on the justices. We include the number of cases heard, the percentage of activist votes, and the percentage of those votes that were handed down in majority or concurring opinions. Arbour, 5, 0.0, 0.0; Bastarache, 10, 0.0, 0.0; Binnie, 9, 11.1, 100.0; Chouinard, 1, 0.0, 0.0; Deschamps, 2, 0.0, 0.0; Estey, 3 0.0, 0.0; LeBel, 6, 16.7; 100.0; Stevenson, 4, 25.0, 0.0.

a The justice's value for this indicator is 2 times the standard deviation from the mean value.

in the last column of Table 6.4). Conversely, justices who are the most restrained in the economic field tend to cast most of their activist votes when joining majority coalitions. Even though this finding is tentative, given the low number of activist opportunities in the economic realm, it lends credence to a pattern found in the two other areas of law, particularly in criminal disputes.

When we compare rates of activism with the ideological patterns found in Table 6.3, it is worth noting that the most liberal and the second most conservative justices, Justices Wilson and Major, appear on opposite ends of the activist continuum in economic cases. This raises the question, posed in Chapters 4 and 5, of whether rates of activism are highly correlated with a priori measures of judicial ideology. The data for justices listed in Table 6.4 give mixed results. In the economic area, the party of prime minister variable produces a statistically significant positive coefficient ($r = .640$, significant at the 99 percent confidence level), suggesting that Liberal Party appointees are more activist in economic cases. On the other hand, the newspaper ideology coefficient, while positive, is not statistically significant, leading to the conclusion that no prominent relationship exists ($r = .447$).[1] One explanation for this bifurcated result may be the much lower number of cases that raise activist possibilities (an average of 19) in relation to the other two areas of law (an average of 47 for criminal cases and 51 for civil rights and liberties). As a result, we regard the connection found between Liberal appointees and activist rulings in the economic area with more suspicion than the connection found in criminal disputes. Overall, the findings from the three areas suggest that while there is an obvious connection between liberalism and activism in criminal post-*Charter* cases, and no significant connection in civil rights and liberties cases, there *may* be a connection in the realm of business law. These broader patterns indicate there is only a small grain of truth to the notion that post-*Charter* Liberal justices are more activist than their Conservative counterparts.

As in Chapters 4 and 5, we turn in Table 6.5 to an analysis of the ideological stability of the justices. One must remember that the left side of the table analyzes the changing pattern of liberal votes of an individual justice from years 1 and 2 to years 5 and 6, while the right side of the table engages in the same analysis for the continuing cohort of justices serving with them. This comparison helps to control for membership change on the Court and issue change over time (see Baum 1988, 1992).[2] The overall findings at the bottom of Table 6.5 suggest that in the economic area, the average ideological change of the justices is a movement of 2 percentage points in the conservative direction, which reflects a fairly stable pattern of attitudinal voting in economic cases.

Regarding specific justices, Justice Sopinka became far more liberal in his first six years on the high court in both the economic and criminal cases, with net changes of 34 and 15 percent, respectively (see Tables 6.5 and 4.5, respectively). Indeed, his ideological shift was 1 full standard deviation beyond the average change of other justices in both areas of law. In contrast,

TABLE 6.5

Changes in ideological voting patterns by Supreme Court justices in economic cases when years 1 and 2 (T1) are compared with years 5 and 6 (T2)

Judge (votes T1, T2, number of continuing judges)	% liberal (T1)	% liberal (T2)	Change in voting	% liberal continuing justices (T1)	% liberal continuing justices (T2)	Change in continuing justices	Difference in value change
Sopinka (20, 21, 3)	45.0	57.1	12.1	68.2	46.4	-21.8	33.9
Dickson (23, 26, 2)	47.8	73.1	25.3	51.0	63.1	12.1	13.2
La Forest (30, 29, 3)	50.0	65.5	15.5	48.4	56.4	8.0	7.5
Gonthier (24, 18, 6)	54.2	38.9	-15.3	55.3	35.6	-19.7	4.4
Wilson (28, 35, 2)	50.0	68.6	18.6	50.0	64.3	14.3	4.3
Binnie (22, 39, 5)	45.5	46.2	0.7	47.1	46.0	-1.1	1.8
Iacobucci (25, 22, 7)	52.0	63.6	11.6	51.4	66.2	14.8	-3.2
L'Heureux-Dubé (30, 30, 2)	80.0	46.7	-33.3	69.7	41.5	-28.2	-5.1
Cory (26, 15, 6)	61.5	33.3	-28.2	54.1	36.6	-17.5	-10.7
Bastarache (23, 40, 5)	60.9	37.5	-23.4	52.8	41.3	-11.5	-11.9
Major (16, 27, 6)	37.5	37.0	-0.5	36.8	53.2	16.4	-16.9
Lamer (21, 30, 2)	52.4	56.7	4.3	49.0	70.5	21.5	-17.2
McLachlin (20, 17, 6)	60.0	23.5	-36.5	54.5	38.5	-16.0	-20.5
Average	53.6	49.8	-3.8	52.9	50.7	-2.2	-1.6
Std. dev.	10.5	15.4	21.1	8.5	12.2	17.5	15.0

NOTE: Justices who appear to display significant ideological shifts from those serving as cohorts on the Court are identified in bold text. A simple rule of thumb was used: if the value difference exceeded 1 standard deviation (15.0) when comparing a justice's ideological change with the change score of other justices on the Court with him or her, that justice was highlighted as exhibiting a significant ideological change. Obviously, changes in ideological scores are more reliable when the comparison groups of justices are larger; thus, we have the most confidence in the change scores for justices McLachlin, Cory, Gonthier, Iacobucci, and Major. These change scores must be interpreted with caution, given the small number of economic cases decided during the years of interest.

both Justices Lamer and McLachlin demonstrated overwhelming shifts in the conservative direction in both economic and civil rights and liberties cases (see Tables 6.5 and 5.5, respectively). It also should be noted that Justice Major, like Justices Lamer and McLachlin, also exhibited a 1 standard deviation swing to the right in economic cases during his first years on the Court. These data clearly demonstrate that a few justices do change their ideological stripes over time while on the bench. The fact that only four of the justices exhibit major shifts in economic liberalism over a six-year span on the Court suggests that the attitudinal model, which assumes ideological stability, might have the same level of explanatory power in economic voting behaviour as it did in the criminal arena. Only a rigorous test of the attitudinal model that simultaneously controls for the influence of multiple variables can shed light on its viability in Canadian economic cases. We turn to this test next.

Union Cases

DATA AND METHODS

Mindful of the earlier work of Schubert (1965, 1974) and other US scholars, and in keeping with Chapters 4 and 5, our test of the attitudinal model in the economic area focused on two areas of law presenting ideological conflicts that can be easily coded along liberal/conservative lines. We looked first at union/management cases, where union efforts were seen as protecting the "have-nots" or societal underdogs against more powerful economic interests, and then turned our attention to tax cases, which readily pitted liberty interests of taxpayers against government efforts to promote economic equality and provide collective goods. We chose these two sets of cases because they comprised the largest percentage of rulings in the post-*Charter* economic area, and they also provided fertile ground for examining the tension between notions of economic liberty and equality.

As in other areas of law, the data for the union cases were derived from decisions argued in the post-*Charter* Canadian Supreme Court (1984–2003) featuring written reasons for judgment. Cases were included in the union area if a labour or workplace issue was central to the Court's analysis. Ultimately, the model analyzing all union cases featured a total of 560 judicial votes in seventy-nine disputes, while that examining non-unanimous cases featured 228 votes in thirty-two disputes.[3] As in Chapters 4 and 5, the dependent variable was a dichotomous measure reflecting whether a justice cast a liberal vote, and was coded as "1" if a justice supported the union's position or "0" if the justice supported management or state interests. We believe that unions represent the economic underdog in these cases because they personify individuals' efforts to secure better working conditions and compensation from employers. The coding scheme utilized here follows a well-established pattern of research analyzing the economic votes of US Supreme Court justices (see Schubert 1965, 1974; Spaeth 1963; Hagle and Spaeth 1992, 1993).

A total of fourteen independent variables were included in the first stage of our analysis, three of which pertained to judge-level characteristics, including newspaper ideology, party of prime minister, and private practice. As in previous chapters, the newspaper ideology score for each justice was derived from our analysis in Chapter 3, and it was expected that justices scoring most positively on this indicator (closest to +2) would be more likely to side with union interests, while those scoring most negatively (closest to –2) would tend to favour corporate and government claims. Similarly, it was thought that justices appointed by Liberal Party prime ministers (+1) would be more prone to favour the economic interests of unions in labour disputes, because they would be more predisposed toward favouring the "have-nots" or underdogs in society. In contrast, Conservative Party appointees (–1) were expected to align themselves with the economic liberty claims of employers and economic elites. For both of these indicators, we anticipated that positive coefficients would emerge in the regression analysis.

The last judge-level variable was a background measure that we thought would be particularly prominent in economic disputes, namely, whether a justice had spent the bulk of his or her career as a lawyer in private practice; we thought that this background variable would correlate well with our measures of ideology. This variable was included in our analysis because it made intuitive sense to believe that justices who arrived on the Court after a long tenure in private practice would tend to favour corporate interests more readily than other justices (for a similar argument, see Tate and Sittiwong 1989). Since most of these justices had worked for top law firms representing leading corporate interests in Canada, we hypothesized that they would be more likely to support the economic liberty claims made by corporate parties. As a result, justices with long private-lawyer track records and less than five years of judicial experience were coded as "1" on this dichotomous variable. All other justices were coded as "0"; most of them came to the Court with five or more years of judicial experience or extensive service as academics, judges, or politicians. Given our coding scheme and directional hypothesis, we expected a negative coefficient for this indicator.

Seven factual circumstances typical in Canadian labour cases were included in the analysis to control for the fact patterns that might trigger attitudinal disagreement among the justices. As in previous chapters, facts were coded as dichotomous variables with a value of "1" if a specific fact pattern occurred in a dispute or a value of "0" for all other circumstances. We reiterate that our coding of the facts in the cases was drawn from the lower appellate court opinions and not from the Supreme Court opinions themselves, to ensure that a priori measures of the facts were obtained. We therefore believe that the dependent variable (the case vote) necessarily came as a response to the facts of a case, not vice versa.

The first set of factual variables pertained to cases involving some form of inequitable treatment of workers by management. These cases included allegations of unfair bargaining by management, claims of wrongful dismissal of employees, and charges of discrimination and harassment. Disputes that featured unfair labour practices by corporations were coded as "1" while all other cases were coded as "0," and it was hypothesized that when companies engaged in foul play at the bargaining table, justices would be more likely to favour the economic claims of unions because management had not sufficiently played by the rules. Similarly, we believed that justices would support the individual in disputes featuring some form of discrimination or sexual harassment claims (1 = harassment/discrimination cases, 0 = all other cases) because we thought that justices would be more inclined to favour parties who had endured discriminatory treatment in the workforce and the justices would be interested in maintaining a fair workplace environment for all. Lastly, it was perceived that in disputes involving the wrongful dismissal of employees (1 = wrongful dismissal cases, 0 = all other cases), justices would tend to favour the worker more readily because he or she had been unfairly treated by management, at least in relation to cases that did not feature a wrongful dismissal claim. Ultimately, we expected the logistic regression equation to produce positive coefficients for each of these factual variables, even when controlling for ideology and other factors in the model.

A second type of factual variable pertained to disputes involving unemployment, sick leave, workers' compensation, and other benefits and working conditions (1 = benefits and conditions cases, 0 = all other cases). We envisaged that the justices would be sympathetic to the arguments advanced by union workers in cases where benefits and working conditions were at issue, because they are essential to the daily economic well-being of the individual and his or her family. For example, cases involving unemployment benefits for individuals who have lost their job or workers' compensation for those temporarily out of work tend to tug at the heartstrings of the justices to a greater degree than cases not raising these issues. We omitted from our analysis cases involving no benefits in order to have a category of comparison for this variable, and expected a positive coefficient for this variable in the model.

Two other factual variables in the equation dealt with whether employees were pursuing a right to strike claim in the courts, and whether the case involved a strike or lockout. Regarding the first variable, since Canada has laws forbidding strikes by certain workers and there is no recognition of a right to strike in the text of the *Charter*, we expected justices to be less favourable to union claims seeking to secure such a constitutional right. We believed that justices would perceive unions as pushing the legal envelope by trying to secure a constitutional right that did not exist. Moreover, it is possible that justices may fear that if such a right were read into the *Charter*, a power imbalance would result between workers and management because unions could simply bypass the negotiation process and use the threat of a strike to achieve their demands. The coding scheme for this variable was "1" if unions sought a right to strike under the *Charter* and "0" in all other cases, and we anticipated a negative coefficient for this variable. In contrast, we expected the justices to be more sympathetic to union workers in cases where a strike or lockout had occurred because of the economic jeopardy striking workers face and the harm such activity causes to the process of reaching a negotiated settlement. In light of our hypothesis, we expected the strike or lockout indicator to feature a positive coefficient.

The last factual variable in the union model takes into consideration the possibility that the justices might defer to the expertise of labour boards, which play a key role in resolving union/management conflicts in Canada. The rationale for this variable is that since labour boards have been established to adjudicate union/management conflicts, and have necessarily developed expertise in resolving such cases, justices would be more likely to defer to their rulings. Indeed, one could persuasively argue that if justices simply substituted their views for the rulings of these specialized bodies, the primary rationale for creating these institutions would be undermined. We therefore coded disputes with a liberal labour board ruling as +1, cases with a conservative ruling by a labour board as −1, and cases with no labour board ruling as 0. In line with our hypothesis, we expected a positive coefficient to appear if the justices were swayed by the expertise of labour board arbitrators.

Two litigant variables included in the regression equation dealt with whether blue collar and public safety workers were parties in the case, and whether the Canadian Labour Congress (CLC) intervened. For the first measure, it was hypothesized that, controlling for all other factors, justices would favour blue collar and public safety workers (coded as "1") more than their white collar counterparts (coded as "0") because they more readily represent the economic underdogs in society. Since blue collar workers are less privileged, face more difficult working conditions, and have fewer job opportunities, we believed that justices would deem them more worthy of protection from economic harm than other types of workers. In essence, even when controlling for judicial ideology, we anticipated that the justices would be more supportive of those who are most vulnerable to the whims of the marketplace. We therefore expected the blue collar variable to produce a positive coefficient in the equation. It is important to note that we included police and public safety workers in the blue collar category. While some may quibble with this classification scheme, most would agree that those employed in the public safety sector face stressful working conditions on par with those of other blue collar workers. We also expected the justices to be more sympathetic to union claims when the CLC provided resources and legal justification in the guise of *amicus* support. Our hypothesis in this area is in line with the work of Brodie (2002), who suggested that some interest groups have received favourable treatment by the Court in the post-*Charter* era. We expected this variable (1 = CLC intervention) to generate a positive coefficient in the equation.

The last two variables in the model assess whether the Lamer and McLachlin Court justices treated union/management claims differently from their Dickson Court predecessors. We did not posit a directional hypothesis for this measure because there is no theoretical justification for expecting that the two latter courts would hand down a statistically significant larger number of liberal or conservative rulings than the Dickson Court when controlling for the ideology of the justices. Having said this, a significant coefficient in the positive direction would signal a liberalizing trend on the part of the latter two courts in union cases, while a negative coefficient would signal the opposite. Ultimately, we included these two variables in order to tease out any ideological differences that may appear between the first three post-*Charter* courts.[4]

RESULTS

All Union/Management Cases

Table 6.6 provides the maximum likelihood coefficients for the cases involving union/management conflicts; model fit statistics are found at the bottom of the table. The results indicate that the fourteen-variable model correctly predicts the ideological direction of the justices' votes 75 percent of the time,

TABLE 6.6

Logistic regression estimates of liberal votes in all union cases, 1984–2003

Variable	b	Statistical significance	Probability of liberal vote when x is low	Probability of liberal vote when x is high	Change in probability
JUDGE-LEVEL VARIABLES					
Private practice	−0.748	.009**	.622	.437	−.185
Newspaper ideology	−0.040	.386	.618	.580	−.038
Party of prime minister	0.085	.243	.577	.618	.041
CASE CHARACTERISTICS					
Unfair labour practice	0.988	.002**	.560	.774	.214
Benefits and conditions	1.312	.000***	.533	.809	.276
Discrimination claim	0.671	.013*	.567	.719	.152
Right to strike	−1.510	.001***	.619	.264	−.355
Strike/lockout	−0.679	.011*	.626	.459	−.167
Wrongful dismissal	−1.227	.000***	.677	.380	−.296
Liberal labour board	0.705	.000***	.361	.698	.337
PARTIES AND INTERVENORS					
Blue collar workers	0.442	.031*	.525	.633	.108
Canadian Labour Congress	2.625	.000***	.518	.937	.419
COURT CONTROL VARIABLES					
Lamer Court	−1.300	.000***	.706	.395	−.311
McLachlin Court	−1.340	.000***	.680	.358	−.322
CONSTANT AND MODEL FIT STATISTICS					
Constant	0.658				
−2 LLR chi-square		596.644***			
Nagelkerke R^2		.348			
Percent correct		74.6%			
Reduction in error		40.8%			

NOTE: $N = 560$.
* $p < .05$, ** $p < .01$, *** $p < .001$

producing a proportional reduction in error (PRE) of 41 percent. Compared with the five other models examining both unanimous and non-unanimous cases, the set of variables in the union area produces one of the strongest prediction rates, second only to the search and seizure model (78 percent; see Table 4.9).

As in the search and seizure area, all the case-level characteristics are significant in the union equation. Moreover, the judge-level indicator tapping extensive experience as a lawyer, the two litigant measures, and both court control variables prove to be statistically significant in the equation. Turning to the judge-level characteristics, it is not surprising that the coefficient for private practice indicates that justices who come to the Court with significant prior experience as private lawyers (five or more years) are 19 percent more likely to side with business interests in union disputes than those who spent a bulk of their careers as judges or academics ($b = -0.75$, significant at the 99 percent confidence level). This makes intuitive sense and coincides with the hypothesis that justices coming to the high court from a privileged legal background will remain more closely affiliated with the corporate interests that they had predominantly represented.

Interestingly, neither the party of prime minister nor newspaper ideology measure proves to be statistically significant in the union area, and only the party indicator's coefficient is in the expected direction ($b = 0.09$ for party of prime minister, $b = -0.04$ for newspaper ideology). The failure of the newspaper ideology measure to achieve significance can be partially explained by the high degree of collinearity between this measure and private practice ($r = -.455$). Because of this collinearity, we explored several different model specifications, including ones where newspaper ideology and party of prime minister were omitted and tested alone. Our comparison of the various models makes it clear that, in the union/management area at least, private legal experience serves as a useful surrogate for explaining ideological conflict on the post-*Charter* Canadian Court. [5]

As mentioned earlier, all seven factual variables are statistically significant in the equation, indicating that, as in the search and seizure area, case facts largely trigger predictable attitudinal responses by the justices in the area of labour law. As expected, justices are 21 percent more likely to favour union litigants in cases where companies are found to engage in unfair labour practices than in all other cases ($b = 0.99$, significant at the 99 percent confidence level). Thus, even when controlling for the ideological proclivities of the justices and other factors, members of the Court show greater sympathy toward union workers when corporations have violated tenets of fair play in the bargaining process or in response to union efforts to represent workers. The Court's rulings in *CBC v. Canada (Labour Relations Board)*, [1995] 1 S.C.R. 157 and *Royal Oak Mines v. Canada (Labour Relations Board)*, [1996] 1 S.C.R. 369 demonstrate this pattern. In the first case, the Court ruled that the Canadian Broadcasting Corporation had engaged in unfair labour practices by forcing a journalist to choose between serving as union president and his job as a radio host after he published articles in a union newsletter that management believed undermined journalistic objectivity. In *Royal Oak Mines v. Canada*, the Court sided forcefully with employees involved in a bitter and violent strike against a mining company that had clearly failed to bargain in good faith and had balked at Labour Relations Board efforts to facilitate the bargaining process. Both cases highlight the Canadian Court's willingness to support union workers in the face of corporate strong-arm tactics. Moreover, the justices are 15 percent more likely to vote liberally in cases where a worker alleges that harassment or discrimination has occurred in the workplace, as opposed to non-discrimination disputes ($b = 0.67$, significant at the 95 percent confidence level). For example, in *Brooks v. Canada Safeway Ltd.*, [1989] 1 S.C.R. 1219, the Court ruled that female employees could not be excluded from sick leave benefits during their pregnancy, while in *Janzen v. Platy Enterprises Ltd.*, [1989] 1 S.C.R. 1252, the Court determined that sexual harassment is a form of sex discrimination that needed to be curtailed by the employer in order to maintain a non-threatening work environment.

The justices of the post-*Charter* Court are also 28 percent more likely to favour union workers when they bring forth claims involving the loss of various benefits and working conditions ($b = 1.31$, significant at the 99.9 percent confidence level). The Court's rulings in *Hills v. Canada*, [1988] 1 S.C.R. 513 and *Caron v. Canada*, [1991] 1 S.C.R. 48 illustrate this pro-worker sentiment. In the former case, the Court determined that employees who were laid off because of a strike by a companion union were not disqualified from receiving unemployment benefits because they were not actively financing or participating in the strike. Meanwhile, in *Caron v. Canada*, the majority ruled that workers who were not immediately recalled to work following a labour settlement remained entitled to unemployment benefits from the time the labour pact was reached. Collectively, these cases suggest that judicial sympathies extend to individuals who are trying to meet basic economic needs when they have faced discrimination, lost their jobs or benefits, or experienced unfair labour practices in contract disputes.

The two variables pertaining to the right to strike and strikes and lock-outs are statistically significant, although only the coefficient for right to strike cases is in the expected direction ($b = -1.51$ for right to strike, significant at the 99.9 percent confidence level; $b = -0.68$ for strike/lockout, significant at the 95 percent confidence level). The findings reveal that in cases where unions seek to advance a constitutional right to strike, justices are 36 percent less likely to rule in their favour compared with other cases, and that they are 17 percent less likely to cast a pro-union vote in cases where a strike or lockout has occurred (see the last column of Table 6.6). In the first instance, the justices appear unwilling to push the legal envelope of the *Charter* right to free expression, as exemplified by a trio of rulings handed down in 1987 (*Reference re Public Service Employee Relations Act*, [1987] 1 S.C.R. 313; *PSAC v. Canada*, [1987] 1 S.C.R. 424; and *RWDSU v. Saskatchewan*, [1987] 1 S.C.R. 460). In the second instance, the justices appear troubled by the degree to which strikes disrupt normal economic activity (for examples, see *Newfoundland (Attorney General) v. NAPE*, [1988] 2 S.C.R. 204 and *BCGEU v. British Columbia (Attorney General)*, [1988] 2 S.C.R. 214). Thus, our results suggest that members of the high court are far less sympathetic to collective efforts by unions to strike than to their efforts to redress individual grievances pertaining to benefits and unfair working conditions.

Contrary to expectations, the coefficient for the wrongful dismissal variable is in the negative direction, indicating that when workers allege that they have been unlawfully fired, the justices are 30 percent less likely to side with the underdog than in all other cases ($b = -1.23$, significant at the 99.9 percent confidence level). This is a counterintuitive finding, but cases like *Bhinder v. Canadian National Railway*, [1985] 2 S.C.R. 561 and *Flieger v. New Brunswick*, [1993] 2 S.C.R. 651 help explain the Court's overall stance. In *Bhinder v. Canadian National Railway*, the Court upheld the dismissal of a Sikh who refused to wear a hard hat in a potentially dangerous work setting. The majority of the Court held that the dismissal was legitimate because Bhinder was unwilling to be reassigned to accommodate his religious objection, and requiring a hard hat was a bona fide occupational requirement. In *Flieger v. New Brunswick*, the Court was unsympathetic to highway patrolmen who argued that they were wrongfully laid off when the province contracted out its services to the RCMP. Ultimately, the Court dismissed their claim because it believed that the province had engaged in a legitimate management decision and had provided them with reasonable notice of their termination and alternative employment as corrections workers. These two cases illustrate that in some wrongful dismissal claims decided by the Court, it was the employee, not management, who presented unreasonable demands in the workplace. The last case-level characteristic, capturing whether a labour board had issued a liberal ruling, indicates that, as expected, the justices are 34 percent more likely to favour the lower labour board's ruling ($b = 0.71$, significant at the 99.9 percent confidence level). This result confirms our hyphothesis that the justices might be willing to defer to the expertise of labour boards and rely on their rulings in most labour/management disputes.

The four remaining variables in the equation prove to be statistically significant predictors of liberal or conservative votes in union/management cases. The coefficients for both blue collar workers and the Canadian Labour Congress are in the expected direction, and indicate that when either of these parties is involved in a dispute, the Court is 11 percent and 42 percent more likely to side with the economic underdog than in all other cases ($b = 0.44$ for blue collar workers, significant at the 95 percent confidence level; $b = 2.63$ for the CLC intervenor, significant at the 99.9 percent confidence level). Indeed, intervention by the CLC produces the largest change in the odds for a liberal vote in the model, and indicates that the organization has been a successful protagonist for union interests (for example, see *UFCW Local 1518 v. KMart Canada, Ltd.*, [1999] 2 S.C.R. 1083 and *Allsco Building Products Ltd. v. UFCW Local 1288P*, [1999] 2 S.C.R. 1136). The impact of the CLC as an intervenor squares well with Brodie's research (2002) suggesting that some key interest groups have attained a privileged status when appearing and arguing before the Canadian Court.

Both the Lamer and McLachlin Court control variables show that these two courts were roughly 30 percent more likely than their Dickson Court predecessor to hand down rulings that favoured management interests, all other things being equal ($b = -1.30$ for Lamer Court, $b = -1.34$ for McLachlin Court, both significant at the 99.9 percent confidence level). These findings suggest that, controlling for all other factors, the zenith of pro-union voting occurred during the *Charter* honeymoon period of the Dickson Court.

Taken together, the fourteen variables in the model provide a powerful explanation for the ideological division found in all post-*Charter* union cases. In the union area, however, it is private practice, not newspaper ideology or party of prime minister, that serves as the most useful surrogate for the ideological proclivities of the justices. The question remains whether this judge-level variable provides even greater explanatory power in a model examining only non-unanimous cases in this area of law. We address this question next.

Non-Unanimous Union/Management Cases
The model for contested union/management cases featured twelve of the variables found in the larger equation, with the exception of the Lamer Court control variable, which was highly collinear with the McLachlin Court indicator ($r = -.520$), and the CLC variable because the CLC appeared in only one case. The results in Table 6.7 provide almost as powerful a prediction rate of judicial votes despite the fact that only five variables attained significance in the model (72 percent of votes correctly predicted, as opposed to 75 percent for all cases). Although there is an overall decrease in the ability to correctly forecast the votes when justices disagree in union/management cases, there is a substantial increase in the relative impact of private practice as an explanatory variable. Indeed, justices who had served the bulk of their career in private practice are 30 percent less likely to rule for economic underdogs than their counterparts who had worked principally as academics or judges. This represents an 11 percent jump in the change in probability over the model for all union/management cases. It is noteworthy that the coefficients for both the newspaper ideology and party of prime minister measures flipped in terms of their directional impact relative to the prior model, which may be attributed to the high collinearity between the private practice and newspaper ideology scores. There is, however, a substantially larger gap between the justices at the two extremes of the newspaper ideology measure in the second model, with liberals on the newspaper measure being 24 percent more likely than conservatives to rule for the economic underdog. The results for private practice and newspaper ideology illustrate not only that private practice remains a useful ideological surrogate in union cases where the justices disagree but also that the newspaper ideology score is more effective at differentiating the voting behaviour of the justices than is the larger set of union cases.

In contrast to the model analyzing all union/management disputes, only three case-level variables are statistically significant, all of them at the 95 percent confidence level. In line with the larger model, both cases involving unfair labour practices and those involving lost benefits and working conditions produce relatively similar positive impacts, with the likelihood of the justices casting a liberal vote increasing 4 percentage points (to 25 percent) in the first instance and with no real change (remaining at 28 percent) in the second instance. Somewhat surprisingly, the coefficient for discrimination claims flips from positive to negative in the second model, and indicates that in discrimination cases where there is disagreement on the Court,

TABLE 6.7

Logistic regression estimates of liberal votes in non-unanimous union cases, 1984–2003

Variable	b	Statistical significance	Probability of liberal vote when x is low	Probability of liberal vote when x is high	Change in probability
JUDGE-LEVEL VARIABLES					
Private practice	−1.242	.007**	.588	.292	−.296
Newspaper ideology	.249	.131	.385	.629	.244
Party of prime minister	−.009	.447	.543	.538	−.005
CASE CHARACTERISTICS					
Unfair labour practice	1.092	.013*	.486	.738	.252
Benefits and conditions	1.273	.027*	.502	.783	.281
Liberal labour board	.251	.198	.451	.576	.125
Wrongful dismissal	.440	.196	.521	.628	.107
Right to strike	−.213	.377	.547	.494	−.053
Strike/lockout	.498	.140	.520	.640	.120
Discrimination claim	−1.171	.031*	.579	.299	−.280
PARTIES AND INTERVENORS[a]					
Blue collar workers	−.555	.081	.627	.491	−.136
COURT CONTROL VARIABLES					
Lamer Court[b]	—	—	—	—	—
McLachlin Court	2.153	.000***	.367	.833	.466
CONSTANT AND MODEL FIT STATISTICS					
Constant	−.613				
−2 LLR chi-square		269.139***			
Nagelkerke R^2		.243			
Percent correct		71.5%			
Reduction in error		38.7%			

NOTE: $N = 228$.

a The indicator for Canadian Labour Congress intervenor status is omitted from the equation because of the low participation rate in non-unanimous cases (only one).

b The Lamer Court indicator is omitted from the equation because of high collinearity with the McLachlin Court.

* $p < .05$, ** $p < .01$, *** $p < .001$

the justices are 28 percent *less* likely to rule for the worker than in all other disputes. Perhaps this anomaly becomes a little more understandable when we examine a few cases where litigants attempted to use novel legal strategies to redress discriminatory action. For example, in *Beliveau-St-Jacques v. FEESP,*

[1996] 2 S.C.R. 345, the Court refused to allow a woman who had already obtained workers' compensation for sexual harassment to pursue civil damages for the same injury. Likewise in *Bhinder v. Canadian National Railway*, [1985] 2 S.C.R. 561, the Court ruled that the dismissal of a Sikh was legitimate because he refused to wear a hard hat at the worksite and was unwilling to accept the employer's efforts to accommodate his religious objections. Thus, a textual analysis of these two cases where litigants were pushing the envelope of the law helps one understand why the impact of this factual variable is not in the hypothesized direction. Overall, when the case-level characteristics of the two union/management models are compared, it is clear that when the justices disagree, facts matter far less in fostering that disagreement than the ideological leanings of the justices. In addition, the one variable included in the equation in an attempt to capture the type of litigant involved in the dispute, namely, blue collar workers, proves not to be statistically significant, and its impact is in the unexpected direction ($b = -0.56$). Thus, when justices disagree, they do not appear predisposed to favour the claims of blue collar and public safety workers over other litigants in the union area.

The most important variable in the non-unanimous model is the McLachlin Court control variable, which is statistically significant at the 99.9 percent confidence level ($b = 2.15$). Indeed, this variable proved to be the most powerful predictor of liberal votes in the equation, and suggests that *when the justices are at odds*, the justices on the McLachlin Court are 47 percent more likely to side with union interests than their colleagues on the two prior Courts. This finding bucks the trend across all union cases that suggests that when the McLachlin Court justices agree, they tend to reach more conservative rulings, which advance business interests more frequently than union demands.

Taken together, the twelve variables in the model tapping ideology, experience in private practice, types of litigants, judicial deference, a court control variable, and factual circumstances in a case provide a powerful explanation for the ideological division found in post-*Charter* union cases. One should keep in mind, however, that it is private practice, not newspaper ideology or party of prime minister, that best captures the ideological leanings of justices in such cases. Overall, we believe that the results confirm the relevance of the attitudinal model for explaining voting behaviour in this area of law, and thus provide evidence of the model's utility beyond the confines of criminal disputes in the modern Canadian context.

Given the importance of ideology in the resolution of disputed union cases, we sought to replicate the bifurcated analysis that we used in the criminal area to assess whether justices on the liberal side of the Canadian high court approach case facts differently from their more conservative colleagues. In step with our earlier analysis, we divided the justices into two ideological camps based on their newspaper ideology scores. Since there were 23 justices in the union dataset (as opposed to 21 in the criminal dataset), the dividing line between the two camps shifts slightly from 0.444 to 0.500 on the ideology scale. Thus, we split the sample of 23 justices into the 11 most liberal-scoring justices (greater than 0.500) and the 12 most conservative-moderate–scoring justices (less than or equal to 0.500). Interestingly, the results in Table 6.8 confirm that justices from the two sides of the ideological spectrum do respond to different case facts in different ways when resolving non-unanimous union cases. For example, it is clear that the liberal justices are prompted to cast more liberal votes when unfair labour practices and benefits and working conditions are at issue (b = 1.39 for unfair labour practices, b = 1.82 for benefits and conditions, both significant at the 95 percent confidence level). Not surprisingly, these findings parallel the statistically significant coefficients that appear in the model for the non-unanimous cases.

These two case facts trigger much more muted ideological responses from the conservative and moderate side of the bench. The only case fact that appears to prompt a substantial conservative attitudinal response is the presence of discrimination claims, which features a change in probability of –47 percent (b = –2.56, significant at the 99 percent confidence level). Although this variable also has a negative effect on the liberal members of the Court, its impact is minimal, with this case fact triggering a more conservative vote only 3 percent of the time (b = –0.13). Remarkably, the McLachlin Court variable proved statistically significant for both sides of the ideological spectrum in union cases. While the liberal members of that Court are 34 percent more likely to side with union claimants than their Lamer and Dickson Court predecessors, the conservative-leaning justices are 51 percent more likely to do so (b = 1.62 for liberals, significant at the 99 percent confidence level; b = 2.26 for conservative-moderates, significant at the 99.9 percent confidence level).

These findings confirm that there is a substantial liberalizing trend in *non-unanimous* union disputes on the McLachlin Court, and that both ideological wings are responsible for this shift. Despite this trend, the findings in Table 6.8 illustrate that justices on both sides of the bench respond to

different characteristics of the non-unanimous union cases. These findings,
like the right to counsel and search and seizure results, lend credence to the
claim that distinctive patterns of ideological voting are evident across the
ideological divide in the post-*Charter* Canadian Court.

Tax Cases

DATA AND METHODS

Following our earlier analyses, cases in the tax area were derived from published decisions in the *Canadian Supreme Court Reports* (1984–2003) that

TABLE 6.8

**Estimates of liberal votes by liberal-moderate and conservative-moderate justices in
non-unanimous union cases, 1984–2003**

	Moderates and liberals		Moderates and conservatives	
	b	Change in probability of a liberal vote (N = 125)	*b*	Change in probability of a liberal vote (N = 103)
CASE CHARACTERISTICS				
Unfair labour practice	1.390*	.289	0.440	.110
Benefits and conditions	1.824*	.329	0.838	.206
Liberal labour board	0.371	.180	0.310	.150
Wrongful dismissal	0.439	.101	0.683	.169
Right to strike	−0.024	−.006	−0.072	−.018
Strike/lockout	0.936	.203	−0.005	−.001
Discrimination claim	−0.131	−.032	−2.559**	−.472
PARTIES AND INTERVENORS				
Blue collar workers	−0.397	−.093	−0.837	−.206
COURT CONTROL VARIABLES				
Lamer Court [a]	—	—	—	—
McLachlin Court	1.616**	.335	2.263***	.512
CONSTANT AND MODEL FIT STATISTICS				
Constant	−0.673		−0.560	
−2 LLR chi-square		149.782*		117.018**
Nagelkerke R^2		.193		.291
Percent correct		69.6%		75.7%
Reduction in error		25.5%		47.9%

a The Lamer Court indicator is omitted from the equation because of high collinearity with the McLachlin
   Court.
* $p < .05$, ** $p < .01$, *** $p < .001$

addressed tax disputes between government and individuals or corporations. The analysis of all the tax cases featured 501 votes across seventy-three disputes, while the non-unanimous dataset focused on 134 votes across nineteen cases.[6] As in our previous tests of the attitudinal model, each justice's vote served as the unit of analysis, with liberal votes coded as "1" whenever a justice endorsed the government's power to tax, and conservative votes coded as "0" when individual or corporate interests prevailed. The rationale behind this coding scheme was that government collects taxes to provide a variety of public goods and services for its citizens, and to ensure a social safety net for the economically disadvantaged. Thus, a liberal vote would favour government's power to deliver more of these services through taxation, while a conservative vote would favour the economic liberty claims of individual taxpayers and companies seeking to protect their resources to pursue their own economic goals.

There were twelve independent variables in our analysis of tax votes, covering judge-level characteristics, case-level facts, parties and litigants, and court control variables. The two judge-level characteristics tap the familiar variables of the party of prime minister and newspaper ideology, and followed a coding scheme identical to that used in the union area, although the hypotheses were recast with a tax focus. Naturally, Liberal Party appointees (+1) were expected to be more favourable than Conservative Party appointees (−1) to the tax arguments advanced by government rather than those advanced by individuals or corporate interests. Similarly, we expected that justices with higher newspaper liberalism scores (closer to +2) would be more prone than their most conservative counterparts (closer to −2) to support the taxation power of government. Thus, these two variables were expected to yield positive coefficients in the logistic regression analysis of tax cases.[7]

Six case-level variables were included in the model, four of which pertain to the type of taxation involved in the dispute: income tax disputes dealing principally with deductions, stock/estate taxes, payroll deductions by companies, and Goods and Services (GST)/sales taxes.[8] All categories were coded as dichotomous variables: "1" if the type of tax was involved in the case and "0" otherwise. We subsequently established a hierarchy for these distinctive tax claims that differentiated between their relative impact on individuals and corporate taxpayers. We placed income taxes, deductions, and exemptions at the top of the hierarchy because we perceived income tax to be the most intrusive type of tax for individuals and companies to pay. Moreover, this type of tax has an impact that is more noticeable from pay period to pay period and financial quarter to financial quarter than other kinds of taxes in the hierarchy. It was hypothesized that justices would be most favourable to the economic liberty claims asserted by taxpayers in cases where government income taxes or tax deductions and exemptions that have been disallowed by government were at issue. We placed stock and estate taxes in the second tier of the tax hierarchy because we perceived their impact to be less central to the day-to-day economic survival of individuals; we placed them in the second tier, however, because they do have material ramifications for surviving dependents. Thus, we anticipated that justices would be *less* favourable to the interests of taxpayers in these cases compared with income tax cases, but still *more* favourable to their claims than in sales tax situations. GST and sales tax cases are found on the third tier of our hierarchy because of the almost invisible impact of this kind of tax on the daily economic fortunes of most people. Thus, we believed that the justices would treat individual challenges to these types of taxes less favourably than challenges to the other taxes in our hierarchy, but more favourably than challenges in either corporate payroll tax collection cases or the excluded category of business licence and property tax cases. Since payroll tax collection cases involve efforts by companies to avoid paying taxes for their respective employees, such cases were found at the bottom of the hierarchy of the variables included in the model. Since these cases feature some of the most egregious forms of tax evasion by corporations, we expected the justices to be less favourable to the economic liberty arguments made in such cases.

Ultimately, the four variables in our tax hierarchy are compared with excluded cases featuring disputes about business licence fees and property taxes. The rationale for using these as a comparison group is that property taxes and business licensing fees are so integral to government collection of revenue that we anticipated very little opposition to government claims in these cases. We believed that justices would view the payment of property taxes and licence fees as just part of the cost of doing business. Ultimately, it was expected that all the coefficients in the tax hierarchy would be negative, with the largest negative impact anticipated for income tax deductions, followed by stock/estate taxes, GST and sales taxes, and corporate payroll tax cases.

Seizure of documents constituted another factual variable in the regression analysis (1 = seizure of materials cases, 0 = all other cases). This variable was included because some cases in the tax area involved the confiscation of financial documents; we believed that justices would be more sympathetic to the taxpayer because of the privacy rights involved. Thus, we hypothesized that seizures of financial records would sway the justices to favour the tax-payer more than government, all other things being equal. Critics might argue, however, that since the government seizes documents only in egregious cases of tax fraud or evasion, the justices could be prone to favour the government and not the taxpayer in such cases. Although this is possible, we believed that the first hypothesis was more credible since privacy interests represent a core value in advanced modern democracies. Assuming that our hypothesis was accurate, we anticipated a negative coefficient for this variable.

As in the union area, a judicial deference measure was included in the analysis, although it was coded slightly differently, with a liberal trial court ruling coded as "1" and a conservative ruling coded as "0." In line with our hypothesis in the union area, we believed that Canadian Supreme Court justices would be prone to defer to trial court judges in tax cases because these lower court judges may have developed more expertise in resolving such claims, especially at the federal level. It makes intuitive sense to believe that justices serving on a generalized high court might be reluctant to go against the rulings of lower court judges in a highly specialized area of law. If this hypothesis held true, we anticipated a positive coefficient in the regression results.

Two party/litigant variables were included in the analysis to determine whether the justices approached individual taxpayers differently from corporate or non-profit agencies, or whether they viewed provincial taxes differently from federal taxes. In the first instance, one might argue that since corporate and non-profit groups are more likely to be involved in tax litigation than the one-shot individual taxpayer, these entities could employ their resource advantage in the legal system to help them win more frequently than their individual counterparts (Galanter 1974, 2003). One might also contend, however, that the justices would be more sympathetic to individual claims in the tax area than to claims by corporate or non-profit entities because of the inherent difficulties individuals might have in understanding the intricacies of the tax code. Although both hypotheses are plausible, we are more persuaded by the first because past scholarship has demonstrated persuasively that repeat players have a distinct advantage in the legal system. Consequently, we created a dichotomous variable to denote individual taxpayers (coded as "1") from their corporate and non-profit counterparts (coded as "0"), and expected a positive coefficient for this indicator. For the second party variable, we believed that justices would be less likely to favour provincial – as opposed to federal – efforts to tax companies and individuals because even though Canada has a federal system where provinces exert independent control over some governmental functions, the national government has premier power to secure taxpayer funds in order to provide public goods and services for the nation as a whole. Indeed, Canada's history of taxing authority since Confederation recognizes a national supremacy in the collection of taxes and the redistribution of resources between the provinces, with the provinces dependent upon tax collections and abatements that are directed by the national government to this day (see Hogg 1997, 143-52). Given this argument, we coded this variable as "1" when provincial taxes were being challenged and "0" if the case involved a federal tax, and expected a negative coefficient for this variable.

The last two variables in the tax model controlled for possible differences in decision-making trends of the first three post-*Charter* courts. In line with our analysis in the union cases, the inclusion of these measures enables us to determine whether the Lamer and McLachlin Courts differed from their Dickson Court predecessor in their ideological approach to tax cases. As in Chapters 4 and 5, we did not posit a directional hypothesis for these two variables, but simply included them to determine whether distinctions exist between these three courts. We now turn to our analysis of the attitudinal model in tax cases decided in the post-*Charter* era.

RESULTS

All Tax Cases

Table 6.9 provides logistic regression estimates for the variables that we believed would explain the voting variance between the justices in tax disputes. The model fit statistics found at the bottom of the table indicate that 74 percent of the justices' votes could be correctly predicted with these variables in the equation. This represents a 43 percent improvement over the modal guessing strategy of 55 percent, and constitutes the largest reduction in error among the models examining all cases in an area of law in our study.

Seven of the twelve variables in the equation proved to be statistically significant, although neither of the two ideology variables provides much explanatory power across all tax cases. Indeed, these variables rank eighth and twelfth in their ability to influence the justices' likelihood of casting a liberal vote ($b = 0.11$ for newspaper ideology and $b = 0.05$ for party of prime minister; see Table 6.9). Thus, as in the equality and free speech areas, the justices do not appear to be heavily influenced by their ideological proclivities across all tax cases. As in the union area, facts play a prominent role in the large model, with five of the six case characteristics being statistically significant at the 99.9 percent confidence level.

The coefficients for the types of tax claims in our four-tier hierarchy match quite well our expectations of tax claim treatment by the justices, with income tax deductions and exemptions generating the most favourable treatment ($b = -3.16$), followed closely by stock/estate taxes ($b = -2.32$). In these

TABLE 6.9

Logistic regression estimates of liberal votes in all tax cases, 1984–2003

Variable	b	Statistical significance	Probability of liberal vote when x is low	Probability of liberal vote when x is high	Change in probability
JUDGE-LEVEL VARIABLES					
Newspaper ideology	0.114	.188	.387	.499	.112
Party of prime minister	0.046	.428	.451	.462	.011
CASE CHARACTERISTICS					
Tax deduction	−3.158	.000***	.844	.187	−.657
Stock dividends/estate	−2.320	.000***	.502	.090	−.412
Payroll tax	−2.168	.000***	.500	.103	−.397
GST/sales tax	−1.483	.001***	.513	.193	−.320
Seizure of documents	1.149	.000***	.424	.699	.275
Deference to trial court	−0.298	.097	.495	.421	−.074
PARTIES AND INTERVENORS					
Individual taxpayer	0.160	.276	.442	.481	.040
Provincial government	−0.731	.014*	.490	.316	−.174
COURT CONTROL VARIABLES					
Lamer Court	−0.759	.005**	.552	.366	−.186
McLachlin Court	0.089	.401	.450	.472	.022
CONSTANT AND MODEL FIT STATISTICS					
Constant	2.722				
−2 LLR chi-square		554.198***			
Nagelkerke R^2		.317			
Percent correct		74.1%			
Reduction in error		42.6%			

NOTE: $N = 501$.
* $p < .05$, ** $p < .01$, *** $p < .001$

two instances, there is a whopping 66 percent and 41 percent greater likelihood that the justices will rule in favour of the taxpayer compared with property tax and business licence cases, the category omitted for comparative purposes. Cases such as *Friesen v. Canada*, [1995] 3 S.C.R. 103 and *Singleton v. Canada*, [2001] 2 S.C.R. 1046 highlight the justices' stance in the area of income tax deductions. In the former case, the majority determined that an individual taxpayer was entitled to an income tax write-off on property that had declined in value for two years prior to its sale. Similarly, in *Singleton v. Canada*, the Court ruled that a lawyer could claim an income tax deduction on the interest of a loan used to refinance his law firm, even though part of the money was also used to purchase a house. In both cases, the Court supported the individual's interpretation of the tax code even though a plausible argument could be made by government that both individuals were obtaining personal gains under the guise of "business" investments. Although the GST/sales tax and payroll tax coefficients have magnitudes that are slightly different from our hypothesized hierarchy, both generate coefficients in the expected direction and have a roughly similar impact on judicial voting patterns (change in odds = –.40 for payroll tax cases and –.32 for GST/sales tax cases). All told, the four variables tapping the type of tax claim had the greatest impact on judicial voting patterns across all tax disputes, demonstrating the importance that justices place on the factual circumstances and the types of claims raised in these cases.

The seizure of financial documents is also an important factual circumstance in tax cases, albeit in the unexpected direction ($b = 1.15$, significant at the 99.9 percent confidence level). The results indicate that justices are 28 percent more likely to support tax authorities when government officials have seized documents and the seizures are being challenged in court (for example, see *Knox Contracting v. Canada*, [1990] 2 S.C.R. 338 and *143471 Canada v. Quebec*, [1994] 2 S.C.R. 339). This counterintuitive finding suggests that justices give less consideration to the privacy interests at stake when documents have been seized in tax investigations.

The two other variables that prove to be statistically significant predictors of tax votes are the provincial government ($b = -0.73$) and the Lamer Court ($b = -0.76$) variables; and the province coefficient is in the expected direction. The results for the first variable indicate that the justices favour the federal government 17 percent more than provincial governments when resolving tax disputes (see Table 6.9), which makes sense given Ottawa's preeminence in securing funds for the federal system. The results for the second variable indicate, however, that, controlling for all other factors, the Lamer Court justices were 19 percent less likely than their Dickson Court predecessors to side with the government in tax cases. The McLachlin Court justices are more prone to walk in step with the Dickson Court tax record. From a broader economic perspective, the findings across all union and tax cases show that the Lamer Court had a decisively conservative strain relative to the Dickson Court, while the contemporary McLachlin Court has taken a more conservative stance in the union area only.

When the full tax model is taken into consideration, the twelve variables successfully explain nearly as many of the case votes as in the union area (74 and 75 percent, respectively). Similarly, almost all the case-level characteristics are statistically significant, which is not surprising given the detailed nature of tax law and the complex interplay of specific facts with disputed interpretations of the tax code. Moreover, this pattern of factual significance is evident in the full panoply of cases decided in the union area, as well as in search and seizure and right to counsel cases. Measures of judicial ideology, however, play a much more muted role in the economic cases, in contrast to their dominance in the two criminal law areas of our study. The relative weakness of ideology in the full tax model raises concerns about the applicability of the attitudinal model in non-unanimous cases as well.

Non-Unanimous Tax Cases

Eleven of the twelve variables in the non-unanimous model are the same as those found in the previous equation, except that payroll cases were omitted because they had to replace the business licence fee and property tax disputes as the excluded category in the tax hierarchy.[9] A new factual variable pertaining to bankruptcy claims was added to the model because of its great prominence in non-unanimous disputes. In essence, these cases featured government efforts to demand priority standing over all other creditors in bankruptcy claims. Whenever this fact appeared in a case, we coded the case as "1"; all other cases were coded as "0." We anticipated that justices would be unlikely to favour governmental priority claims in bankruptcy cases because to do so would be to give government an unwarranted advantage. Indeed, if governments were given priority in such cases, private creditors and banks would be less willing to lend money and invest in economic enterprises because of the increased economic risk in the event of a bankruptcy. We therefore expected a negative coefficient for the bankruptcy/government priority measure. A potential counter-argument to this hypothesis is the notion that justices might believe that government should have priority in bankruptcy cases simply because it has a paramount interest in securing timely payment of debts to the public treasury, and because government provides public goods and services to society at large. Although this is plausible, we did not think it was as convincing because we believed that justices are more prone to treat people who are owed money on equal footing, rather than automatically support the government interest in collecting debts.

The results in Table 6.10 indicate that, as in the union area, there is a reduction in the ability to predict judicial votes in tax cases when there is disagreement on the Court (68 percent versus 74 percent in the larger model, with a proportional reduction in error of 27 percent). Thus, contrary to expectations, in four of the six areas of law studied in this book, there is a reduction, not an increase, in predictive accuracy when we look solely at non-unanimous cases. We expected that when the justices were at odds with each other, the various independent variables would collectively do a better job of accounting for the variance in voting behaviour, simply because the outcomes were not diluted by unanimous votes cast by the justices. As it turns out, the judge-level variables do explain better the variance in voting behaviour in non-unanimous cases, but this is not the case with fact-level variables, which perform less well in the non-unanimous models. Ultimately, the lower predictive accuracy of the models can be attributed to this loss of predictive power from the case facts.

One unique feature that separates the tax cases from the other five areas of law is the fact that newspaper ideology is transformed from a relatively weak explanatory variable in all tax cases into the most important explanatory variable when the justices disagree ($b = 0.60$, significant at the 99 percent confidence level). Indeed, the most liberal justices are 50 percent more likely to rule in favour of the government's authority to tax than their most conservative counterparts, and the magnitude of the coefficient in non-unanimous cases is over four times the size of that found in the first model (0.11; see Table 6.9). This finding indicates that the principal source of disagreement between the justices in the tax area is one that is grounded in ideological differences. Although the impact of the ideology variable increases dramatically across all six areas of law, the tax cases present the only example where the influence changes from not significant to most profound when looking solely at non-unanimous cases. Taken together, the findings provide compelling evidence that when the justices are at odds, their ideological proclivities have a profound impact on their voting behaviour, indicating that attitudinal decision making, at least in the Canadian context, does matter when justices disagree. The more mixed results when analyzing all cases indicate, however, that attitudinal behaviour may not be as pervasive in other court settings as it is in the US.

Only two of the factual variables are statistically significant in both levels of analysis, although the variable tapping seizure of documents is now found in the expected direction in the non-unanimous model, with

TABLE 6.10

Logistic regression estimates of liberal votes in non-unanimous tax cases, 1984–2003

Variable	b	Statistical significance	Probability of liberal vote when x is low	Probability of liberal vote when x is high	Change in probability
JUDGE-LEVEL VARIABLES					
Newspaper ideology	0.597	.009**	.145	.649	.504
Party of prime minister	−0.621	.117	.473	.326	−.148
CASE CHARACTERISTICS					
Bankruptcy/priority	−1.800	.011*	.527	.155	−.371
Seizure of documents	−1.453	.040*	.470	.172	−.298
Tax deduction	−1.912	.022*	.606	.185	−.421
Stock dividends/estate	−0.952	.138	.474	.258	−.216
GST/sales tax	0.017	.489	.432	.436	.004
Deference to trial court	0.282	.297	.391	.460	.069
PARTIES AND INTERVENORS					
Individual taxpayer	−1.055	.045*	.505	.262	−.243
Provincial government	−0.597	.148	.491	.346	−.144
COURT CONTROL VARIABLES					
Lamer Court	0.394	.254	.377	.473	.096
McLachlin Court	1.025	.145	.407	.657	.250
CONSTANT AND MODEL FIT STATISTICS					
Constant	0.980				
−2 LLR chi-square		164.860*			
Nagelkerke R^2		.177			
Percent correct		67.9%			
Reduction in error		27.0%			

NOTE: $N = 134$.
* $p < .05$, ** $p < .01$, *** $p < .001$

the justices being 30 percent less likely to side with the government in such cases (b = −1.45, significant at the 95 percent confidence level). Similarly, the justices are 42 percent less likely to rule in favour of the government in cases involving tax deductions or exemptions (b = −1.91, significant at the 95 percent confidence level). The only other case-level characteristic that proved statistically significant was the newly added bankruptcy variable, indicating that justices are 37 percent less likely to give the government priority in debt collection in bankruptcy claims (b = −1.80, significant at the 95 percent confidence level). The rulings in *British Columbia v. Henfrey Samson Belair Ltd.*, [1989] 2 S.C.R. 24 and *Husky Oil Operations Ltd. v. M.N.R.*, [1995] 3 S.C.R. 453 are indicative of the justices' approach to these disputes. In the former case, a majority of the Court rejected the argument that the federal *Bankruptcy Act* allowed the province of British Columbia to give itself priority over other creditors by passing its own legislation. In *Husky Oil Operations Ltd. v. M.N.R.*, the Court used a similar line of reasoning when it determined that the province of Saskatchewan could not invoke priority over other debtors for unpaid taxes in a bankruptcy proceeding. Clearly, a majority of the justices in both cases did not want to give government priority consideration in bankruptcy claims, instead viewing all creditors as equally worthy.

The only other non-ideological variable to achieve significance is the one denoting an individual taxpayer, which is no longer in the anticipated direction (b = −1.06, significant at the 95 percent confidence level). While the change in probability score for individual taxpayers was insignificant in the large model (.04), in non-unanimous cases, the government is 24 percent less likely to prevail when facing an individual taxpayer as opposed to other types of taxpayers. This suggests that although individuals are not repeat players in the legal system, the justices appear to be more sympathetic to their underdog status given the complex nature of such disputes. Collectively, the twelve variables in the model are able to accurately forecast more than two-thirds of the votes cast in non-unanimous tax cases.

Since ideology is the fulcrum in non-unanimous tax cases, it is important to determine whether factual circumstances have a distinctive impact on the justices at the two ideological extremes. To test for this impact, we divided the twenty justices involved in these cases into the same two blocs as in the criminal law area. Thus, the ten justices scoring 0.444 or less on the newspaper ideology measure were classified as conservative-moderates, while the ten ranking above this cut-off were classified as liberals. The most significant finding from Table 6.11 is that the liberal members of the post-*Charter*

Court responded to cases involving bankruptcy claims ($b = -3.20$), the seizure of documents ($b = -2.47$), and income tax deductions ($b = -3.89$, all significant at the 95 percent confidence level). In cases featuring these three factual circumstances, the liberal justices were at least 50 percent more likely to support the tax claimants, compared with cases not featuring these characteristics. In contrast, their moderate and conservative colleagues were not motivated by any of the factual circumstances in our model; rather, they were 39 percent more likely to side with individual taxpayers advancing a tax claim. Taken as a whole, the results in Table 6.11 suggest that the conservative justices on the post-*Charter* Court are more motivated by their ideological leanings when deciding tax cases, while their liberal colleagues are more responsive to the unique factual circumstances of tax disputes. The fact that the justices at the two ideological extremes do respond differently to factual circumstances and litigants in non-unanimous tax cases provides further evidence that complex patterns of attitudinal decision making take place on opposite ends of the ideological continuum of the Canadian Supreme Court.

Overall, the results across all union and tax cases are mixed with regard to the impact that ideology has on the voting behaviour of post-*Charter* justices in the economic area. Although the impact of ideology in the union and tax area ranked ninth and eighth, respectively, compared with other variables in the model, our results indicate that liberal justices are far more likely to be at odds with their conservative colleagues in union cases than in tax disputes (see Tables 6.6 and 6.9). Ideology becomes one of the most prominent explanatory variables when looking at non-unanimous cases in these two economic areas, however. Specifically, in contested, or non-unanimous, tax cases, the newspaper ideology measure has the most significant impact on whether a justice will cast a liberal vote, while in contested union cases, the ideological surrogate of private practice is the second strongest variable in the equation. Taking a broader look across all the equations, the impact of ideology in tax and union cases falls somewhere between its more prominent profile in two key areas of criminal law and its almost imperceptible role in two fields of civil rights and liberties litigation.

Conclusion

This chapter has provided a review of Supreme Court activity in economic cases decided during the first twenty years of the post-*Charter* experience. The tables in the first portion of the chapter indicate that disputes in the economic area feature panel sizes that are roughly the same as those in all other

TABLE 6.11

Estimates of liberal votes by liberal-moderate and conservative-moderate justices in non-unanimous tax cases, 1984–2003

	Moderates and liberals		Moderates and conservatives	
	b	Change in probability of a liberal vote $(N = 125)$	b	Change in probability of a liberal vote $(N = 103)$
CASE CHARACTERISTICS				
Bankruptcy/priority	-3.195*	-.622	-0.462	-.091
Seizure of documents	-2.465*	-.502	-1.269	-.201
Tax deduction	-3.889*	-.729	-0.299	-.062
Stock dividends/estate	-2.676	-.541	-0.064	-.013
GST/sales tax	0.796	.190	-1.529	-.251
Deference to trial court	-0.369	-.091	1.316	.247
PARTIES AND INTERVENORS				
Individual taxpayer	-0.015	-.004	-2.300*	-.388
Provincial government	-1.964*	-.455	1.284	.283
COURT CONTROL VARIABLES				
Lamer Court	0.994	.243	-0.797	-.171
McLachlin Court	1.526	.313	-0.328	-.065
CONSTANT AND MODEL FIT STATISTICS				
Constant	3.144		-0.318	
-2 LLR chi-square		86.499		67.367
Nagelkerke R^2		.258		.194
Percent correct		70.3%		70.0%
Reduction in error		37.2%		9.9%

* $p < .05$

cases, yet these disputes generated higher rates of unanimity among the justices than did criminal and civil rights and liberties disputes. Justices Iacobucci and Estey stood fully 2 standard deviations above the average in terms of majority opinion authorship, while the bulk of the remaining justices are clustered within 9 percentage points of the mean. The opinion leadership of these two justices is not surprising given their prior expertise in the realm of business law. In contrast, Justice Stevenson stood out as the sole economic outsider on the post-*Charter* Court, authoring concurring or dissenting opinions in almost 30 percent of the cases he heard in this area during his brief stay on the Court. Justice Stevenson's extreme conservatism in economic decisions was counterbalanced by Justice Wilson's overwhelming tendency to cast liberal votes in this area. Most of the justices appeared to cluster around the moderate middle of the Court. Unlike in the other two areas of law, the connection between activism and liberalism in economic cases is more uncertain, perhaps because of the small number of rulings handed down by the Court. As mentioned earlier, while there is a clear connection between liberalism and activism in criminal cases, the insignificant connection in the civil rights and liberties area and the murky findings in the economic area suggest that any criticism of "liberal activist" judges ought to be muted. As in the civil rights and liberties area, a few of the justices do not exhibit strong patterns of attitudinal stability over time in the economic area, in contrast to the more stable record for post-*Charter* justices in the criminal area. The findings across two of the three substantive areas suggest that lawyers and court watchers must recognize that several individual justices might change their ideological stripes over time in different legal areas, and in the process might alter the direction of law in subtle or substantial ways.

The second half of the chapter provides compelling evidence that when justices do disagree in tax and union disputes, ideology plays an integral role in triggering such conflict. Moreover, in both areas of law, there were a few factual variables that triggered attitudinal responses on the part of the justices, with liberal justices being more responsive than their conservative colleagues to particular factual scenarios in both sets of cases. Thus, in contrast to our findings in the two areas of criminal law, conservative justices on the post-*Charter* Court are more animated by their ideological proclivities in the economic area than by the particular case facts in legal disputes. The findings also suggest that members of the McLachlin Court have a greater propensity than members of the Dickson Court to side with the government in non-unanimous tax cases (25 percent more likely) and with the underdog in non-unanimous union cases (47 percent more likely).

From a broader theoretical standpoint, our cumulative findings make it clear that ideology plays a more muted role in the post-*Charter* Canadian setting than in the US Supreme Court. For instance, when looking across the six regression models assessing all cases, the ideology measure ranks among the top three explanatory variables in only one model (right to counsel cases), and consistently falls somewhere between eighth and thirteenth in importance compared with indicators tapping factual circumstance, litigants, and controls for different post-*Charter* courts.[10] Similar studies of the US Supreme Court find a much more powerful role for ideological forces (see Segal and

Spaeth 1993, 2002). When the focus is on cases in which the Canadian justices disagree, however, ideology does have a predictable and prominent impact on judicial voting activity across five of the six areas of law analyzed, and it ranks as the top predictor of liberal voting behaviour across four of the six regression models. Having said this, the fact that ideology's impact runs contrary to expectations in the free expression area highlights the importance of conducting comparative research across high courts in different cultural contexts. While the attitudinal model may provide a viable account of judicial behaviour in general, distinctive cultural factors in other countries may require a more nuanced understanding of its applicability abroad.

7
Attitudinal Consistency in the Post-*Charter* Supreme Court

Chapters 4 to 6 have shown that judicial attitudes and values constitute one of the most powerful predictors of voting behaviour in most of the non-unanimous cases decided by the Supreme Court of Canada, and play a significant role in several of the equations examining all cases. They have also demonstrated that it is the newspaper ideology measure, not the party of prime minister measure, that most accurately taps the attitudinal proclivities of the justices in the Canadian setting. The chapters have also indicated that most of the justices engaged in relatively stable attitudinal behaviour over a six-year period. One question that remains, however, is whether, and to what extent, the justices engage in consistent ideological voting behaviour across the three distinct areas of law examined in this book. In other words, do justices who vote most liberally in the criminal area do so in economic and civil liberties cases as well? Similarly, do justices at the other end of the ideological continuum vote conservatively across all types of legal disputes? What about those found in the ideological middle? Do they remain centrist in all areas of law, or are they more likely to exhibit ideologically inconsistent behaviour than their more extreme colleagues? In the course of answering these questions, this chapter assesses whether, and to what degree, a theoretical construct borrowed from the US public opinion literature informs our understanding about the patterns of ideological consistency found in the voting behaviour of modern Canadian justices. Specifically, we examine whether a theoretical paradigm outlining four distinct archetypes of political ideology help us understand judicial behaviour in the years since the adoption of the *Canadian Charter of Rights and Freedoms*.

Issue Consistency and Four Ideological Archetypes
According to attitudinal theorists, justices come to the high court with well-established beliefs that have been honed through years of scholarship and

training and, in most cases, through prior judicial rulings. These scholars maintain that a justice's voting behaviour should remain fairly consistent across time and issue area. Specifically, we believe that justices found at the two ideological extremes will cast consistently liberal or conservative votes across criminal, economic, and civil rights and liberties cases, while those in the middle will take an ideologically centrist position across these issues.

Having said this, we are aware that our expectations might need to be tweaked a bit because even though ideologues are most likely to exhibit attitudinal consistency, those found in the ideological middle are less likely to do so for several reasons. First, even though justices found at the ideological poles almost always conceptualize issues through a clear ideological prism, the voting behaviour of centrist justices may be inconsistent simply because they often approach the issues in a piecemeal, case-by-case practical fashion. If this holds true, any inconsistency on their part is more likely a byproduct of their attention to the particular legal and factual considerations in a given case rather than an overarching commitment to a certain ideological outcome. Second, given that centrist justices are more likely to act strategically because they often hold the swing vote on the Court, they are more prone to alter their policy position in different issue areas for bargaining purposes in an effort to build majority coalitions. In such situations, the apparent inconsistency of a centrist justice would make intuitive sense and might be a hallmark of strategic activity that provides them with considerable leverage over the direction the Court may take. Lastly, inconsistent voting activity by centrist justices might occur because they are acting as opinion followers on the Court; thus, they are more willing to suppress their own weakly held policy preferences in order to go along with the ideological preferences of the majority coalition. Given these alternative theoretical explanations for attitudinal consistency and inconsistency, it is important to examine judicial voting behaviour across different issue areas to determine the general contours of a particular justice's ideology and voting consistency.

One of the most effective ways to do this is to plot each justice in a two-dimensional ideological space. Our decision to analyze the post-*Charter* justices in this manner fits nicely with the intellectual legacy established in the United States by Schubert (1965, 1974) and more recently in the Canadian context by Morton et al. (1994). Our approach here is animated, however, by a contemporary framework of attitudinal research outlined by Janda and colleagues (2004) in the US public opinion literature. They suggest that attitudinal responses to specific political controversies may fall along two separate ideological continua, one featuring a tension between the values of freedom and order along the x-axis, and the other featuring a tension between freedom and equality along the y-axis. Specifically, they contend that in a democracy, all citizens must determine how much freedom they are willing to sacrifice in order for government to ensure public safety and traditional modes of behaviour. They must also identify how much freedom they are willing to forgo in the marketplace in an effort to achieve progress toward economic and social equality for all. Janda and colleagues (2004, 26) suggest that the balance struck between these conflicting core values by individuals and politicians yields four distinct ideological archetypes: liberals, conservatives, communitarians, and libertarians. Individuals who endorse economic and social equality over freedom, and freedom over social order, fit into the liberal category, while those taking the opposite stance fall into the conservative camp. Although most people think they fit into one of these two classifications, Janda and colleagues (2004, 26) point out that individuals who support equality and order over freedom should be labelled communitarians, while those who value freedom above all else would be libertarians. The four ideological archetypes that they use to gauge public sentiment in a democracy provide a convenient barometer for assessing the ideological proclivities of post-*Charter* Canadian justices as well. By plotting the ideological location of the justices, we are able to assess the attitudinal consistency of members of the post-*Charter* Court across different sets of issue comparisons.

Our effort to spatially plot the post-*Charter* justices is not a new endeavour in the judicial literature or the Canadian setting.[1] In 1994, Morton and colleagues engaged in a similar enterprise when they examined the first ten years of *Charter* rulings. In their analysis, they also plotted the justices' *Charter* votes in two-dimensional space, with one axis assessing legal rights claims in criminal disputes and the second axis addressing "court party" cases that dealt with a host of equality rights cases, discrimination claims, privacy interests, freedom of expression, and religious concerns (Morton et al. 1994, 44-45). Their assessment led them to conclude that the Canadian Court was unified in one centrist, amorphous bloc rather than divisive ideological camps (49-50). Although their findings were important for understanding early post-*Charter* behaviour, we believe that a more fine-tuned and comprehensive analysis of judicial rulings is needed for several reasons. First, the analysis by Morton and colleagues (1994) was *Charter*-centred, and we are interested in capturing important judicial voting trends in both *Charter* and non-*Charter* legal areas. An examination of economic disputes may unmask ideological behaviour on the part of some justices that is distinctive from their patterns in the *Charter* area. Moreover, we believe that Morton and colleagues' two-dimensional analysis actually conflated issues in civil rights and liberties because they placed cases pertaining to discrimination and Aboriginal rights in the same category as cases involving freedom of expression, religion, and abortion. As Janda and colleagues (2004) would point out, cases in the first category (discrimination cases) should be placed along the freedom versus equality continuum, rather than the freedom versus order continuum, because they generally trigger value conflicts involving a tension between equality rights and liberty interests. Ultimately, our analysis seeks to evaluate the decisions of the first twenty years of the post-*Charter* era following Janda and colleagues' more refined categorization scheme, because it may identify justices who approach civil rights and liberties in a distinctive fashion and also provide a more complex and complete understanding of the ideological value conflicts that have emerged between the post-*Charter* justices.

Before actually plotting each of the Canadian justices' ideological stances in the different legal areas, we need to explain how cases addressing various types of issues fit along Janda and colleagues' two attitudinal continua. In line with their categorization scheme, we placed criminal cases along the freedom-order dimension because these disputes necessarily pit the liberty interest of the accused against government's interest in ensuring public safety and order (the x-axis). Economic cases, in turn, fit nicely along Janda and colleagues' freedom-equality continuum because they create a tension between an individual's interest to be free from governmental regulation and government's interest in promoting economic equality and providing collective goods for society at large (the y-axis). Unlike criminal and economic disputes, civil rights and liberties cases could not all be neatly placed along either of Janda and colleagues' two distinct dimensions. While most disputes in this area set an individual's liberty interests against societal efforts to uphold traditional norms of social behaviour (the x-axis), a few, namely, those relating to discrimination and Aboriginal land and treaty claims, fall more readily along the freedom-equality dimension (the y-axis) because the litigants seek to obtain greater social and economic equality for various disadvantaged groups. Given the disparate treatment of these two types of civil rights and liberties claims, we chose to split the civil rights and liberties issues between Janda and colleagues' two continua by placing discrimination and Aboriginal claims along the freedom-equality continuum (on the y-axis) and placing all other civil liberties disputes along the freedom-order continuum (the *x*-axis). Once we reclassified the civil rights and liberties issues in this manner, we could assess the post-*Charter* justices' ideological proclivities in a two-dimensional space because two of the sets of issues in the study dealt with freedom-order concerns, while two others dealt with freedom-equality concerns.

One important limitation to utilizing Janda and colleagues' framework is that the plot of each of the justices' ideological stance is necessarily an artifact of the two issue areas under comparison. Thus, the placement of a particular justice within the two-dimensional framework may change as the issue areas being compared are changed. Although we acknowledge this limitation, it is precisely these types of comparisons that enable us to gauge the relative ideological consistency of a given justice across different sets of issues. We believe that utilizing Janda and colleagues' framework makes sense because we are actually assessing relationships across broad areas of law that account for over 80 percent of the post-*Charter* docket. As a result, we can distinguish justices who are ideologically consistent from those who are not, and can assess whether the fickle are found at the ideological poles or centre of the Court.

Our analysis of voting patterns using Janda and colleagues' two-dimensional framework is featured in Figures 7.1 to 7.4. These figures plot the justices' votes on two issue dimensions in the following sequence: criminal versus economic cases (Figure 7.1), criminal versus discrimination cases (Figure 7.2), civil liberties versus discrimination cases (Figure 7.3), and civil liberties versus economic cases (Figure 7.4). Judicial scores along a particular continuum were calculated based on the percentage of times a justice supported the values of equality, freedom, or order depending on the legal issues under comparison. For example, when judicial votes in the criminal area were compared with economic cases, voting behaviour along the *x*-axis was scored based on the percentage of times a justice supported the government in criminal prosecutions, while the *y*-axis featured scores based on the percentage of times a justice supported an economic underdog or supported government efforts to raise taxes for public goods (see Figure 7.1). Using this scoring method, each justice would necessarily have an *x* and *y* coordinate reflecting his or her support for order and equality over freedom, or vice versa. This same scoring technique was utilized for all four figures.

Figure 7.1 compares judicial votes in criminal cases along the *x*-axis with economic cases along the *y*-axis. Overall, the plot reveals that the post-*Charter*

FIGURE 7.1

Ideological support for order and equality in criminal and economic cases decided by the Supreme Court of Canada, 1984–2003

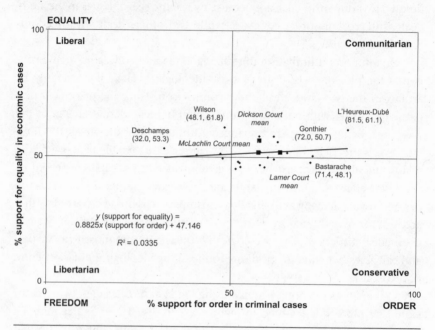

justices are widely dispersed in their support for order in criminal cases, but narrowly dispersed and relatively moderate in their support for equality in economic cases. This distinction can be seen in the wide gap between Justices Deschamps and L'Heureux-Dubé in the criminal dimension, whereas the distance between the most extreme justices is much smaller in the economic dimension. Given the lack of variance in economic voting behaviour, we are not surprised that the line of best fit for this specific set of data is relatively flat. If both issue dimensions reflected a particularly strong ideological chasm between the justices, the data points would cluster along a diagonal slope running at or near a 45-degree angle in either the positive or negative direction. Since the regression line is relatively flat in Figure 7.1, we know that economic cases do not generate a great deal of ideological conflict among the post-*Charter* justices, whereas criminal cases do. This finding is significant because it suggests that even though Morton and colleagues' study (1994) focused exclusively on *Charter* voting patterns, they did not miss any important evidence of distinct ideological voting behaviour between the justices in the economic area.

Turning to the data points for individual members of the Court along these two dimensions, it is clear that Justice L'Heureux-Dubé stands out as an outlier in her voting behaviour, fitting squarely into Janda and colleagues' communitarian box (2004) (see Figure 7.1). Although Justices Gonthier and Bastarache also exhibit high levels of support for upholding the conviction of criminals along the freedom-order continuum, their moderate support for economic equality along the *y*-axis places them well below Justice L'Heureux-Dubé, and has them straddling the communitarian-conservative quadrants when these two issues are compared. In contrast, Justice Deschamps anchors the liberal end of the criminal continuum, supporting the rights of the criminally accused in 68 percent of the cases she heard during her first two years on the Court.

In economic-equality cases, Justices Wilson and L'Heureux-Dubé stand out, if at all, only as weak outliers, with both supporting the equality position over 61 percent of the time. Since Justice Wilson's voting behaviour is far more moderate than that of Justice L'Heureux-Dubé in criminal cases, she falls into Janda and colleagues' liberal camp when these two areas of law are compared (Figure 7.1). Aside from this, most of the justices on the Court take a relatively centrist position on these two issues, although there is a slight tendency for the Court as a whole to fall on the communitarian-conservative side of the ideological divide in their approach toward criminal cases.

A comparison of the aggregate patterns of case outcomes across the Dickson, Lamer, and McLachlin Courts (denoted by the squares in the scatterplot) indicates that mean levels of support for both criminal convictions and economic equality claims have remained relatively stable over the first twenty years under the *Charter*. This fact is reflected in the tight clustering of the means for the three courts in Figure 7.1, two of which happen to fall directly on the regression line. The tendency to side with the government in criminal cases across all three courts suggests that despite some movement in the direction of the due process model after the introduction of the *Charter*, the Canadian Court has been, for much its post-*Charter* history, remarkably consistent in the way it strikes a balance between the crime control model and due process concerns (see Packer 1968).

Figure 7.2 assesses the relationship between voting in criminal cases along the *x*-axis and discrimination cases along the *y*-axis. One is immediately

FIGURE 7.2

Ideological support for order and equality in criminal and discrimination cases decided by the Supreme Court of Canada, 1984–2003

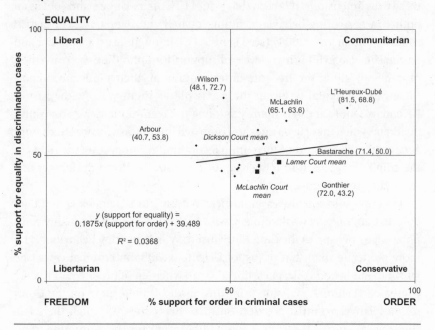

struck by the similarity between the overall patterns found in Figures 7.2 and 7.1. Like the earlier figure, Figure 7.2 shows only a slight libertarian-communitarian trend among the post-*Charter* justices in these two areas of law; again, many of the justices fall fairly close to the regression line. The over-all findings in the first two figures suggests that many of the post-*Charter* justices like to strike a consistent moderate balance when weighing values along the freedom-equality dimension, regardless of whether they are dealing with discrimination or economic concerns. While the voting dispersion in the criminal area, found along the *x*-axis, is identical in the two figures, the greater dispersion of a few of the justices' votes in discrimination suits in Figure 7.2 makes it easier to identify judicial outliers and moderates in that plot.

One of the most striking features of Figure 7.2 is that it highlights the distinctive pro-equality character of the female justices who decided more than ten discrimination cases in the post-*Charter* era. Echoing themes from our analysis in Chapter 5, three of the four female justices included in the figure (Justices Wilson, McLachlin, and L'Heureux-Dubé) exhibit distinctive outlier activity in support of civil rights claimants, and their behaviour is in stark contrast to the relatively moderate record of most of the male justices in such cases. Indeed, these three justices sided with the equality claims advanced by minority interests over 63 percent of the time (see Figure 7.2). While Justices McLachlin and L'Heureux-Dubé fall squarely into Janda and colleagues' communitarian archetype because of their more conservative stance in criminal cases, not surprisingly, Justice Wilson falls into the liberal archetype because of her more liberal stance in such disputes. Although Justice Arbour is more moderate than her three female colleagues in her support of discrimination claims, she stands alone as the most liberal outlier in the criminal dimension because she is willing to support the defendant 59 percent of the time. In contrast to Justice Arbour, Justices Bastarache and Gonthier are found at the opposite end of the criminal spectrum, along with Justice L'Heureux-Dubé. Unlike the communitarian-minded L'Heureux-Dubé, however, they again straddle the communitarian-conservative divide.

Thus, regardless of whether one is comparing criminal cases along the *x*-axis with either economic or discrimination disputes along the *y*-axis, both Justices Bastarache and Gonthier demonstrate remarkably consistent patterns of ideological voting behaviour. When looking holistically at the case outcomes in the three post-*Charter* courts (denoted as squares in the scatterplot), it is remarkable how similar the aggregate data are for the Dickson, Lamer, and McLachlin Courts across the two plots (Figures 7.2 and 7.1). These data suggest that a strong pattern of ideological consistency plays out within each court across two different sets of issue comparisons. Moreover, the aggregate data also indicate that there is a substantial degree of attitudinal stability over time, because all three court values are found in close proximity to each other. Collectively, these two features provide strong evidence that theories of attitudinal consistency and stability are germane in explaining post-*Charter* voting behaviour across these first two graphs.

The scatterplot in Figure 7.3 assesses the patterns of voting in civil liberties cases along the *x*-axis and discrimination cases along the *y*-axis. The overall pattern in this graph suggests that the scores for the justices are widely dispersed in both dimensions, which is not surprising given the contentious nature of the issues raised in both civil liberties and discrimination suits. Unlike in Figures 7.1 and 7.2, the line of best fit shows a marginal ideological trend in a liberal-conservative rather than libertarian-communitarian direction). The change in the direction of the regression line featured in Figure

FIGURE 7.3

Ideological support for order and equality in civil liberties and discrimination cases decided by the Supreme Court of Canada, 1984–2003

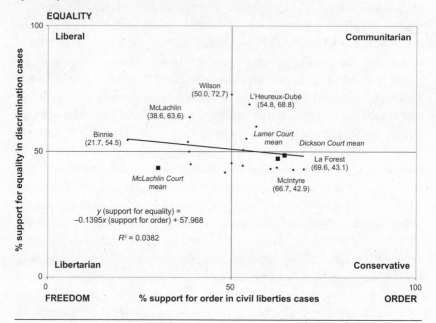

7.3 should not be taken too seriously, however, since it is necessarily an artifact of the two dimensions being compared and, like its predecessors, shows only a slight linear trend of ideological conflict among the justices across these two issue areas.

An examination of the individual justices indicates that the same three female justices who appeared as outliers in the criminal and discrimination graph (Figure 7.2) also occupy extreme positions when civil liberties are compared with discrimination suits (see Justices L'Heureux-Dubé, Wilson, and McLachlin at the top of Figure 7.3). This finding is not surprising since these three women also took strong equality stances in the discrimination area. One notable change between Figures 7.2 and 7.3, however, is that Justice McLachlin, unlike the more ideologically consistent Justices Wilson and L'Heureux-Dubé, has moved from a communitarian stance in the criminal area to a liberal stance in civil liberties cases. This dramatic shift in her ideological location is indicative of someone harbouring conservative values in the area of criminal law while promoting more libertarian values in cases that raise free speech, press, religion, and privacy concerns. The extreme liberal behaviour of Justice McLachlin is outstripped by that of Justice Binnie, who is the most supportive of individual freedom in civil liberties cases (supporting the individual 78 percent of the time). Unlike that of Justice McLachlin, however, his ideological position is found directly on the regression line because of his more moderate treatment of discrimination suits (Figure 7.3). Justices La Forest and McIntyre, on the other hand, are found at the most conservative end of the civil liberties spectrum, taking the position held by Justices Bastarache and Gonthier in the two criminal scatterplots. Finally, the greater degree of overall dispersion reflected in the judicial voting records in Figure 7.3 illustrates that the ideological centre of the Court is more fluid and less compact than in the two earlier scatterplots.

The results in Figure 7.3 illustrate the importance of placing discrimination and Aboriginal land and treaty claims on the y-axis and comparing them with civil liberties disputes on the x-axis. Ultimately, if all the justices viewed the two types of civil rights and liberties issues through the same ideological prism, the line of best fit would be at a 45-degree angle running from the liberal to conservative corners of the plot. The fact that the line is relatively flat, and that some of the justices are located in each of the four ideological quadrants, demonstrates the validity of separating how justices approach some discrimination cases from how they approach civil liberties cases. Consider Justice L'Heureux-Dubé, for example, whose behaviour is indicative of a communitarian when these two issue areas are compared, because she strongly supports equality interests but does not strongly support civil liberties claims. Since Morton and colleagues (1994) conflated these two issue areas, they understandably misclassified her as a liberal because of her progressive record in *Charter* discrimination suits. When one places discrimination and civil liberties claims on two distinct axes, however, one realizes that she has exhibited more moderate behaviour in civil liberties disputes than these authors might have anticipated. In addition, we believe that our classification of Justices Cory and Dickson as communitarians (not identified in Figure 7.3) and Justice McLachlin as a liberal provides a more accurate description of the long-term ideological behaviour of these justices when these two issue areas are compared. Needless to say, Janda and colleagues' refined classification scheme (2004) enables scholars to obtain a more nuanced understanding of the ideological orientation of the justices in these overarching, complex areas of law.

One other significant element in Figure 7.3 becomes apparent when we look at the aggregate comparisons for the Dickson, Lamer, and McLachlin Courts. One may be surprised to find such a dramatic libertarian shift taking place in the McLachlin Court in the civil rights and liberties area relative to the criminal area. In order to understand this change, we conducted a regression analysis of non-unanimous cases raising free speech, press, and association claims (not reported in any of the tables presented here). The results of our analysis, like the data in Figure 7.3, revealed that the McLachlin Court was 25 percent more liberal than the Dickson Court, and nearly 8 percent more liberal than the Lamer Court in civil liberties cases when controlling for case facts and the ideological proclivities of individual justices. While Justices Binnie and McLachlin are key players in the McLachlin Court's dramatic shift in this issue area, these regression results and the plot of justices in Figure 7.3 confirm that this transformation is due more to the McLachlin Court as a whole. The recent ideological shift under Chief Justice McLachlin's early tutelage should send a strong signal to civil liberties litigants that their claims will be taken seriously by a Court whose attitudinal alignment is more receptive to their arguments.

The last plot, in Figure 7.4, compares civil liberties cases along the x-axis with economic cases along the y-axis. The regression line mirrors the slight libertarian- communitarian trends found in Figures 7.1 and 7.2. From a holistic perspective, given the more moderate approach taken by the post-Charter justices in economic cases, it is not surprising that the plot of justices in Figure 7.4 is more tightly clustered around the regression line than in Figure 7.3. Overall, the outliers found in Figure 7.4 are virtually identical to those found in a comparison of civil liberties and discrimination claims (Figure 7.3). As in Figure 7.3, Justices Binnie and La Forest naturally occupy the two poles in civil liberties cases (see the x-axis in Figure 7.4). Justices Wilson and L'Heureux-Dubé anchor the equality end of the economic continuum (see the y-axis), while the remaining justices appear to fall relatively close to the regression line, with no real extremist outliers found on the freedom side of the economic continuum.

Looking at all four scatterplots collectively, one is struck by the relative flatness of the four regression lines and by the absence of any consistently strong ideological dimensions dominating the post-Charter Court in these issue areas. Although three of the four plots identify a slight libertarian- communitarian trend at work in the Court, the institution as a whole has been relatively moderate and centrist in its aggregate ideological orientation,

FIGURE 7.4

Ideological support for order and equality in civil liberties and economic cases decided by the Supreme Court of Canada, 1984–2003

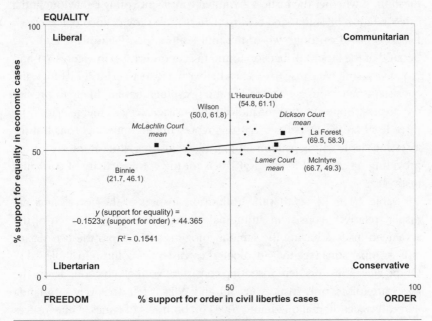

despite the increased contentiousness of post-*Charter* disputes. This finding may surprise US scholars but it is in line with Morton and colleagues' depiction (1994, 49-50) of the first ten years of *Charter* jurisprudence. Moreover, although judicial outliers do appear within the four scatterplots, the moderate behaviour exhibited by the bulk of the justices across the four graphs makes sense in light of some of the theoretical arguments laid out in Chapter 2. For example, given the low profile of ideological considerations in the judicial selection process, and the institutional norms of deference and collegiality, it is not surprising that the justices of the Canadian Supreme Court have engaged in more moderate voting activity. The scatterplots confirm, however, that when the justices do disagree, they act in accordance with attitudinal theory and display relatively consistent issue stances across disparate areas of law.

To organize the data found in the four scatterplots, we present summary data in Table 7.1, highlighting the ideological orientation of individual justices across two different sets of issues (see the "Ideological category when comparing criminal and discrimination" and "Ideological category when comparing civil liberties and discrimination" columns), followed by an indication of whether the justices exhibited consistent voting behaviour and a categorization of outlier and centrist patterns. We provide ideological classifications based on only two of the four scatterplots (Figures 7.2 and 7.3) because of the lack of dispersion found in economic cases in Figures 7.1 and 7.4. As a result, we chose to assess whether the justices exhibit ideologically consistent behaviour by comparing the two plots that are likely to present the greatest opportunities for judicial inconsistencies to emerge across the three legal areas. We believe that this represents the most rigorous test for assessing stable voting patterns among all the justices while at the same time providing meaningful ideological labels for the voting activity of particular justices.

Table 7.1 indicates that the bulk of the justices of the post-*Charter* era display relatively consistent attitudinal voting patterns, with eleven of the seventeen justices having the same ideological label across the two sets of issue comparisons (see the "Ideological consistency" column in Table 7.1).[2] Of the eleven justices demonstrating consistent voting behaviour across the two scatterplots, only Justices Arbour and Wilson fell decisively into Janda and colleagues' liberal quadrant (2004) on both sets of issues, while Justices Beetz, Gonthier, La Forest, Lamer, and McIntyre fell into the conservative camp on both plots. While Justices Cory, Dickson, and L'Heureux-Dubé earned the communitarian label across both sets of issues, Justice Iacobucci is found squarely on the communitarian-conservative divide in both graphs. Overall, we believe that these ideological classifications accord well with how political science and legal scholars in Canada would categorize the justices.

It is interesting to note that five of the six justices who exhibit ideologically inconsistent voting patterns across these two sets of cases are members of the McLachlin Court, which is captured nicely by the change in labels that appear for these justices in the "Ideological category" columns of Table 7.1. One should note that Justices McLachlin, Bastarache, and Binnie register the most dramatic ideological shifts from a pro-government stance to a pro-litigant stance when civil liberties claims are substituted for criminal cases on the freedom-order continuum. Although Justices Major and LeBel also move in a libertarian direction, their inconsistency is far less dramatic since they move from a weak conservative stance in criminal cases to a weak libertarian position in civil liberties cases. Justice Sopinka's inconsistent behaviour

TABLE 7.1

Ideological orientation and attitudinal consistency of post-Charter justices, 1984–2003

Justice	Ideological category when comparing criminal and discrimination	Ideological category when comparing civil liberties and discrimination	Ideological consistency?	Outlier or centrist pattern?
Arbour	Liberal	Liberal	Yes	Outlier – criminal
Bastarache	Conservative (on line)	Libertarian (on line)	No	Outlier – criminal
Beetz	Conservative	Conservative (on line)	Yes	Centrist
Binnie	Communitarian	Liberal	No	Outlier – civil liberties
Cory	Communitarian	Communitarian	Yes	Centrist
Dickson	Communitarian	Communitarian	Yes	Centrist
Gonthier	Conservative	Conservative	Yes	Outlier – criminal
Iacobucci	Communitarian (on line)	Communitarian (on line)	Yes	Centrist
La Forest	Conservative	Conservative	Yes	Outlier – civil liberties
Lamer	Conservative	Conservative	Yes	Centrist
LeBel	Conservative	Libertarian	No	Centrist
L'Heureux-Dubé	Communitarian	Communitarian	Yes	Outlier – criminal, discrimination
Major	Conservative	Libertarian	No	Centrist
McIntyre	Conservative	Conservative	Yes	Outlier – civil liberties
McLachlin	Communitarian	Liberal	No	Outlier – discrimination
Sopinka	Libertarian	Conservative	No	Centrist
Wilson	Liberal	Liberal (on line)	Yes	Outlier – discrimination

moves in the opposite ideological direction, however, shifting from a weak libertarian stance in the criminal area to a solid conservative position in the area of civil rights and liberties. Even though some of the justices are ideologically inconsistent, a majority take issue stands that validate the theoretical contention in the public opinion literature that political elites think about issues in an ideological manner, possess stable attitudes over time, and cast relatively consistent votes across different issue domains (see Campbell et al. 1960).

The last column in Table 7.1 reveals that roughly half of the post-*Charter* justices (nine of seventeen) exhibit some form of outlier behaviour in one of the three areas of law. Clearly, six of these nine are engaging in behaviour consistent with attitudinal theory because they are found in the same ideological quadrant in both sets of issue comparisons (see the entries for Justices Arbour, Gonthier, La Forest, L'Heureux-Dubé, McIntyre, and Wilson in the last two columns of Table 7.1). The three outliers who do not fall into the same ideological quadrant across these two issue comparisons are Justices Bastarache, Binnie, and McLachlin. Since they stake out different strong ideological positions in both the criminal and civil liberties areas, we believe that they are also engaging in attitudinal decision making but simply hold different ideological stances across the two distinct issue domains.

Five of the remaining eight justices who are found in the relative centre of the Court exhibit consistent ideological voting patterns across both sets of issue comparisons (see the entries for Justices Beetz, Cory, Dickson, Iacobucci, and Lamer). The fact that they appear as consistent centrists, not only in this table but across all four scatterplots, strongly suggests that they are acting in line with the attitudinal theory of judicial decision making and simply have moderate attitudes across all the issue areas studied. We cannot rule out the possibility, however, that these justices may also be engaging in strategic activity from the centre, especially the two chief justices (Dickson and Lamer), who might have chosen to join majority coalitions in order to become opinion leaders and guide the legal direction of the courts that bear their names.[3]

It is much more difficult to label the three remaining centrists (Justices LeBel, Major, and Sopinka) because they exhibit inconsistent behaviour in these two issue comparisons. Given their inconsistent tendencies, one is tempted to label them as strategic actors. Since the earlier chapters portrayed Justice LeBel as an opinion leader in civil rights and liberties cases, and Justice Sopinka as one in criminal cases, we believe that they are more likely driven by attitudinal motivations than strategic interests, at least in the legal area where they author large numbers of opinions. Having said this, these three justices, along with some of the other centrists, may be ultimately engaging in both strategic and attitudinal behaviour. Alternatively, it may also be that they approach cases in more of a piecemeal, practical fashion, paying greater attention to the particular facts and legal precedents at hand than to overarching ideological concerns. Unfortunately, we are unable to definitively label these justices as attitudinalists, strategists, or legal pragmatists until more research is done that sheds light on the inner workings of the Canadian Supreme Court. Overall, the data demonstrate that the bulk of the justices engage in consistent ideological behaviour – whether from ideologically remote or moderate positions – with a few defying clear-cut classification given their inconsistent moderate tendencies. We believe that this consistency provides further evidence that attitudinal decision making is prominent in the first twenty years of the post-*Charter* Court.

Conclusion

An analysis of patterns of ideological consistency in the Supreme Court of Canada points to two broad conclusions about post-*Charter* voting behaviour. First, many of the justices are ideologically consistent when their voting behaviour in criminal, economic, and civil rights and civil liberties disputes are examined. The substantial degree of attitudinal agreement fits well with theoretical accounts in the US public opinion literature anticipating that political elites will possess coherent ideological beliefs across disparate issue areas. Second, the fact that some justices cast ideologically disparate votes across different issue dimensions paints a more subtle portrait of attitudinal voting behaviour in the Canadian context. For example, the voting behaviour of Chief Justice McLachlin reflects an approach that is simultaneously tough on the criminally accused but favourable toward the civil liberties advocate. This example illustrates a level of ideological complexity that is typically absent from the voting patterns of justices of the US Supreme Court. Ultimately, her voting behaviour, along with the distinctive and moderate stances of others, demonstrates the utility of conducting cross-national comparisons of voting consistency in national high courts.

8
The Political and Social Implications
of Post-*Charter* Judicial Behaviour

Our study of the Supreme Court of Canada has enabled us to examine research questions about changing patterns of judicial activity in several areas of law over the course of the last twenty years, while simultaneously examining the broader viability of the attitudinal model of judicial decision making outside the United States. The first portion of Chapters 4, 5, and 6 assessed a host of judicial activities in the period following the adoption of the *Canadian Charter of Rights and Freedoms*, including the voting and writing patterns of the justices and their activist tendencies in three areas of law, while the second portion examined the applicability of the attitudinal model in six specific legal fields. Chapter 7 catalogued the degree of ideological consistency exhibited by the justices across criminal, economic, and civil rights and liberties cases, and the extent to which the justices endorsed the values of freedom, order, and equality in their rulings. In this chapter, we review some of the overarching findings of our study and draw some conclusions about the broader implications of these findings for the Canadian political system, comparative legal scholarship, and the ability of the attitudinal model to serve as a more global explanation of judicial decision making.

Leadership and Patterns of Judicial Activism
One of the goals of this study was to determine which of the post-*Charter* justices were leaders, followers, and outsiders in the criminal, civil rights and liberties, and economic areas of law. Looking across the three areas simultaneously, there are a few notable trends. First, Justices Lamer and Cory wrote disproportionately large numbers of opinions in both criminal and civil rights and liberties cases, and thus acted as opinion workhorses on the Court in two prominent areas of law that constituted 58 percent of the Court's docket. Neither of these justices took a lead role in the economic area, however, with Justice Lamer acting as an opinion follower and Justice Cory authoring only

a moderate number of majority opinions. The other justice who emerged as an opinion leader in the civil rights and liberties area was Chief Justice Dickson, whose opinion leadership in this area, like Justice Lamer's, may have been motivated by the desire to lead the Court as chief justice in high-profile *Charter* disputes. In contrast, Justice Estey was a notable follower in both criminal and civil rights and liberties cases, but his expertise in business law enabled him to serve with Justice Iacobucci as an opinion leader in economic disputes. Meanwhile, Justice Gonthier appeared to be the quintessential follower in all three issue areas because he registered one of the lowest majority opinion authorship rates in both criminal and civil rights and liberties disputes, and was found only in the middle of the pack in the economic area. Three of the five females serving during the first twenty years of the post-*Charter* period acted as outsiders, with Justices L'Heureux-Dubé and McLachlin dissenting most frequently in the civil rights and liberties cases, and Justices L'Heureux-Dubé and Deschamps in criminal cases. Justice Stevenson was the lone maverick in economic disputes.

The opinion authorship data indicate that members of the Canadian Court are very willing to share leadership positions by deferring majority authorship to their colleagues, particularly in their areas of expertise. These findings provide Canadian scholars with insight on how members of the Canadian Court interact with their colleagues on the bench in the modern era. The fact that different justices occupy opinion leadership positions in distinct fields of law suggests that the Canadian Supreme Court is a collegial institution that is willing to work as a coordinated team when resolving cases, and that individual justices may be willing to sacrifice the overt expression of their own attitudes and values more readily than their US counterparts, for the good of the team. This greater willingness to function as a coherent unit is highlighted not only in opinion authorship patterns but also in the significant number of unanimous decisions handed down by the post-*Charter* Court, at least compared with its US counterpart.

Several conclusions can be drawn from our study relating to patterns of leadership behaviour exhibited by the chief justices in the post-*Charter* period. First, it is clear that the two male chief justices believed that it was important for them to author a large number of majority opinions in high-profile cases. Indeed, both were opinion leaders in their own courts in civil rights and liberties cases. Chief Justice Lamer was also an opinion leader in the field of criminal law, which coincided with his area of legal specialization. In contrast, Chief Justice McLachlin does not stand out as a majority opinion leader in any of the three areas of law studied in this book. In addition, our prior research suggests that she has undergone a strategic shift in behaviour since she was elevated to the helm of the Court in January 2000 (Wetstein and Ostberg 2005, 666-68). Specifically, she has moved from being a decisive outsider on the Lamer Court to being a social leader who is more interested in consolidating the Court by letting others shoulder the majority opinion workload, and in casting fewer dissenting votes and writing fewer dissenting opinions as chief. Her effort to unify the Court is not surprising, given the criticism levelled at the Court in the 1990s, and fits well with her initial proclamation upon becoming chief justice that she intended to build greater consensus within the Court (Schmitz 1999).

The fact that Canadian chief justices possess the power of panel assignment has important ramifications in the post-*Charter* era, when the Court has come to play a critical policy oversight role. Since the Court is addressing an increasing number of highly controversial issues, the chief justice could strategically use the power of panel assignment to potentially shape a policy outcome that he or she desires. This can be done either by assigning like-minded justices to a panel or by striking a smaller panel, which is less likely to produce a divided ruling. Scholarship by others suggests that post-*Charter* chief justices have utilized this power to their advantage in *Charter* cases (Hausegger and Haynie 2003). Although our data do not directly address this question, our findings regarding panel size imply that post-*Charter* chief justices do not appear to be overtly abusing their panel assignment power. For example, panel sizes in the civil rights and liberties area are larger by an average of one justice, suggesting that the post-*Charter* chiefs recognize the need to strike larger panels in cases that have broader social significance for Canadians. Moreover, the fact that average panel size across all cases has increased to 7.7 justices during Chief Justice McLachlin's tenure reflects her interest in fostering a sense of participation on the Canadian high court, rather than in trying to strategically control the outcome of cases. Needless to say, the panel assignment power that exists in the Canadian setting stands in marked contrast to the situation in the US Supreme Court, and provides Canadian chief justices with a unique institutional mechanism that they could use to potentially direct the course of law. Ultimately, if this power is used strategically, it could have profound implications for the debate over the Court's legitimacy as a policy-making institution in the Canadian political system.

Our findings in the area of authorship and panel assignments suggest that comparative scholars should pay particular attention to the impacts of legal specialization and the power that chief justices might have to shape work assignments in other high courts. The fact that a justice's specialization is directly correlated with opinion leadership should not escape the attention of Justice Department officials or the prime minister, because specialized appointments to the Court could have a profound impact on the direction taken in a particular area of Canadian law. We also believe that the legal specialization of potential nominees should remain a central consideration in the appointment process, because having justices with diverse legal expertise can help the Court function more effectively as a collegial body with a balanced workload in terms of panel and opinion assignment.

In light of the heated debate in the Canadian literature over the degree of judicial activism in the post-*Charter* era, we were interested in examining the percentage of cases in which justices voted to strike down laws and the degree to which activist behaviour was correlated with indicators of judicial liberalism in the criminal, economic, and civil rights and liberties areas. The findings from the three main legal areas of this study suggest that Justice Wilson was the most activist justice in the criminal and economic areas, voting to overturn statutes 37 and 47 percent of the time, respectively. Both Justices LeBel and McLachlin outstripped her level of activism in the civil rights and liberties field, voting to nullify statutes 50 percent of the time. In contrast, Justice Major was one of the most deferential justices across all three issue areas, with only Justice L'Heureux-Dubé and Gonthier exhibiting more deferential behaviour in the criminal and civil rights and liberties areas, respectively. In Chapter 4, 5, and 6, we examined bivariate correlations between our two ideology measures and judicial activism to see whether there was a strong relationship between these two concepts. The findings from the three main chapters yielded mixed results. While a clear linkage existed between judicial liberalism and activism in criminal cases and a tenuous connection appeared in economic cases, there was no significant link between the two in civil rights and liberties cases.[1] Given the discrepancies reported in our analysis, we contend that court critics need to be careful not to link all activist behaviour with the rulings of liberal-leaning justices. Indeed, when it comes to some of the most high-profile legal controversies, conservative justices are just as likely as their liberal colleagues to be activists.

Prime ministers and members of Parliament from both sides of the aisle should be aware that justices of all stripes are going to invoke their legitimate judicial power to scrutinize the actions of legislative and executive officials. Policy makers would be wise, therefore, to subject policy proposals to their own exacting *Charter* scrutiny before they leave the legislative and cabinet chambers (see Kelly 2005). Our findings on judicial activism also have important implications for the Supreme Court appointment process: prime ministers should be mindful that, outside the area of criminal law, rates of activism in the post-*Charter* era have been roughly equal for both liberal and conservative justices. Thus, it may be prudent to pay particular attention to the criminal law rulings of a lower court judge before making an appointment to the bench because such rulings may reveal the intersection between liberalism and activist tendencies most readily. Lastly, our findings suggest that it may be fruitful for comparative scholars to study the relationship between judicial ideology and rates of activism to see whether ideological tendencies align with the pattern of activism displayed by justices serving on high courts in other cultural contexts. In other words, can the mixed results found in the Canadian Supreme Court be documented in other democratic societies, or are there other distinctive patterns of judicial power in such societies?

The Importance of Judicial Ideology

One of the most important aspects of our study is the analysis of several a priori measures of liberalism and their ability to predict subsequent ideological voting patterns of the justices. In Table 8.1, we provide a summary that rank-orders the relative impact of the two measures of ideology used in the various regression equations in this book (the newspaper ideology and party of prime minister indicators). Looking at the results, one is immediately struck by the more powerful impact that the newspaper ideology measure has for explaining liberal voting behaviour in the post-*Charter* context, compared with the party of prime minister measure. Overall, the newspaper ideology measure had a statistically significant impact in the hypothesized direction in three of the six areas of law when looking at all cases, with the strongest impact occurring in right to counsel cases, followed by search and seizure and then union cases in order of magnitude (see the "Change in probability" column under "All cases" in Table 8.1). The impact of newspaper ideology became significant in four of the six equations when looking at non-unanimous cases, with tax cases joining the list (see the "Change in probability" column under "Non-unanimous cases" in Table 8.1). These findings suggest that when the justices are at odds, their conflict is driven principally by ideological differences in the criminal and economic areas. The sharp jump in the probability scores across the two levels of analysis provides strong

TABLE 8.1

Impact of newspaper ideology and party of prime minister on judicial voting behaviour in six areas of law, 1984–2003

Model	All cases		Non-unanimous cases	
	Change in probability	Expected direction?	Change in probability	Expected direction?
NEWSPAPER IDEOLOGY				
Right to counsel model	.398**	Yes	.719***	Yes
Search and seizure model	.245**	Yes	.439***	Yes
Union (private practice)	−.185**	Yes	−.296**	Yes
Tax model	.112	Yes	.504**	Yes
Equality model	.101	Yes	.326	Yes
Free expression model	−.070	No	−.450	No
PARTY OF PRIME MINISTER				
Right to counsel model	−.101	No	−.094	No
Search and seizure model	−.096*	No	−.138	No
Union model	.041	Yes	−.005	No
Tax model	.011	Yes	−.148	No
Equality model	.046	Yes	−.089	No
Free expression model	−.094	No	−.225*	No

* $p < .05$, ** $p < .01$, *** $p < .001$

SOURCE: Derived from logistic regression results shown in Tables 4.6, 4.7, 4.9, 4.10, 5.6, 5.7, 5.8, 5.9, 6.6, 6.7, 6.9, and 6.10.

evidence that attitudinal decision making is prevalent in the post-*Charter* Court. The newspaper ideology measure does not perform well in equality and free speech cases, however, and its impact is in the unexpected negative direction in the latter (see Table 8.1).

As was suggested in Chapter 5, these findings might surprise readers familiar with the US Supreme Court literature, where measures of ideology and party are the most dominant predictors of voting behaviour in emotionally charged cases that touch on fundamental questions of freedom and human dignity. The findings provide an intriguing quandary for comparative scholars because one is uncertain whether the Canadian results represent the exception to the rule or are in line with patterns that would appear in other high courts outside the US context. Only future systematic studies of ideological decision making in high courts with similar and different institutional and cultural norms will provide a more complete answer to the question of how well the attitudinal model can ultimately serve as a useful global theory of judicial decision making.

The disparate impact of ideology on judicial voting behaviour in these three distinct categories of Canadian law raises the question of why attitudes and values matter so much in the two fields of criminal law but less so in the economic cases, and why their influence is negligible, even counterintuitive, in the two civil rights and liberties areas studied. We believe that the ideological divisions that appear so readily in the search and seizure and right to counsel disputes reflect a larger ideological divide in Canadian society between a crime control or a due process approach toward those charged with crimes. Echoing some of the themes laid out in Chapter 2, the justices on the post-*Charter* Court are at odds over the degree to which the criminal justice system should cater to the desire for tougher sentences in the name of public safety as opposed to placing greater emphasis on procedural due process protections of the criminally accused even at the expense of public safety. These competing visions of the criminal justice system split naturally along liberal and conservative lines, and are clearly reflected in the criminal decisions of the Court. The ideological split in the economic area is less visceral, but it seems that the post-*Charter* justices have come of age in an era when conflict has emerged over employee wages and benefits and the degree to which government should redistribute wealth. Once again, ideological differences on economic issues are commonplace in an advanced industrial society like Canada, and it is not surprising to find some judicial divisions on these issues as well. In contrast, we believe that the failure of ideology to emerge as an important predictor of attitudinal voting in the civil rights and liberties areas may be explained by the overriding significance of gender in the discrimination cases and by the appointment of civil libertarians by Prime Minister Mulroney in the 1980s. Taken together, these findings suggest that while the attitudinal model has relevance in the post-*Charter* Court, its importance in the Canadian setting is more complex and less pronounced than found in the United States, particularly in light of its negligible explanatory power in civil rights and liberties cases, where most attitudinalists would expect a high degree of ideological decision making. One must note that the impact of the Mulroney appointments may be a time-bound phenomenon and that ideology may have a more prominent impact in civil liberties cases in future years.

Turning to the party of prime minister measure in Table 8.1, it is clear that it is woefully inadequate at predicting liberal voting behaviour in the six areas of law. In fact, this measure is statistically significant in only two of the twelve equations – all search and seizure cases and non-unanimous free expression cases – and its coefficient was not in the expected direction in either model. Overall, the disparate nature of the findings for the party and newspaper ideology measures in these six areas of law highlight the relative crudeness of the former indicator and the viability of the latter, more sophisticated one for measuring ideological behaviour. Ultimately, we believe that the newspaper ideology measure is able to capture more nuanced ideological distinctions because it is based on journalistic interviews with legal experts in the field and so provides a more accurate, fine-tuned account of the true ideological tendencies of individual justices once they are on the high court.

The differential impact of the party and ideology measures in our regression models of judicial behaviour has broader theoretical implications for comparative law scholars. Our research suggests that the party of prime minister indicator, which has proved to be such a convenient and fruitful measure in a plethora of US studies, may not perform as well in other democratic societies where more moderate justices are appointed to the bench. Since justices appointed to the US Supreme Court are so ideologically polarized and are willing to express their views forcefully and without reservation, it is not surprising that even a crude measure such as party identification proves statistically significant in most regression analyses of the US Supreme Court. In countries like Canada, however, where prime ministers have avoided making such blatant political appointments to the bench, a more stringent measure of ideology may be needed to capture any true ideological differences that may exist between the justices. Consequently, our research leads us to believe that comparative law scholars should be guided by a research strategy that, wherever possible, incorporates a multiple-method approach to the measurement of judicial liberalism in other high courts. If such an approach is not taken, important conclusions about attitudinal behaviour may be overlooked.

The presence of attitudinal decision making on the post-*Charter* Canadian Supreme Court has important implications for the Canadian political system. First, our findings are particularly timely given the continuing debate over reforming the judicial appointment process. Some scholars and court critics have argued that because of the increased political power of the Court in the post-*Charter* period, there needs to be greater parliamentary oversight of nominations to the high court (see Morton 1989; Ziegel 2001). Our findings indicate that recent efforts to revamp the process to allow for greater parliamentary input are not misguided. The establishment of some form of legislative questioning of judicial nominees in a public manner provides

politicians, journalists, and the Canadian citizenry an opportunity to understand the core beliefs of a potential justice before he or she takes a seat on the
Court. It also provides a forum for developing a better understanding of why
the prime minister has chosen a particular nominee for a coveted high court
seat. One scholar has pointed to the advantages of such legislative participation, largely because it "injects a democratic and balancing process" into the
selection of justices and because it helps educate politicians and the public
on the importance of the *Charter* and the political significance of the high
court (Ziegel 2001, 147). Since our study demonstrates the importance of
judicial ideology in several important areas of law, allowing this type of questioning might shed light on important transitions that may result from a
particular Supreme Court appointment. Seen in this light, the hearing that
Prime Minister Stephen Harper allowed for the Court's newest justice, Marshall
Rothstein, in early 2006 may reflect a willingness to soothe some political
concerns about the attitudes and values that justices can bring to the Court.

The danger that might flow from parliamentary questioning of judicial
nominees is that the process may become excessively politicized, like the US
appointment process. Moreover, some have argued that it is politically un-
seemly for judges to submit to a public inquiry from politicians (for criticisms of this argument, see Ziegel 2001). Some believe that allowing members
of Parliament to probe the ideological underpinnings of a nominee's thinking might cause the hearings to become a partisan forum where the nominee
is grilled in a manner that denigrates his or her character and degrades the
appointment process (Hunter 1989). Additionally, overt political partisan-
ship might filter into the nomination process, encouraging prime ministers
to become even more focused on selecting a future justice who possesses the
"right" ideological makeup to appease his or her partisan base and perhaps
steer the Court back in the "right" direction. If this plays out, opposition
members of Parliament and critics of the party in power are likely to use the
parliamentary review process to try to score political points with their supporters. This would indeed reflect the worst elements of the polarized US
process. The ultimate fear is that judicial hearings might foster greater emphasis on ideology at the expense of a broader host of factors that are currently taken into consideration, such as regional balance, legal specialization,
gender, bilingual skills, and overall judicial temperament.

The degree to which the appointment process becomes more politicized
depends upon both the strategic choices made by prime ministers regarding
future nominees and the type of legislative oversight adopted by Parliament.

For example, legislative oversight could range from a formal majority vote of confirmation, similar to the US approach, at one extreme, to a simple informational hearing before a small parliamentary committee selected by the prime minister. We believe that the type of legislative oversight that is ultimately chosen will have a profound impact on the degree to which ideological wrangling emerges in the Canadian appointment process. If Parliament engages in a formal background investigation and publicly televised hearings, we would not be surprised if the polarizing features that dominate the US appointment process materialize in the Canadian setting. If members of Parliament and prime ministers develop a more informal and less confrontational system, however, it is unlikely that the appointment process will reach the level of political rancour seen in the US. Moreover, if a less combative system emerges, the prime minister has a greater opportunity to continue a tradition of taking into consideration a host of nomination factors that are critical to maintaining a more collegial, less ideologically polarized court. Regardless of which route is taken, since our findings show that ideological behaviour is prominent in the post-*Charter* Court, we believe that some type of parliamentary oversight can serve the important function of teasing out judicial viewpoints before nominees are elevated to such a prominent policy-making institution.

We believe that attitudinal decision making in the post-*Charter* Court has been a partial byproduct of the rise of interest group activity in recent decades and the fact that members of the Court have taken their new *Charter* mandate seriously. The addition of the *Charter* to the Constitution enabled the Court to become a much stronger policy player in the modern Canadian political system. The *Charter* transformed the Court from a relatively passive tribunal that principally settled jurisdictional disputes into an activist defender of newly entrenched individual rights and freedoms (see Morton 1987; Morton et al. 1991; Knopff and Morton 1992; Manfredi 1993, 2001). This transformation, coupled with interest group pressures that originated before the *Charter*'s adoption, provided a mechanism for increased interest group activity in the form of litigation and third-party intervention before the Supreme Court (see Brodie 2002; Epp 1998). The legal mobilization of various groups has fostered the natural tendency of these organizations to make the most of the rights language found in the *Charter*. Our regression results indicate that the Women's Legal Education Action Fund and the Canadian Labour Congress were particularly successful in advancing their agendas in the high court, while the Canadian Civil Liberties Association has been much less successful. We believe that the attitudinal responses by the justices are partially a byproduct of the types of claims advanced by some interest groups, and that future scholarship should devote greater attention to understanding the discrepancies in the success rates of various groups.

The political ascendance of the Supreme Court in the post-*Charter* period has triggered a debate in the larger body politic over whether the locus of power in Canada has shifted away from a system based on parliamentary supremacy to one of judicial supremacy (Manfredi 1993, 2001; Morton and Knopff 2000). Our research adds fuel to the fire by demonstrating that justices on the post-*Charter* Court are influenced by their own attitudes and values in four of the six areas of law studied, which, for some, might raise further doubt about the legitimacy of the Court in the Canadian political system. The central contention of those criticizing the Court's increased judicial review power is that the values of elected majorities have been usurped and supplanted by the values of unelected judges. Recent scholarship by Kelly (2005) takes issue with the argument that the power structure has dramatically changed in the Canadian system since the adoption of the *Charter*. At the heart of Kelly's argument is the claim that Parliament and cabinet remain supreme within the Canadian system because they have institutionalized a process of subjecting proposed legislation to "constitutional vetting" within the cabinet and the Department of Justice. Thus, he argues that it is bureaucratic activism, not judicial activism, that structures the "*Charter* dialogue" between the Court and other political institutions (Kelly 2005, 256). According to Kelly, the bottom line is that the elected arm of the government has learned to govern under the *Charter*, and has become effective at crafting laws aligned with *Charter* values. Regardless of which branch dominates the continuing "*Charter* dialogue," it is clear from our research that attitudinal decision making is prevalent on the Court within two of the three broad areas of law studied, and that the Supreme Court is bound to remain a central political player in the dialogue concerning the scope and limits of *Charter* principles well into the future. Ultimately, we believe that interaction between different institutions in a democratic system are essential to the development of law over time, and ensure that the principles enshrined in the Constitution evolve with the changing needs of society. As a result, the Supreme Court's occasional nullification of laws should be seen as a healthy sign for Canadian democracy and should not be portrayed as necessarily undermining democratic values.

The Importance of Gender

Moving beyond ideological concerns, one of the most important findings from our study pertains to the powerful impact that a justice's gender has in the resolution of civil rights and liberties disputes during the post-*Charter* era. Regardless of their partisan background or ideological predisposition, female members of the post-*Charter* Court have been far more likely than their male colleagues to protect the interests of vulnerable minorities in all equality cases and in non-unanimous equality and free expression cases. These findings suggest that the prime minister and Justice Department officials, as well as members of Parliament, need to be aware that female justices on the modern Canadian Court do speak in a different voice from their male counterparts on some critical civil rights and liberties issues. In other words, appointing a female justice to the high court can have a profound impact on judicial decision making in at least two significant areas of law. Moreover, our results suggest that comparative scholars should pay more attention to the role that gender differences might have in the rulings of other high courts, particularly in equality and fundamental freedoms disputes. Our findings trigger several important empirical questions for comparative scholars to consider: Do pervasive gender differences emerge in other modern high courts with similar democratic common law traditions? Are gender differences prevalent in high courts with different democratic legacies? If gender differences do exist in several high courts, is a critical mass of women needed on a given court before fundamental male/female differences become salient in their rulings? Answers to these and other questions will become increasingly important to the field of comparative judicial behaviour as more women are elevated to democratic high courts around the world and more women assume leadership roles in these judicial forums.

The Importance of Factual Circumstances

The regression models in the various areas of law in our study indicate that factual circumstances do trigger attitudinal responses in the minds of the post-*Charter* justices. This overall finding is in line with attitudinal accounts of recent US Supreme Court behaviour (Segal and Spaeth 1993, 2002). Although case facts have a significant impact on liberal voting patterns in all six areas of law in Canada, the greatest impact was felt when unanimous and non-unanimous decisions in a particular area were analyzed together; the impact was less when only non-unanimous decisions were examined. We contend that this discrepancy is due to the fact that ideological differences are bound to be the primary source of disagreement when the justices are at odds.

When examining the results across all cases in the six areas of law, one is struck by the fact that case facts play a much stronger role in search and seizure, right to counsel, union, and tax disputes than in the two civil rights and liberties areas. Indeed, every factual scenario that was included in the full search and seizure and union models was statistically significant, as were most factual scenarios in the right to counsel and tax realm. The importance of case facts in the criminal areas makes intuitive sense given the vast number of circumstances that police encounter in the course of making an arrest that might influence whether or not a Supreme Court justice believes that the individual has been rightly convicted. Similarly, it is not surprising that factual scenarios are prominent in the minds of the justices in the tax area, given the highly technical nature of Canada's revenue code and the types of issues that emerge in tax litigation. A similar argument can be made in the collective bargaining arena, where a variety of distinctive workplace issues can provoke attitudinal responses on the part of the justices. We believe that the weak performance of many of the case facts in the equality and free speech areas is due to the overwhelming effect of the gender variable in triggering voting behaviour in discrimination cases, and is attributable to the assumption that even though *Charter* violations have occurred, they may be justified in a free and democratic society. The cumulative body of findings across all the models in our study indicates that facts do play an important role in influencing judicial decision making in the Canadian context, although the impact is much more noticeable when the justices agree on the outcome than when they do not.

Another significant finding of our study is that even though ideology is the dominant factor influencing judicial voting when the justices disagree, justices on different sides of the ideological spectrum do respond to case facts in different ways when they are at odds. In four of the six areas where ideological differences emerged, the justices on the liberal side of the spectrum tended to focus on different factual cues to guide their voting behaviour than their conservative colleagues. This finding reinforces the claims made by attitudinal theorists that justices at the two political extremes are motivated to view cases through distinctive ideological prisms. Moreover, our findings indicate that conservative-leaning justices respond to fewer factual cues in three of the four non-unanimous models. We therefore conclude that in the post-*Charter* Court, conservative justices are more prone than their liberal colleagues to base their votes on their ideological predispositions. Ultimately, our results suggest that comparative scholars need to carefully consider the complex role that factual circumstances might play in relation to ideology in the minds of high court justices in other countries.

Collectively, the findings surrounding case facts have both practical and theoretical implications for legal practitioners in Canada and for public law scholars. From a practical standpoint, litigators working in the Canadian justice system should realize that post-*Charter* justices are indeed responding to certain case facts in predictable ways. Thus, the presence or absence of particular case stimuli could provide attorneys with valuable information on how to craft their legal arguments before an appeals court or the Supreme Court, which, in turn, might influence their odds of prevailing on appeal. In addition, knowledge of judicial predispositions toward case facts in different areas of law might serve as important cues for litigants and intervenors in assessing whether or not to devote time, energy, and resources to pursue an appeal. From a broader theoretical perspective, our findings suggest that attitudinal scholars need to test whether and to what degree justices of other high courts respond to factual stimuli, and if they do, whether justices at different ends of the ideological spectrum also react differently to those case facts. Answers to these types questions may be critical to the development of a more global understanding of attitudinal decision making in high courts in different cultural settings.

The Importance of Court Dynamics and Institutional Norms

The inclusion of court control variables enabled us to gain a more holistic understanding of whether the three post-*Charter* courts were unique or similar in their approach to cases in the six areas of law. One should keep in mind that data limitations prevented us from testing for Lamer and McLachlin Court effects in every statistical model, so our results should be interpreted with some caution. Still, we were able to demonstrate that the Lamer Court justices were 24 percent more likely than their Dickson Court counterparts to side with the accused in all right to counsel cases, but no more likely to do so across all search and seizure cases (see Table 8.2). The pattern was reversed in both of the economic areas of law studied, with Lamer Court justices 31 and 19 percent more conservative in all union and tax cases, respectively. Thus, when controlling for the fact patterns and the ideological leanings of the justices, the Lamer Court as an institution did cast distinctively different

TABLE 8.2

The impact of court control variables in the regression equations

| | Change in probability | |
Model	All cases	Non-unanimous cases
LAMER COURT		
Right to counsel	.240*	.200
Search and seizure	.020	—
Equality	—	—
Free expression	.128	−.052
Union	−.311***	—
Tax	−.186**	.096
MCLACHLIN COURT		
Right to counsel	—	—
Search and seizure	.013	.236*
Equality	.265***	.217*
Free expression	.078	—
Union	−.322***	.466***
Tax	.022	.250

* $p < .05$, ** $p < .01$, *** $p < .001$
SOURCE: Derived from logistic regression results shown in Tables 4.6, 4.7, 4.9, 4.10, 5.6, 5.7, 5.8, 5.9, 6.6, 6.7, 6.9, and 6.10.

votes from its Dickson Court predecessor in two key areas of economic law and one of criminal law. The results for the McLachlin Court show that in four of the five models where a significant voting pattern appears, the McLachlin Court justices tend to be more liberal than their Dickson Court counterparts; this pattern is more noticeable when the justices are at odds (see Table 8.2). This is true even when controlling for case facts and the ideological tendencies of the justices. Thus, the first four years of the McLachlin Court as a whole have been marked by an institutional shift in the liberal direction in some key areas of law.

Given the liberal voting trends for the Lamer and McLachlin Courts relative to the Dickson Court, we were interested in seeing whether these results roughly matched the liberal voting patterns found in *Charter* disputes across the three courts. This analysis is important because *Charter* cases represent some of the most politically charged disputes heard by the Court since 1984. Figure 8.1 presents the percentage of liberal rulings across two-year increments in all *Charter* disputes featuring written reasons for judgment.[2] It demonstrates that the first two years of *Charter* jurisprudence can be considered a

"*Charter* honeymoon" period, and that pro-rights decisions exceeded 50 percent in the 1984-86 time frame. In the subsequent two-year period, support for *Charter* liberalism on the Dickson Court plummeted to less than 30 percent, although it rebounded in the last two years of his tenure. We believe that the dramatic rise in liberal outcomes in the latter years of the Dickson Court was due to the arrival of Justices Sopinka, Gonthier, Cory, and McLachlin. *Charter* liberalism remained fairly constant throughout the Lamer Court, with the justices favouring the rights claimant an average of 39 percent across the 1990-99 period. In the first four years of Chief Justice McLachlin's tenure, however, there was a decisive upward surge in rulings favouring the *Charter* rights claimant, peaking at 53 percent in 2002. Overall, the early McLachlin Court average of favouring the rights claimant 48 percent of the time is substantially higher than either the Dickson or Lamer Court averages of 42 and 39 percent, respectively. The upward slope of *Charter* liberalism depicted for the McLachlin Court is entirely consistent with the positive coefficients found for the McLachlin Court control variables in Table 8.2.

FIGURE 8.1

Two-year moving average of *Charter* liberalism in cases with written reasons for judgment, 1984–2003

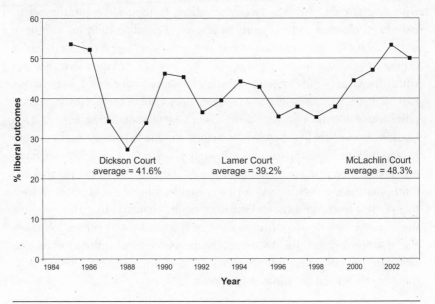

One might wonder why the early McLachlin Court moved so decisively to the left in both *Charter* and some non-unanimous rulings. One plausible explanation is that members of the current Court are responding to post-materialist, progressive norms that are taking root in Canadian society on such issues as the death penalty, marijuana liberalization, and gay rights. If this is the case, the justices' rulings might simply reflect the larger attitudinal shifts taking place in the body politic. Alternatively, one could argue that Prime Minister Chrétien appointed a more libertarian group of justices to the early McLachlin Court. Regardless of which explanation is correct, the cumulative body of evidence presented here shows that the justices' attitudes provide a powerful theoretical explanation for the liberal shift taking place on the McLachlin Court, particularly in the field of civil liberties.

Implications of Our Findings for the Attitudinal Model

Although a substantial amount of attitudinal decision making appears in diverse areas of law in the post-*Charter* Court, especially in non-unanimous cases, the impact of ideology is not as crystal-clear or as systematic as that found in the US context. The fact that judicial ideology weaves a more complex tapestry in the Canadian setting flows, in part, from the different institutional structures and norms that operate in the high court. For example, historical patterns of judicial selection in Canada have ensured that justices with diverse characteristics, largely unrelated to their ideological leanings, have been elevated to the Court. As a result, Canadian judicial nominees, unlike their US counterparts, are not as overtly ideological once they arrive on the bench. Additionally, the pervasive norm of consensus that operates within the Court naturally deflates the level of attitudinal discord that emerges in the justices' written opinions. Moreover, since Canadian chief justices maintain control over panel assignments, and can strike smaller panels or assign like-minded justices to particular cases, they are able to foster greater unanimity and help mitigate the role that ideology plays in the Canadian context to a greater degree than their US counterparts. Ultimately, we believe that the attitudinal model would play an even smaller role in democratic systems that possess fewer political and institutional mechanisms that allow justices the freedom to vote according to their own attitudes and values. We think that there is a direct positive relationship between institutional traits that safeguard judicial independence and the degree of ideological decision making that will appear in courts of last resort.

Since attitudinal decision making is less overt than one might have expected in the modern Canadian Supreme Court, some might contend that our results raise doubts about the broader applicability of the attitudinal model to other cultural settings. The presumption here is that since Canada represents one of the easiest test cases for the applicability of this paradigm outside the US, it may be natural to question the degree to which the model will apply systematically across different legal fields in more divergent cultural, political, and institutional contexts. The fact that ideology did not prove salient in Canadian civil rights and liberties cases, an area where US public law scholars would expect judicial attitudes and values to dominate, indicates that it is wrong to assume that the power of ideology would necessarily apply neatly and completely to other cultural settings, even one so similar to the United States. Our findings suggest that it is critical for comparative scholars to explore how other high courts operate in their own unique environments, because any systematic differences that appear can further inform our understanding of the features that promote or mitigate ideological decision making. Accounting for these differences is pivotal, because they may reveal the existence of even more complex patterns of judicial voting behaviour across high courts. We believe that this deeper analysis is necessary before a more cogent, global theoretical account of judicial behaviour can be developed.

Notes

CHAPTER 1: MODELS OF JUDICIAL BEHAVIOUR AND THE CANADIAN SUPREME COURT

1   We present data on only seventeen of the post-*Charter* justices in this analysis because they have the most substantial voting records for comparison across our scatterplots. We omit from our analysis Justices Chouinard, Estey, Le Dain, Stevenson, Deschamps, and Fish.

CHAPTER 2: THE VIABILITY OF THE ATTITUDINAL MODEL IN THE CANADIAN CONTEXT

1   Our arguments in this chapter expand upon our earlier discussions of attitudinal decision making in the Canadian Supreme Court. For these earlier works, see Ostberg 1995; Ostberg and Wetstein 1998, 2003, 2005; Wetstein and Ostberg 1999, 2005; Ostberg et al. 2001, 2002; and Ostberg, Johnson et al. 2004.

2   This brief discussion of the history of the Canadian Supreme Court draws heavily on material presented in Ostberg 1995, ch. 1.

3   McCormick (1994b, 109) provides a counter-argument, suggesting that political party ties have motivated judicial appointments in contemporary Canada: "Most judges appointed by both federal and provincial Liberal governments are Liberal, judges appointed by Conservative governments are Conservative."

4   One should note that the Canadian Court also cites US case law in non-*Charter* cases, although not as frequently. In decisions handed down outside the *Charter* area between 1984 and 1995, the justices cited US precedents 22 percent of the time, which is 26 percent less than in *Charter* cases (Ostberg et al. 2001, 392).

CHAPTER 3: MEASURING JUDICIAL IDEOLOGY

1   This pitfall is precisely what one encounters when examining the appointments of the post-*Charter* Canadian justices, because only one justice (Justice Chouinard, appointed by Joe Clark) was labelled as ideologically conservative. Thus, there was not enough variance in this variable to distinguish it from the party of prime minister variable.

2   In this analysis, we omit scores for Justices Fish and Deschamps because of their recent appointment to the Supreme Court.

3   The high correlation between prime minister ideological motivation and party of prime minister may be an artifact of the time period and data used in this study. Since the measure of prime minister motivation looked only at justices serving in the post-*Charter* period, there was only one appointed by a highly conservative prime minister, namely, Justice Chouinard. Thus, there was insufficient variance in the scores between party of prime minister and prime minister motivation to generate more distinct measures. A listing of all the justices' scores on the prime minister ideological motivation indicator is found earlier in this chapter.

4   Due process cases that were categorized as civil rights and liberties disputes did not include criminal due process concerns.

5   The career scores tabulated for the twenty-three justices examine cases argued from 1973, when Justice Dickson was elevated to the Court, through 2003. The calculation of the number of criminal cases for each justice is based on whether a criminal issue was identified as the principal issue of a given dispute. Cases in which criminal issues were subordinate to another issue were not identified as criminal cases for the purpose of this study. We applied a similar line of reasoning to the two other areas of law. The total number of cases analyzed for the three issue areas is 1,275 in the criminal area, 259 in the civil rights and liberties area, and 1,037 in the economic area.

6   We replicated the analysis for the prime minister ideological motivation indicator and obtained results that were virtually identical with those for the party of prime minister variable. Because the results were so similar, we omitted them from Table 3.4.

7   While our findings did not turn up significant relationships with career liberalism in civil rights and liberties cases, analyses conducted by other scholars on a different database have turned up significant results at the 95 percent confidence level (see Ostberg, Johnson et al. 2004). The results we report here are significant only at the 80 percent confidence level, which is below the customary standard accepted by quantitative scholars. We believe that the counterfactual findings are due to different weighting values used in the regression analyses, selection of case votes from a different time frame in the other analysis (1984-2002), and slight differences in the coding of case issues and liberal votes across the two datasets.

CHAPTER 4: ATTITUDINAL CONFLICT IN CRIMINAL CASES

This chapter contains material from our previously published study on judicial decision making in search and seizure cases ("Search and Seizure Cases in the Supreme Court of Canada," *Social Science Quarterly* 80 (4): 757-74, copyright © 1999 by the University of Texas Press, all rights reserved). The data analysis is greatly revised and expanded. We are grateful for permission from the editors of

Social Science Quarterly and the University of Texas Press to reproduce some of the material. We are also grateful for the permission to reprint some of our theoretical arguments and data description from "Judicial Behavior on the Canadian Supreme Court: Attitudinal Conflict in Right to Counsel Cases, 1984–2001," *Political Science Quarterly* 121 (Winter 2006–07).

1   These averages for the three courts are calculated from the mean annual percentages that comprise the Court's criminal share of the docket, with figures for the Dickson Court averaged from 1984 to 1989, the Lamer Court from 1990 to 1999, and the McLachlin Court from 2000 to 2003.

2   Indeed, oral judgments in criminal cases feature average panels of 6.2 justices, a decrease of one justice for every two non-oral cases heard (6.2 versus 6.9).

3   We excluded Justices Ritchie and Fish from this analysis because they participated in ten or fewer criminal cases during the 1984–2003 period.

4   When the analysis was also conducted for all twenty-three post-*Charter* justices, regardless of the number of panels participated in, the results were still statistically significant for both ideological measures in the criminal area (r = .563 for newspaper liberalism, significant at the 99 percent confidence level; r = .422 for the party of prime minister, significant at the 95 percent confidence level).

5   The six-year time frame was chosen to permit examination of the largest pool of justices in the dataset, while at the same time providing a sufficient time gap for allowing possible ideological differences to emerge. For most of the justices in the table, the data for time period 1 reflect their first two years of service on the Court. As previous scholarship suggests, these first two years are typically characterized as a "freshman" acclimation period, when justices are trying to adapt to the Court's workload and institutional norms (Snyder 1958; Heck and Hall 1981; Dudley 1993; McCormick 1993). Some scholars speculate that freshmen voting patterns will be different from those of their latter years of service on the bench (Snyder 1958; Brenner 1983; Hagle 1993; Wood et al. 1998; but see Ostberg et al. 2003 for a counter-argument). Given this contention, we thought it would be worthwhile to separate out the first two years of service for the post-*Charter* justices whenever it was possible. For the four justices who joined the Court prior to the *Charter*'s enactment – Dickson, McIntyre, Lamer, and Wilson – their first two years of data encompassed the first two years of *Charter* litigation (1984-85) because those years constituted their "freshman" years in terms of assessing *Charter* litigation. Ultimately, Table 4.5 features fourteen justices who had judicial tenures that spanned at least a six-year time frame in the post-*Charter* period.

6   We began our analysis with a set of hypotheses that parallel the discussion of prominent factual circumstances identified in a leading constitutional law text in Canada (see Hogg 1997, 1149-65). We subsequently relied on stepwise regression procedures to help identify the most prominent factual circumstances in right to counsel disputes. Thus, our results represented the most parsimonious

model to explain variance in the dependent variable when examining right to counsel cases. The eight factual variables included in our study are salient ones that most scholars would identify as typical fulcrums of attitudinal conflict in the right to counsel area.

7   In general, we excluded variables from the model whenever the frequency of that variable was equal to or less than 10 percent, unless there was a compelling theoretical reason to include the variable and/or it achieved statistical significance in the model. Although the "no warning" variable comprised 12 percent of all right to counsel cases, its frequency fell to only 7 percent in the smaller subset of non-unanimous cases. We decided to include the measure in both equations, however, because of the obvious theoretical power this variable would have in right to counsel cases. Its ability to achieve statistical significance in both equations attests to its theoretical importance.

8   A measure for the McLachlin Court was not included in the analysis because there were no right to counsel cases argued during the 2000–03 period.

9   The calculation of the proportional reduction in error measure (PRE) is modelled after prior work by Hagle and Spaeth (1992) and Brenner et al. (1990).

10 We examined the impact of the party of prime minister variable in a separate equation, leaving out newspaper ideology. The results also indicate that there is no significant impact of the party measure on judicial decision making. This pattern of insignificance also plays out for the party of prime minister measure in the search and seizure area.

11 The bivariate correlation between arrests made late at night and warnings after detention is –.722, while the correlation between impaired driving and after-detention warnings is –.592. Given this high collinearity, we chose to include the after-detention indicator because it was the most inclusive measure and appeared to capture elements of all three variables.

12 Six search and seizure cases were omitted from the analysis because the published opinions did not contain enough factual material to warrant inclusion in the study (*R. v. Meltzer*, [1989] 1 S.C.R. 1764; *R. v. Heikel*, [1989] 1 S.C.R. 1776; *R. v. Oullette*, [1989] 1 S.C.R. 1781; *Dersch v. Canada*, [1990] 2 S.C.R. 1505; *R. v. Zito*, [1990] 2 S.C.R. 1520; and *Smith v. Canada*, [2001] 3 S.C.R. 902).

13 Border searches are uncommon in the Canadian setting, appearing only 5 percent of the time in both the large and small search and seizure models. Despite this low frequency, it was included in the regression models for obvious theoretical reasons, and its coefficient happened to be significant in the model for all search and seizure cases.

14 Although breathalyzer cases (6 percent) did not meet our 10 percent criterion for inclusion in the model, we added it to the small equation for several reasons. First, it was not highly correlated with any other variable in the model (unlike the larger equation). Second, it made intuitive theoretical sense to maintain that

breathalyzer cases would trigger conservative votes. Third, it achieved statistical significance in the equation, which further justified its inclusion despite its low frequency.

CHAPTER 5: ATTITUDINAL CONFLICT IN CIVIL RIGHTS AND LIBERTIES CASES

1   Justices Ritchie, Stevenson, and Fish were excluded from Tables 5.2 through 5.4 because they cast ten or fewer votes in civil rights and liberties cases during their tenure on the post-*Charter* Court.

2   We excluded the statistics for ten justices in Table 5.4 because none of them addressed more than ten cases where potential activism came into play. The justices are Dickson, Wilson, McIntyre, Beetz, Chouinard, Le Dain, Estey, Stevenson, Deschamps, and Fish. Their data are provided in a note to Table 5.4.

3   In the course of this analysis, we utilized weighted regression techniques to control for case participation variances between the justices. We opted not to create tables for this analysis; the data are presented in the text herewith and in note 4 below.

4   When justices who heard only a few activist cases were included in the analysis, the correlations between the ideology indicators and activist rulings were statistically significant for the party of prime minister measure ($r = .369$, $p = .042$) but not for the newspaper ideology measure ($r = .130$, $p = .277$). Because of the very low levels of case participation for some of these justices, we do not put much stock in the findings, although we would have to acknowledge a slight activist tendency among Liberal Party appointees.

5   We omitted from the analysis cases that involved Aboriginal rights and language claims because they featured different types of legal and constitutional claims than those grounded in section 15 of the *Charter* and/or provincial human rights legislation. We also excluded three cases involving prisoner rights and race/ethnic discrimination claims because the number of cases falling into these areas of law were very low in the 1984–2003 period (*R. v. Williams*, [1998] 1 S.C.R. 1128; *Sauvé v. Canada*, [2002] 3 S.C.R. 519; and *Quebec (Human Rights Commission) v. MakSteel Quebec, Inc.*, [2003] 3 S.C.R. 228).

6   The Lamer Court control variable was omitted from this analysis because of its high collinearity with the McLachlin Court ($r = -.566$).

7   The analysis of all equality disputes omitted seven cases that some would classify as raising equality issues. Three of these cases, dealing with prisoner rights and racial/ethnic claims, were mentioned in note 5, and were excluded from our models because they appeared so infrequently. Four other cases were excluded because the equality claim was tangential to the central legal issues raised in the disputes: *Rudolf Wolff Co. v. Canada*, [1990] 1 S.C.R. 695; *Dywidag Systems International Canada v. Zuthpen Brothers Construction*, [1990] 1 S.C.R. 705; *Re: Therrien*, [2001] 2 S.C.R. 3; and *Siemens v. Manitoba (Attorney General)* [2003] 1 S.C.R. 6.

8   This variable was not included in the other areas of law because we could not come up with valid theoretical reasons to justify its inclusion in the model. In the realm of discrimination, this variable made obvious sense as a potentially significant variable for explaining disparate voting patterns on the Canadian high court.

9   We acknowledge that the Court's ruling in *Egan v. Canada*, [1995] 2 S.C.R. 513 read sexual orientation into section 15 of the *Charter*, which extended constitutional protection to this class of citizens. Since roughly half of the cases included in our analysis were handed down in this area before the *Egan* ruling, however, our hypothesis pertaining to gay rights cases was based on the initial scope of protections explicitly identified in section 15 of the *Charter*, which did not give sexual orientation protected status.

10 In contrast to these two forms of discrimination, the justices do not treat bias on the basis of age, sex, disability, and citizenship in a dramatically different manner from marital status, although two of the model coefficients (age and sex) are in the unexpected direction.

11 Although it makes theoretical sense to include family law cases as an independent variable in the equality area, we omitted it from the larger equation because it appeared so infrequently in the dataset (9.5 percent). Although the frequency of these cases is only slightly larger in the non-unanimous subset, the fact that the measure was more highly correlated with the dependent variable led us to include it in the smaller equation. We want to reiterate that our general rule of thumb was to exclude variables if their frequency fell below 10 percent, unless there was a compelling theoretical rationale for including them in the model. For example, in the equality area, we included religious (9.5 percent), gay (7.5 percent), and citizenship (5.6 percent) discrimination despite their low frequencies because of their obvious relevance to section 15 concerns, and we wanted to test whether any of these *Charter* circumstances led to differential treatment by the justices.

12 We excluded three cases from the analysis that some might characterize as free expression disputes. First, *Canadian Egg Marketing Agency v. Richardson*, [1998] 3 S.C.R. 157 was excluded because it is primarily a mobility rights case. *Harper v. Canada (Attorney General)*, [2000] 2 S.C.R. 764 was excluded because it was a motion for a stay and the Court did not decide the free speech issue on the merits. *MacKay v. Manitoba*, [1989] 2 S.C.R. 357 was excluded because there was no factual basis for the allegation that section 2(b) of the *Charter* had been infringed.

13 This variable essentially compares provincial cases with all other cases, with disputes featuring the federal government representing the bulk of the comparison group (54 percent). Indeed, the federal government is a party in twenty-four of the forty-four disputes in the dataset, while provinces were involved in ten of the cases. It should be noted that two of the suits dealt with local government ordinances, and fall into the residual category left out of the equation (see *Ramsden v.*

Peterborough, [1993] 2 S.C.R. 1084 and *R. v. Guignard*, [2002] 1 S.C.R. 472). A small number of libel and obscenity cases make up the rest of the dataset and feature individual or corporate entities as litigants.

14 Readers should note that the weak performance of ideology in free speech cases was also seen in a larger analysis of speech, press, and association cases. In logistic regression results for this larger analysis, both newspaper ideology and party of prime minister were insignificant and had coefficients in the negative, unexpected direction (*b* for newspaper ideology = –0.10, *b* for party of prime minister = –0.04).

15 The individual rights claimant variable was highly collinear with criminal charge (*r* = .682), obscenity (*r* = –.596), McLachlin Court (*r* = –.596), and commercial advertising (*r* = –.552). The McLachlin Court variable was omitted because of its high collinearity with individual claimant (*r* = –.596) and with obscenity, which featured a perfect 1.0 correlation. This last score indicates that the McLachlin Court decided all of the non-unanimous obscenity cases.

CHAPTER 6: ATTITUDINAL CONFLICT IN ECONOMIC CASES

1 When the analysis was conducted for twenty-two post-*Charter* justices who had had an opportunity to strike down a law in economic cases, the equations produced the same bifurcated results. In the party of prime minister equation, *r* = .386 (significant at the 95 percent confidence level); for the newspaper ideology measure, *r* = .355 (not statistically significant).

2 For justices appointed prior to the *Charter* – Dickson, Lamer, and Wilson – the first two years of data are taken from 1984 and 1985 because these represent the first two years of post-*Charter* jurisprudence.

3 Three cases that some would classify as union/management disputes were omitted from the analysis because we were unable to determine what constituted a liberal outcome in the case (see *CMSG. v. Gagnon*, [1984] 1 S.C.R. 509; *Hémond v. Coopérative Fédérée du Québec*, [1989] 2 S.C.R. 962; and *CUPE v. Canadian Broadcasting Corp.*, [1992] 2 S.C.R. 7). A fourth case was excluded because a jurisdictional issue was central to the case, rather than a labour dispute (*Supermarchés Jean LaBrecque Inc. v. Flamand*, [1987] 2 S.C.R. 219). We also omitted five cases where federalism issues were the dominant theme in the case (*Sobeys Stores Ltd. v. Yeomans and Labour Standards Tribunal (Nova Scotia)*, [1989] 1 S.C.R. 238; *IBEW v. Alberta Government Telephones*, [1989] 2 S.C.R. 318; *PIPSC v. Northwest Territories (Commissioner)*, [1990] 2 S.C.R. 367; *United Transportation Union v. Central Western Railroad Corporation*, [1990] 3 S.C.R. 1112; and *Ontario Hydro v. Ontario Labour Relations Board*, [1993] 3 S.C.R. 328).

4 Note that our model does not test for the impact of government parties as litigants, in large part because initial data runs indicated that these variables had no influence on patterns of voting in union cases. Given their statistically weak

impact, we opted for a more parsimonious model that omitted them from the equation.

5 When newspaper ideology was omitted from the equation, private practice yielded a coefficient of –0.71, significant at the 99 percent confidence level, and the model correctly predicted 75.2 percent of the judicial votes, producing a PRE of 42.2 percent. Conversely, when private practice was omitted, newspaper ideology produced a coefficient of .11 and the model predicted 74.8 percent of the judicial votes, with a PRE of 41.3 percent. One should note that the coefficient for newspaper ideology is in the expected positive direction once private practice is eliminated from the model. While the private practice model slightly outperforms the model that we include in Table 6.6, we believe that it is imperative to present the larger equation, which includes both ideology measures, for theoretical reasons that lie at the foundation of this book.

6 Two unanimous cases were excluded from the analysis because there was too little information to code the case: *City of Montreal v. Steckler*, [1986] 2 S.C.R. 571 and *Quebec (Deputy Minister of Revenue) v. Nolisair International Inc.*, [1999] 1 S.C.R. 759. A third case, *National Corn Growers Association v. Canada (Import Tribunal)*, [1990] 2 S.C.R. 1324, was excluded because it featured a complex international trade dispute over customs fees between Canadian and US corn growers and the issues made it difficult to code the case along liberal/conservative lines. A fourth case, *Slattery (Trustee of) v. Slattery*, [1993] 3 S.C.R. 430, was excluded because it was a dispute over the confidentiality of records and the powers of tax investigators in a divorce bankruptcy case; as such, it was difficult to code along liberal/conservative lines.

7 Private practice, which appeared as a significant judge-level characteristic in the union area, was excluded from the analysis in tax cases because of the relatively high degree of collinearity between it and the newspaper ideology measure ($r = -.473$) and because it had a much weaker correlation with the dependent variable. When we performed the regression analysis with all three judge-level variables in the equation, or with private practice substituted for the newspaper ideology indicator, the explanatory power of the model was not improved. Given our efforts to assess the attitudinal model in the Canadian context and to be consistent with our earlier models in this book, we included newspaper ideology instead of the private practice indicator in the equation.

8 Our coding scheme parallels the types of facts that Howard (2004) has used in his studies of US tax courts.

9 It was necessary to omit business licence and property tax cases because none of these cases appeared in the non-unanimous cases database.

10 In this analysis, we are using the private practice measure as our indicator of ideology in the union cases.

CHAPTER 7: ATTITUDINAL CONSISTENCY IN THE POST-*CHARTER* SUPREME COURT

1   There is a striking parallel between Janda and colleagues' two-dimensional ideological framework (2004) for assessing public opinion and Schubert's early assessment (1965) of judicial liberalism in the US Supreme Court from the 1940s to 1960s. In his pioneering research, Schubert (1965, 199-202) concluded that three dominant ideological dimensions could be found underlying his scales of political and economic liberalism: (1) collectivism versus individualism, (2) libertarianism versus authoritarianism, and (3) equalitarianism versus traditionalism. Schubert's first ideological dimension squares nicely with Janda and colleagues' continuum reflecting the tension between freedom and equality, particularly as it relates to economic issues. We also believe that the other two continua identified by Schubert fit within Janda and colleagues' framework, although Schubert's choice of language and labels skews the comparative dimensions somewhat. In short, the four ideological archetypes drawn from the public opinion literature are not far removed from the pioneering attitudinal work that Schubert applied to the judicial decision-making patterns of the US Supreme Court in the 1950s and 1960s. Thus, we believe that these archetypes are useful constructs for understanding how US justices approach criminal, economic, and civil rights and liberties disputes, and for assessing how Canadian justices have done so in the post-*Charter* era.

2   Six of the justices are excluded from the analysis because they participated in ten or fewer cases in the civil liberties or discrimination areas. They are Justices Deschamps, Fish, Stevenson, Le Dain, Chouinard, and Estey.

3   Although uncommon, this behaviour is not unheard of. For example, Woodward and Armstrong (1979, 70-73) provide several classic illustrations of US Chief Justice Burger's switching of his votes in order to control opinion assignment.

CHAPTER 8: THE POLITICAL AND SOCIAL IMPLICATIONS OF POST-*CHARTER* JUDICIAL BEHAVIOUR

1   Since there were too few opportunities for activist behaviour in the economic cases ($N = 19$), we are less confident with the correlation findings in that area of law, especially since we obtained statistically significant results for one measure of ideology (party of prime minister) but not the other (newspaper ideology score).

2   We measured liberalism as a moving average across two-year increments to help smooth out the undulations in the trend that appear if one reports yearly rates. This allows one to more readily see the differences between the courts.

References

BOOKS AND ARTICLES

Aldrich, John H., and Forrest D. Nelson. 1984. *Linear Probability, Logit, and Probit Models.* Sage University Paper Series on Quantitative Applications in the Social Sciences, series no. 07-045. Beverly Hills, CA: Sage.

Bain, George. 1990. "Trust Us. We Know: Ottawa's Rationale Made Little Sense." *Maclean's,* 15 October, 24-25.

Baum, Lawrence. 1988. "Measuring Policy Change in the US Supreme Court." *American Political Science Review* 82: 905-12.

—. 1992. "Membership Change and Collective Voting Change in the United States Supreme Court." *Journal of Politics* 54: 3-24.

—. 1997. *The Puzzle of Judicial Behavior.* Ann Arbor: University of Michigan Press.

—. 2001. *American Courts: Process and Policy,* 5th ed. Boston: Houghton Mifflin.

Bender, Paul. 1983. "Canadian Charter and US Bill of Rights." *McGill Law Journal* 28: 811-66.

Bindman, Stephen. 1990. "Surprise Pick Gets Rave Reviews." *Ottawa Citizen,* 22 December.

Blackshield, A.R. 1972. "Quantitative Analysis: The High Court of Australia, 1964-1969." *Lawasia* 3 (April): 1-66.

Brenner, Saul. 1983. "Another Look at Freshman Indecisiveness on the United States Supreme Court." *Polity* 16: 320-28.

Brenner, Saul, Timothy Hagle, and Harold J. Spaeth. 1990. "Factors Affecting the Size of the Final Coalition on the Warren Court." *Polity* 23: 309-18.

Brodie, Ian. 2002. *Friends of the Court: The Privileging of Interest Group Litigants in Canada.* Albany: State University of New York Press.

Bushnell, Ian. 1986. "The Use of American Cases." *University of New Brunswick Law Review* 35: 157-81.

Calgary Herald. 2003. Quebecer Elevated to Top Court. 1 August, A4.

Came, Barry. 1990. "The FLQ Crisis: Quebec and Canada 20 Years Later." *Maclean's,* 15 October, 18-20.

Cameron, Charles M., Albert D. Cover, and Jeffrey A. Segal. 1990. "Senate Voting on Supreme Court Nominees: A Neo-Institutional Model." *American Political Science Review* 84: 525-34.

Campbell, Angus, Philip E. Converse, Warren E. Miller, and Donald E. Stokes. 1960. *The American Voter.* Chicago: University of Chicago, Midway Reprint ed.

Canadian Centre for Justice Statistics (CCJS). 1999. *The Juristat Reader: A Statistical Overview of the Canadian Justice System.* Toronto: Thompson Educational Publishing.

Centre for Research and Information on Canada (CRIC). 2002. *The Charter: Dividing or Uniting Canadians?* Montreal: CRIC; McGill University.

Chambers, Tom. 1996. *Canadian Politics: An Introduction.* Toronto: Thompson Educational Publishing.

Danelski, David J. 1969. "The Supreme Court of Japan: An Exploratory Study." In *Comparative Judicial Behavior,* edited by Glendon Schubert and David Danelski, 121-56. New York: Oxford University Press.

—. 1989. "The Influence of the Chief Justice in the Decisional Process of the Supreme Court." In *American Court Systems,* edited by Sheldon Goldman and Austin Sarat, 486-99. New York: Longman.

Dator, James A. 1969. "Measuring Attitudes across Cultures: A Factor Analysis of the Replies of Japanese Judges to Eysenck's Inventory of Conservative-Progressive Ideology." In *Comparative Judicial Behavior,* edited by Glendon Schubert and David Danelski, 71-102. New York: Oxford University Press.

DesBarats, Peter. 2003. "A Judge with Literary Flair." *The Gazette* (Montreal), 17 August, A13.

DiFrederico, Giuseppe, and Carlo Guarnieri. 1988. "The Courts in Italy." In *The Political Role of Law Courts in Modern Democracies,* edited by J. Waltman, and K. Holland, 153-80. London: Macmillan.

Ducat, Craig R. 2004. *Constitutional Interpretation,* 8th ed. Belmont, CA: Thomson/West.

Ducat, Craig R., and Robert L. Dudley. 1987. "Dimensions Underlying Economic Policymaking in the Early and Late Burger Courts." *Journal of Politics* 49: 521-39.

Ducat, Craig R., and Victor E. Flango. 1976. *Leadership in State Supreme Courts: Roles of the Chief Justices.* Beverly Hills, CA: Sage.

—. 1985. "The Outsider on the Court." *Journal of Politics* 47: 282-89.

Dudley, Robert L. 1993. "The Freshman Effect and Voting Alignments: A Reexamination of Judicial Folklore." *American Politics Quarterly* 21 (3): 360-67.

Dudley, Robert L., and Craig R. Ducat. 1986. "The Burger Court and Economic Liberalism." *Western Political Quarterly* 38: 236-49.

Emerson, Thomas I. 1970. *The System of Freedom of Expression.* New York: Random House.

Epp, Charles. 1996. "Do Bills of Rights Matter? The Canadian Charter of Rights and Freedoms." *American Political Science Review* 90: 765-79.

—. 1998. *The Rights Revolution: Lawyers, Activists, and Supreme Courts in Comparative Perspective.* Chicago: University of Chicago Press.

Esptein, Lee, and Jack Knight. 1998. *The Choices Justices Make*. Washington, DC: CQ Press.

Epstein, Lee, and Carol Mershon. 1996. "Measuring Political Preferences." *American Journal of Political Science* 40: 261-94.

Epstein, Lee, Jeffrey A. Segal, Harold J. Spaeth, and Thomas G. Walker. 1996. *The Supreme Court Compendium: Data, Decisions and Developments*. Washington, DC: CQ Press.

Epstein, Lee, Thomas G. Walker, and William J. Dixon. 1989. "The Supreme Court and Criminal Justice Disputes: A Neo-Institutional Perspective." *American Journal of Political Science* 33: 825-41.

Fine, Sean. 1997. "Search for Judge Turns to Atlantic." *Globe and Mail*, 28 August, A1, A7.

Fisher, William W., Morton J. Horowitz, and Thomas A. Reed, eds. 1993. *American Legal Realism*. New York: Oxford University Press.

Flango, Victor E., and Craig R. Ducat. 1977. "Toward an Integration of Public Law and Judicial Behavior." *Journal of Politics* 39: 41-72.

Flango, Victor E., and Glendon Schubert. 1969. "Two Surveys of Simulated Judicial Decision-Making: Hawaii and the Philippines." In *Comparative Judicial Behavior*, edited by Glendon Schubert and David Danelski, 197-220. New York: Oxford University Press.

Flemming, Roy B. 2004. *Tournament of Appeals: Granting Judicial Review in Canada*. Vancouver: UBC Press.

Flemming, Roy B., and Glenn S. Kurtz. 2002a. "Selecting Appeals for Judicial Review in Canada: A Replication and Multivariate Test of American Hypotheses." *Journal of Politics* 64: 232-48.

—. 2002b. "Repeat Litigators and Agenda Setting on the Supreme Court of Canada." *Canadian Journal of Political Science* 35: 811-33.

Fletcher, Joseph F., and Paul Howe. 2000. "Canadian Attitudes toward the Charter and Courts in Comparative Perspective." *Choices: Courts and Legislatures* 6 (3): 4-29.

Fouts, Donald E. 1969. "Policy Making in the Supreme Court of Canada, 1950–1960." In *Comparative Judicial Behavior*, edited by Glendon Schubert and David Danelski, 257-92. New York: Oxford University Press.

Frank, Jerome. 1930. *Law and the Modern Mind*. New York: Coward-McCann.

Galanter, Marc. 1974. "Why the 'Haves' Come Out Ahead: Speculations on the Limits of Legal Change." *Law and Society Review* 9: 95-160.

—. 2003. "Why the 'Haves' Come Out Ahead: Speculations on the Limits of Legal Change." In *In Litigation Do the "Haves" Still Come Out Ahead*, edited by Herbert Kritzer and Susan Silbey, 13-81. Stanford, CA: Stanford University Press.

Galligan, Brian, and David R. Slater. 1995. "Judicial Intrusion into the Australian Cabinet." In *The Global Expansion of Judicial Power*, edited by Neal Tate and Torbjörn Vallinder, 81-100. New York: New York University Press.

The Gazette (Montreal). 2003. "Fish Brings Right Balance to Court Bench." 4 August, A18.

Geddes, John. 2000. "The Legal Eagles: As the Debate over Judicial Activism Continues, Canada's Supreme Court Justices Are under Scrutiny." *Maclean's*, 10 January, 30-32.

Gewirtz, Paul, and Chad Golder. 2005. "So Who Are the Activists?" *New York Times*, 6 July, A23.

Gibbins, Roger. 1993. "The Impact of the American Constitution on Contemporary Canadian Constitutional Politics." In *The Canadian and American Constitutions in Comparative Perspective*, edited by Marian McKenna, 131-45. Calgary: University of Calgary Press.

Gilligan, Carol. 1982. *In a Different Voice: Psychological Theory and Women's Development.* Cambridge, MA: Harvard University Press.

—. 1987. "Moral Orientation and Moral Development." In *Women and Moral Theory*, edited by Eva F. Kittay and Diana T. Myers, 19-33. New York: Rowman and Littlefield.

Glendon, Mary Ann. 1991. *Rights Talk: The Impoverishment of Political Discourse.* New York: Free Press.

Globe and Mail. 2003. "Welcome to the Court, but Fix the Entrance." 2 August, A16.

Gordon, Mary. 2003. "New Judge 'Phenomenal Human Being.'" *Toronto Star*, 1 August, A4.

Greene, Ian, Carl Baar, Peter McCormick, George Szablowski, and Martin Thomas. 1998. *Final Appeal: Decision-Making in Canada's Courts of Appeal.* Toronto: James Lorimer.

Gruhl, John, Cassia Spohn, and Susan Welch. 1981. "Women as Policymakers: The Case of Trial Judges." *American Journal of Political Science* 25: 308-22.

Hagle, Timothy M. 1993. "'Freshman Effects' for Supreme Court Justices." *American Journal of Political Science* 37: 1142-57.

Hagle, Timothy, and Harold J. Spaeth. 1992. "The Emergence of a New Ideology: The Business Decisions of the Burger Court." *Journal of Politics* 54: 120-34.

—. 1993. "Ideological Patterns in the Justices' Voting in the Burger Court Business Cases." *Journal of Politics* 55: 492-505.

Hausegger, Lori, and Stacia Haynie. 2003. "Judicial Decisionmaking and the Use of Panels in the Canadian Supreme Court and the South African Appellate Division." *Law and Society Review* 37: 635-58.

Hausegger, Lori, and Troy Riddell. 2004. "The Changing Nature of Public Support for the Supreme Court of Canada." *Canadian Journal of Political Science* 37 (1): 23-50.

Heard, Andrew. 1991. "The Charter in the Supreme Court of Canada: The Importance of Which Judges Hear an Appeal." *Canadian Journal of Political Science* 24: 290-307.

Heck, Edward V., and Melinda Gann Hall. 1981. "Bloc Voting and the Freshman Justice Revisited." *Journal of Politics* 43: 852-60.

Hennigar, Matthew A. 2004a. "Expanding the Dialogue Debate: Canadian Federal Government Responses to Lower Court Charter Decisions." *Canadian Journal of Political Science* 37: 3-21.

—. 2004b. "The Canadian Government's Litigation Strategy in Sexual Orientation Cases." Paper presented at the annual meeting of the Canadian Political Science Association, Winnipeg, 4 June 2004.

Hiebert, Janet. 2002. *Charter Conflicts: What Is Parliament's Role?* Montreal and Kingston: McGill-Queen's University Press.

Hirschl, Ran. 2004. *Towards Juristocracy: The Origins and Consequences of the New Constitutionalism.* Cambridge, MA: Harvard University Press.

Hogg, Peter W. 1987. "The Charter of Rights and American Theories of Interpretation." *Osgoode Hall Law Journal* 25: 87-113.

—. 1997. *Constitutional Law of Canada,* 4th ed. Toronto: Carswell.

Hogg, Peter W., and Allison Bushell. 1997. "The Charter Dialogue between Courts and Legislatures." *Osgoode Hall Law Journal* 35: 75-124.

Hogg, Peter W., and Allison Thornton. 1999. "Reply to Six Degrees of Dialogue." *Osgoode Hall Law Journal* 37: 529-36.

Holmes, Oliver Wendell Jr. 1881. *The Common Law.* Boston: Little Brown.

—. 1897. "The Path of the Law." *Harvard Law Review* 10: 457-78.

Howard, Robert M. 2004. "Specialized Federal Courts versus General Courts: Ideology and Expertise in Tax Decisions." Paper presented at the annual meeting of the American Political Science Association, Chicago, 2-5 September 2004.

Hunter, Ian. 1989. "Confirmation Hearings for Judges Would Lower Quality of Court." *Financial Post,* 27 March, 16.

Iacobucci, Frank. 2002. Remarks delivered at a conference commemorating the twentieth anniversary of the *Charter of Rights and Freedoms,* Association of Canadian Studies, Ottawa, March 2002.

Jackson, Robert J., and Doreen Jackson. 1994. *Politics in Canada: Culture, Institutions, Behaviour, and Public Policy.* Scarborough, ON: Prentice Hall Canada.

Janda, Kenneth, Jeffrey Berry, and Jerry Goldman. 2004. *The Challenge of Democracy,* 8th ed. Boston: Houghton Mifflin.

Johnson, Janet Rudolph, and H.T. Reynolds. 2005. *Political Science Research Methods,* 5th ed. Washington, DC: CQ Press.

Kawashima, Takeyoshi. 1969. "Individualism in Decision-Making in the Supreme Court of Canada." In *Comparative Judicial Behavior,* edited by Glendon Schubert and David Danelski, 103-20. New York: Oxford University Press.

Kelly, James B. 2005. *Governing with the Charter: Legislative and Judicial Activism and Framers' Intent.* Vancouver: UBC Press.

Knopff, Rainer, and F.L. Morton. 1992. *Charter Politics.* Toronto: Nelson Canada.

242

REFERENCES

Kritzer, Herbert. 2003. "The Government Gorilla: Why Does Government Come Out Ahead in Appellate Courts?" In *In Litigation Do the "Haves" Still Come Out Ahead*, edited by Herbert Kritzer and Susan Silbey, 342-70. Stanford, CA: Stanford University Press.

LeBlanc, Daniel, and Campbell Clark. 2003. "Quebec Anglophone Joins Supreme Court." *Globe and Mail*, 1 August, A1.

Levy, Harold. 2003. "A Judge Who Has Always Made a Difference." *Toronto Star*, 10 August, A4.

L'Heureux-Dubé, Madame Justice Claire. 1993. "Two Supreme Courts: A Study in Contrast." In *The Canadian and American Constitutions in Comparative Perspective*, edited by Marian McKenna, 149-65. Calgary: University of Calgary Press.

Lipset, Seymour Martin. 1990. *Continental Divide: The Values and Institutions of the United States and Canada*. London: Routledge.

—. 1996. *American Exceptionalism*. New York: Norton.

Llewellyn, Karl. 1931. "Some Realism about Realism: Responding to Dean Pound." *Harvard Law Review* 44: 1237.

Lyons, Nona Plessner. 1988. "Two Perspectives: On Self, Relationships and Morality." In *Mapping the Moral Domain*, edited by Carol Gilligan and Hanis Ward, 221-45. Cambridge, MA: Harvard University Press.

McCormick, Peter. 1993. "Assessing Leadership on the Supreme Court of Canada: Towards a Typology of Chief Justice Performance." *Supreme Court Law Review* 4 (2): 409-29.

—. 1994a. "Career Patterns and the Delivery of Reasons for Judgment in the Supreme Court of Canada (1949-1993)." *Supreme Court Law Review* 5 (2): 499-521.

—. 1994b. *Canada's Courts*. Toronto: James Lorimer.

—. 2000. *Supreme at Last: The Evolution of the Supreme Court of Canada*. Toronto: James Lorimer.

McCormick, Peter, and Twyla Job. 1993. "Do Women Judges Make a Difference?" *Canadian Journal of Law and Society* 8: 135-47.

MacDonald, Ian. 2003. "Morris Fish Is a Supremely Wise and Popular Choice." *The Gazette* (Montreal), 4 August, A19.

MacKay, Wayne. 1983. "Judicial Process in the Supreme Court of Canada: The Patriation Reference and Its Implications for the Charter of Rights." *Osgoode Hall Law Journal* 21: 55-81.

MacKinnon, Catharine. 1993. *Only Words*. Cambridge, MA: Harvard University Press.

McLachlin, Honourable Beverley. 2001. "Courts, Legislatures and Executives in the Post-Charter Era." In *Judicial Power and Canadian Democracy*, edited by Paul Howe and Peter Russell, 63-72. Montreal and Kingston: McGill-Queen's University Press.

—. 2004. "Protecting Constitutional Rights: A Comparative View of the United States and Canada." Remarks of the Right Honourable Beverley McLachlin at the Center for the Study of Canada, Plattsburgh State University, Plattsburgh, NY, 5 April 2004.

MacNeil, Robert. 1991. "Looking for My Country." *American Review of Canadian Studies* 21: 409-21.

MacQueen, Ken. 1987. "Second Woman Takes Supreme Court Seat." *Ottawa Citizen,* 16 April, A1.

Makin, Kirk, and Margaret Polanyi. 1988. "Inexperience as Judge No Handicap, Sopinka Says." *Globe and Mail,* 25 May, A5.

Maltzman, Forrest, James F. Spriggs II, and Paul Wahlbeck. 2000. *Crafting Law on the Supreme Court: The Collegial Game.* Cambridge: Cambridge University Press.

Manfredi, Christopher P. 1990. "The Use of United States Decisions by the Supreme Court of Canada under the *Charter of Rights and Freedoms.*" *Canadian Journal of Political Science* 23: 499-518.

—. 1993. *Judicial Power and the Charter: Canada and the Paradox of Liberal Constitutionalism.* Norman: University of Oklahoma Press.

—. 2001. *Judicial Power and the Charter: Canada and the Paradox of Liberal Constitutionalism,* 2nd ed. Oxford: Oxford University Press.

—. 2002. "Strategic Behaviour and the Canadian Charter of Rights and Freedoms." In *The Myth of the Sacred: The Charter, the Courts, and the Politics of the Constitution in Canada,* edited by Patrick James, Donald E. Abelson, and Michael Lusztig, 147-67. Montreal and Kingston: McGill-Queen's University Press.

—. 2004. *Feminist Activism in the Supreme Court.* Vancouver: UBC Press.

Manfredi, Christopher P., and James B. Kelly. 1999. "Six Degrees of Dialogue: A Response to Hogg and Bushell." *Osgoode Hall Law Journal* 37: 513-27.

—. 2001. "Dialogue, Deference, and Restraint: Judicial Independence and Trial Procedures." *Saskatchewan Law Review* 64: 323-46.

Manheim, Jarol B., and Richard C. Rich. 1991. *Empirical Political Analysis,* 3rd ed. White Plains, NY: Longman.

Massey, Calvin R. 1990. "The Locus of Sovereignty: Judicial Review, Legislative Supremacy, and Federalism in the Constitutional Traditions of Canada and the United States." *Duke Law Journal* (1990): 1229-1310.

Morton, F.L. 1987. "The Political Impact of the Canadian Charter of Rights and Freedoms." *Canadian Journal of Political Science* 20: 31-55.

—. 1989. "Charter Changed Judges' Roles: Their Selection Needs Review." *Financial Post,* 20 February, 16.

—. 1992. *Law, Politics, and the Judicial Process in Canada,* 2nd ed. Calgary: University of Calgary Press.

Morton, F.L., and Rainer Knopff. 2000. *The Charter Revolution and the Court Party.* Peterborough, ON: Broadview Press.

Morton, F.L., Peter H. Russell, and Troy Riddell. 1994. "The Canadian Charter of Rights and Freedoms: A Descriptive Analysis of the First Decade." *National Journal of Constitutional Law* 5: 1-58.

Morton, F.L., Peter H. Russell, and Michael Withey. 1991. "Judging the Judges: The Supreme Court's First One Hundred Charter Decisions." In *Politics: Canada*, 7th ed.,
edited by Paul W. Fox and Graham White, 59-79. Toronto: McGraw-Hill Ryerson.

Murphy, Walter. 1964. *Elements of Judicial Strategy*. Chicago: University of Chicago Press.

Neubauer, David W., and Stephen S. Meinhold. 2004. *Judicial Process: Law, Courts, and
Politics in the United States*, 3rd ed. Belmont, CA: Thomson/Wadsworth.

O'Brien, David M. 1996. *Storm Center: The Supreme Court in American Politics*, 4th ed.
New York: Norton.

Ostberg, C.L. 1995. "A Comparison of US and Canadian Supreme Court Decisions
after the Addition of the Charter of Rights and Freedoms to the Canadian Constitution." PhD dissertation, Northern Illinois University, DeKalb, IL.

Ostberg, C.L., Susan Johnson, Donald R. Songer, and Matthew E. Wetstein. 2004. "The
Nature and Extent of Attitudinal Decision Making in Canada." Paper presented at
the annual meeting of the American Political Science Association, Chicago, 2 September 2004.

—. n.d. "Attitudinal Decision Making in the Supreme Court of Canada: The Lamer
Court, 1992-1997." Unpublished manuscript.

Ostberg, C.L., and Matthew E. Wetstein. 1998. "Dimensions of Attitudes Underlying
Search and Seizure Decisions of the Supreme Court of Canada." *Canadian Journal
of Political Science* 31: 767-87.

Ostberg, C.L., Matthew E. Wetstein, and Craig R. Ducat. 2001. "Attitudes, Precedents
and Cultural Change: Explaining the Citation of Foreign Precedents by the Supreme Court of Canada." *Canadian Journal of Political Science* 32: 377-99.

—. 2002. "Attitudinal Dimensions of Supreme Court Decision Making in Canada: The
Lamer Court, 1991-1995." *Political Research Quarterly* 55: 237-58.

—. 2003. "Acclimation Effects on the Supreme Court of Canada: A Cross-Cultural
Examination of Judicial Folklore." *Social Science Quarterly* 84: 704-22.

—. 2004. "Leaders, Followers, and Outsiders: Task and Social Leadership on the
Supreme Court of Canada in the Early Nineties." *Polity* 36: 505-28.

Ottawa Citizen. 1984. "PM Names Le Dain to High Court." 30 May, A1, A12.

—. 1998. "Judge: Critics Argue Time for Another Woman." 9 January, D2.

Packer, Herbert L. 1968. *The Limits of the Criminal Sanction*. Stanford, CA: Stanford
University Press.

Peck, Sidney R. 1967a. "A Behavioural Approach to the Judicial Process: Scalogram
Analysis." *Osgoode Hall Law Journal* 5: 1-28.

—. 1967b. "The Supreme Court of Canada, 1958-1966: A Search for Policy through
Scalogram Analysis." *Canadian Bar Review* 45: 666-725.

—. 1969. "A Scalogram Analysis of the Supreme Court of Canada, 1958-1967." In *Comparative Judicial Behavior*, edited by Glendon Schubert and David Danelski, 293-
334. New York: Oxford University Press.

Power, John. 1995. "The Executive, the Judiciary, and Immigration Appeals in Austra-lia." In *The Global Expansion of Judicial Power*, edited by Neal Tate and Torbjörn Vallinder, 101-14. New York: New York University Press.

Pritchett, C. Hermann. 1941. "Division of Opinion among Justices of the Supreme Court." *American Political Science Review* 35: 890-98.

—. 1948. *The Roosevelt Court*. New York: Macmillan.

Roach, Kent. 2001. *The Supreme Court on Trial: Judicial Activism or Democratic Dialogue*. Toronto: Irwin Law.

Rohde, David W., and Harold J. Spaeth. 1976. *Supreme Court Decision Making*. San Fran-cisco: Freeman.

Romanow, Roy. 1986. "And Justice for Whom?" *Manitoba Law Journal* 16: 102-22.

Russell, Peter H. 1982. "The Effect of a Charter of Rights on the Policy-Making Role of Canadian Court." *Canadian Public Administration* 25: 1-33.

—. 1987. *The Judiciary in Canada*. Toronto: McGraw-Hill Ryerson.

—. 1988. "Canada's Charter of Rights and Freedoms: A Political Report." *Public Law* 385-401.

—. 1992. "Standing Up for Notwithstanding." In *Law, Politics, and the Judicial Process in Canada*, 2nd ed., edited by F.L. Morton, 474-85. Calgary: University of Calgary Press.

Samonte, Abelardo G. 1969. "The Philippine Supreme Court: A Study of Judicial Back-ground Characteristics, Attitudes, and Decision-Making." In *Comparative Judicial Behavior*, edited by Glendon Schubert and David Danelski, 157-95. New York: Oxford University Press.

Schattschneider, E.E. 1960. *The Semisovereign People*. New York: Holt, Rinehart and Winston.

Schmitz, Cristin. 1999. "Communication, Consensus among McLachlin's Targets." *Lawyer's Weekly*, 19 November. Available online at Lexis/Nexis.

—. 2000. "Powerful New Chief Justice of the Supreme Court Opens Up." *Hill Times*, 17 January. Available online at Lexis/Nexis.

Schubert, Glendon. 1965. *The Judicial Mind: Attitudes and Ideologies of Supreme Court Justices, 1946-1963*. Evanston, IL: Northwestern University Press.

—. 1969a. "The Dimensions of Decisional Response: Opinion and Voting Behavior of the Australian High Court." In *Frontiers of Judicial Research*, edited by Joel B. Grossman and Joseph Tannenhaus, 163-95. New York: John Wiley and Sons.

—. 1969b. "Two Causal Models of Decision-Making by the High Court of Australia." In *Comparative Judicial Behavior*, edited by Glendon Schubert and David Danelski, 335-66. New York: Oxford University Press.

—. 1974. *The Judicial Mind Revisited*. New York: Oxford University Press.

—. 1977. "Political Culture and Judicial Ideology: Some Cross-Cultural and Sub-cultural Comparisons." *Comparative Political Studies* 9 (January): 363-408.

—. 1980. "Subcultural Effects on Judicial Behavior: A Comparative Analysis." *Journal of Politics* 42: 951-92.

Segal, Jeffrey A. 1984. "Predicting Supreme Court Cases Probabilistically: The Search and Seizure Cases, 1962-1981." *American Political Science Review* 78: 891-900.

—. 1986. "Supreme Court Justices as Human Decision Makers: An Individual-Level Analysis of the Search and Seizure Cases." *Journal of Politics* 48: 938-55.

Segal, Jeffrey A., and Albert D. Cover. 1989. "Ideological Values and Votes of US Supreme Court Justices." *American Political Science Review* 83: 557-65.

Segal, Jeffrey A., and Harold J. Spaeth. 1993. *The Supreme Court and the Attitudinal Model.* Cambridge: Cambridge University Press.

—. 2002. *The Supreme Court and the Attitudinal Model Revisited.* Cambridge: Cambridge University Press.

Slattery, Brian. 1987. "A Theory of the Charter." *Osgoode Hall Law Journal* 25: 701-47.

Smith, Charles. 2000. "A New Sensationalism? Media Coverage of Supreme Court Appointments: The Chrétien Period." Paper presented at the annual meeting of the Canadian Political Science Association, Quebec, June 2000.

Sniderman, Paul M., Joseph F. Fletcher, Peter H. Russell, and Philip E. Tetlock. 1996. *The Clash of Rights: Liberty, Equality and Legitimacy in a Pluralist Democracy.* New Haven, CT: Yale University Press.

Snyder, Eloise C. 1958. "The Supreme Court as a Small Group." *Social Forces* 36: 232-58.

Songer, Donald R., and Kelley Crews-Meyer. 2000. "Does Judge Gender Matter? Decision Making in State Supreme Courts." *Social Science Quarterly* 81: 750-62.

Songer, Donald R., and Susan W. Johnson. 2002. "Attitudinal Decision Making in the Supreme Court of Canada." Paper presented at the annual meeting of the Midwest Political Science Association, Chicago, April 2002.

Songer, Donald R., Jeffrey A. Segal, and Charles M. Cameron. 1994. "The Hierarchy of Justice: Testing a Principal-Agent Model of Supreme Court-Circuit Court Interactions." *American Journal of Political Science* 38: 673-96.

Songer, Donald R., Reggie S. Sheehan, and Susan Brodie Haire. 2003. "Do the 'Haves' Come Out Ahead Over Time: Applying Galanter's Framework to Decisions of the US Court of Appeals, 1925-1988." In *In Litigation Do the "Haves" Still Come Out Ahead,* edited by Herbert Kritzer and Susan Silbey, 85-107. Stanford, CA: Stanford University Press.

Spaeth, Harold J. 1963. "An Analysis of Judicial Attitudes in the Labor Relations Decisions of the Warren Court." *Journal of Politics* 2: 290-311.

Spaeth, Harold J., and David J. Peterson. 1971. "The Analysis and Interpretation of Dimensionality: The Case of Civil Liberties Decision Making." *American Journal of Political Science* 15: 415-41.

Spaeth, Harold J., and Jeffrey A. Segal. 1999. *Majority Rule or Minority Will: Adherence to Precedent on the US Supreme Court.* Cambridge: Cambridge University Press.

Steffensmeier, Darrell, and Chris Hebert. 1999. "Women and Men Policymakers: Does the Judge's Gender Affect the Sentencing of Criminal Defendants?" *Social Forces* 77: 1163-80.

Stephenson, Carol A. 1991. "Religious Exercises and Instruction in Ontario Public Schools." *University of Toronto Faculty of Law Review* 49: 82-105.

Stuart, Don. 1987. "Four Springboards from the Supreme Court of Canada: *Hunter, Therens, Motor Vehicle Reference,* and *Oakes* – Asserting Basic Values of Our Criminal Justice System." *Queen's Law Journal* 12: 131-54.

Tate, C. Neal. 1995. "The Philippines and Southeast Asia." In *The Global Expansion of Judicial Power,* edited by Neal Tate and Torbjörn Vallinder, 463-84. New York: New York University Press.

Tate, C. Neal, and Roger Handberg. 1991. "Time Binding and Theory Building in Personal Attribute Models of Supreme Court Voting Behavior." *American Journal of Political Science* 35: 460-80.

Tate, C. Neal, and Panu Sittiwong. 1989. "Decision Making in the Canadian Supreme Court: Extending a Personal Attributes Model across Nations." *Journal of Politics* 51: 900-16.

Tate, C. Neal, and Torbjörn Vallinder, eds. 1995. *The Global Expansion of Judicial Power.* New York: New York University Press.

Tibbetts, Janice. 2003a. "Judicial Friend of the Underdog Finally Named to Supreme Court." *Ottawa Citizen,* 1 August, A1.

—. 2003b. "Anglophone Montrealer Appointed to High Court." *Edmonton Journal,* 1 August, A6.

—. 2003c. "A New Order in the Court." *Vancouver Sun,* 22 November, C3.

Ulmer, Sidney. 1973. "Social Background as an Indicator to the Votes of Supreme Court Justices in Criminal Cases, 1947–1956 Terms." *American Journal of Political Science* 17: 622-30.

Vancouver Sun. 2003. "Anglophone Gets High Court Seat." 1 August, A5.

Verney, Douglas. 1987. "Parliamentary Supremacy versus Judicial Review: Is a Compromise Possible?" *Journal of Commonwealth and Comparative Politics* 29: 185-200.

Wallace, Bruce. 1999. "Activists in Black Robes." *Maclean's,* 6 September, 14-15.

Ward, John. 2003. "Quebec Anglophone Named to Top Court." *Halifax Herald,* 1 August, C16.

Wasby, Stephen L. 1993. *The Supreme Court in the Federal System,* 4th ed. Chicago: Nelson-Hall.

West, Robin. 1991. "Jurisprudence and Gender." In *Feminist Legal Theory,* edited by Katharine T. Bartlett and Rosanne Kennedy, 201-34. Boulder, CO: Westview Press.

Wetstein, Matthew E., and C.L. Ostberg. 1999. "Search and Seizure Cases in the Supreme Court of Canada: Extending an American Model of Judicial Decision Making across Countries." *Social Science Quarterly* 80: 757-74.

—. 2005. "Strategic Leadership and Political Change on the Canadian Supreme Court: Analyzing the Transition to Chief Justice." *Canadian Journal of Political Science* 38: 653-73.

White, Candace C. 1998. "Gender Differences in the Supreme Court." In *Law, Politics, and the Judicial Process in Canada*, 3rd ed., edited by F.L. Morton, 85-90. Calgary: University of Calgary Press.

Wilson, Bertha. 1990. "Will Women Judges Really Make a Difference?" *Osgoode Hall Law Journal* 28: 507-22, as published in *Law, Politics, and the Judicial Process in Canada*, 2nd ed., edited by F.L. Morton, 92-97. Calgary: University of Calgary Press.

—. 2001. "We Didn't Volunteer." In *Judicial Power and Canadian Democracy*, edited by Paul Howe and Peter Russell, 73-79. Montreal and Kingston: McGill-Queen's University Press.

Wilson-Smith, Anthony. 1999. "The Art of Judge-Making." *Maclean's*, 29 November, 17.

Wood, Sandra L., Linda Kamp Keith, Drew Noble Lanier, and Ayo Ogundele. 1998. "'Acclimation Effects' for Supreme Court Justices: A Cross-Validation, 1888–1940." *American Journal of Political Science* 42: 690-97.

Woodward, Bob, and Scott Armstrong. 1979. *The Brethren: Inside the Supreme Court.* New York: Avon Books.

Ziegel, Jacob. 2001. "Merit Selection and Democratization of Appointments to the Supreme Court of Canada." In *Judicial Power and Canadian Democracy*, edited by Paul Howe and Peter H. Russell, 131-64. Montreal and Kingston: McGill-Queen's University Press.

JURISPRUDENCE

143471 Canada v. Quebec, [1994] 2 S.C.R. 339

Allsco Building Products Ltd. v. UFCW Local 1288P, [1999] 2 S.C.R. 1136

Andrews v. Law Society of British Columbia, [1989] 1 S.C.R. 143

Baron v. Canada, [1993] 1 S.C.R. 416

BCGEU v. British Columbia (Attorney General), [1988] 2 S.C.R. 214

Beliveau-St-Jacques v. FEESP, [1996] 2 S.C.R. 345

Bhinder v. Canadian National Railway, [1985] 2 S.C.R. 561

British Columbia v. Henfrey Samson Belair Ltd., [1989] 2 S.C.R. 24

Brooks v. Canada Safeway Ltd., [1989] 1 S.C.R. 1219

Canada (Human Rights Commission) v. Taylor, [1990] 3 S.C.R. 892

Canadian Egg Marketing Agency v. Richardson, [1998] 3 S.C.R. 157

Caron v. Canada, [1991] 1 S.C.R. 48

Carroll v. United States, 267 U.S. 132 (1925)

CBC v. Canada (Labour Relations Board), [1995] 1 S.C.R. 157

Chaoulli v. Quebec (Attorney General), [2005] 1 S.C.R. 791

City of Montreal v. Steckler, [1986] 2 S.C.R. 571

CMSG. v. Gagnon, [1984] 1 S.C.R. 509

Commission Scolaire Régionale de Chambly v. Bergevin, [1994] 2 S.C.R. 525

CUPE v. Canadian Broadcasting Corp., [1992] 2 S.C.R. 7

Dersch v. Canada, [1990] 2 S.C.R. 1505

Dywidag Systems International Canada v. Zuthpen Brothers Construction, [1990] 1 S.C.R. 705

Egan v. Canada, [1995] 2 S.C.R. 513

Flieger v. New Brunswick, [1993] 2 S.C.R. 651

Ford v. Quebec (Attorney General), [1988] 2 S.C.R. 712

Friesen v. Canada, [1995] 3 S.C.R. 103

Harper v. Canada (Attorney General), [2000] 2 S.C.R. 764

Hémond v. Coopérative Fédérée du Québec, [1989] 2 S.C.R. 962

Hills v. Canada, [1988] 1 S.C.R. 513

Hunter v. Southam, [1984] 2 S.C.R. 145

Husky Oil Operations Ltd. v. M.N.R., [1995] 3 S.C.R. 453

Hy and Zels Inc. v. Ontario (Attorney General), [1993] 3 S.C.R. 675

IBEW v. Alberta Government Telephones, [1989] 2 S.C.R. 318

Janzen v. Platy Enterprises Ltd., [1989] 1 S.C.R. 1252

Katz v. United States, 389 U.S. 347 (1967)

Knox Contracting v. Canada, [1990] 2 S.C.R. 338

Kourtessis v. Minister of National Revenue, [1993] 2 S.C.R. 53

Little Sisters Book and Art Emporium v. Canada (Minister of Justice), [2000] 2 S.C.R. 1120

M. v. H., [1999] 2 S.C.R. 3

MacKay v. Manitoba, [1989] 2 S.C.R. 357

National Corn Growers Association v. Canada (Import Tribunal), [1990] 2 S.C.R. 1324

Native Women's Association of Canada v. Canada, [1994] 3 S.C.R. 627

Newfoundland (Attorney General) v. NAPE, [1988] 2 S.C.R. 204

Ontario Human Rights Commission v. Simpsons-Sears, [1985] 2 S.C.R. 536

Ontario Hydro v. Ontario Labour Relations Board, [1993] 3 S.C.R. 328

OPSEU v. Ontario (Attorney General), [1987] 2 S.C.R. 2

PIPSC v. Northwest Territories (Commissioner), [1990] 2 S.C.R. 367

PSAC v. Canada, [1987] 1 S.C.R. 424

Quebec (Deputy Minister of Revenue) v. Nolisair International Inc., [1999] 1 S.C.R. 759

Quebec (Human Rights Commission) v. MakSteel Quebec, Inc., [2003] 3 S.C.R. 228

R. v. Andrews, [1990] 3 S.C.R. 870

R. v. Collins, [1987] 1 S.C.R. 256

R. v. Dyment, [1988] 2 S.C.R. 417

R. v. Elshaw, [1991] 3 S.C.R. 24

R. v. Feeney, [1997] 2 S.C.R. 13

R. v. Garofoli, [1990] 2 S.C.R. 1421

R. v. Golden, [2001] 3 S.C.R. 679

R. v. Grant, [1993] 3 S.C.R. 223

R. v. Greffe, [1990] 1 S.C.R. 755

R. v. Guignard, [2002] 1 S.C.R. 472

R. v. Heikel, [1989] 1 S.C.R. 1776

R. v. Jacoy, [1988] 2 S.C.R. 548

R. v. Jones, [1994] 2 S.C.R. 229

R. v. Keegstra, [1990] 3 S.C.R. 697

R. v. Kokesch, [1990] 3 S.C.R. 3

R. v. LaChance, [1990] 2 S.C.R. 1490

R. v. Manninen, [1987] 1 S.C.R. 1233

R. v. Marshall, [1999] 3 S.C.R. 456

R. v. McKinlay Transport Ltd., [1990] 1 S.C.R. 627

R. v. Meltzer, [1989] 1 S.C.R. 1764

R. v. Ouellette, [1989] 1 S.C.R. 1781

R. v. Plant, [1993] 3 S.C.R. 281

R. v. Pohoretsky, [1987] 1 S.C.R. 945

R. v. Ross, [1989] 1 S.C.R. 3

R. v. Simmons, [1988] 2 S.C.R. 495

R. v. Stillman, [1997] 1 S.C.R. 607

R. v. Therens, [1985] 1 S.C.R. 613

R. v. Wiley, [1993] 3 S.C.R. 263

R. v. Williams, [1998] 1 S.C.R. 1128

R. v. Wise, [1992] 1 S.C.R. 527

R. v. Zito, [1990] 2 S.C.R. 1520

Ramsden v. Peterborough, [1993] 2 S.C.R. 1084

Re: Therrien, [2001] 2 S.C.R. 3

Reference re Public Service Employee Relations Act, [1987] 1 S.C.R. 313

RJR-MacDonald Inc. v. Canada (Attorney General), [1995] 3 S.C.R. 199

Rodriguez v. British Columbia (Attorney General), [1993] 3 S.C.R. 519

Royal Oak Mines v. Canada (Labour Relations Board), [1996] 1 S.C.R. 369

Rudolf Wolff Co. v. Canada, [1990] 1 S.C.R. 695

RWDSU v. Saskatchewan, [1987] 1 S.C.R. 460

Saint-Romuald v. Olivier, [2001] 2 S.C.R. 898

Sauvé v. Canada, [2002] 3 S.C.R. 519

Siemens v. Manitoba (Attorney General), [2003] 1 S.C.R. 6

Singleton v. Canada, [2001] 2 S.C.R. 1046

Slattery (Trustee of) v. Slattery, [1993] 3 S.C.R. 430

Smith v. Canada, [2001] 3 S.C.R. 902

Sobeys Stores Ltd. v. Yeomans and Labour Standards Tribunal (Nova Scotia), [1989] 1 S.C.R. 238

Supermarchés Jean LaBrecque Inc. v. Flamand, [1987] 2 S.C.R. 219

Symes v. Canada, [1993] 4 S.C.R. 695

Thibaudeau v. Canada, [1995] 2 S.C.R. 627

Thomson Newspapers Ltd. v. Canada, [1990] 1 S.C.R. 425

UFCW Local 1518 v. KMart Canada, Ltd., [1999] 2 S.C.R. 1083

United Transportation Union v. Central Western Railroad Corporation, [1990] 3 S.C.R. 1112

U.S. v. Montoya de Hernandez, 473 U.S. 531 (1985)

U.S. v. Ramsey, 431 U.S. 606 (1977)

Vriend v. Alberta, [1998] 1 S.C.R. 493

Winters v. Legal Services Society, [1999] 3 S.C.R. 160

Index

intervenors, 13, 19, 32-33, 131-32, 133, 138, 140, 142, 145, 149, 151, 169, 175, 178, 223

Jackson, Doreen, 23
Jackson, Robert J., 23
Janda, Kenneth, 20, 194-97, 199, 201, 203, 206, 236n1
Janzen v. Platy Enterprises Ltd., 171
Johnson, Janet R., 59
Johnson, Susan W., 6, 33, 45, 62-63, 65, 128, 134
judges as "fair arbiters," 44-45
judicial activism: in civil rights and liberties cases, 122-23, 126, 152, 213, 232n2, 232n4; connection with ideology, 17-18, 21-22, 77-79, 113, 122-23, 126, 152, 161-62, 191, 213-14, 232n4; connection with task leadership, 77; in criminal cases, 16, 69, 77-79, 113, 213; criticism of, 14, 29-31, 42(t), 117, 135, 191, 219; debate concerning 18, 31, 77, 222; in economic cases, 18, 159-62, 191, 213, 236n1 (Ch. 8); feminist strand of, 136; implications for politicians, 213-14; in *Little Sisters* case, 136; measurement of, 77; in *Vriend* case, 135. *See also* patterns of activism *under names of specific justices*
judicial appointment process, 34-35, 44, 214, 217-19, 226
Judicial Committee of the Privy Council (JCPC), 23-24
judicial ideology. *See* ideology
judicial independence, 10, 14, 33-34, 41, 42(t), 226
judicialization of politics, 3-4
judicial power, 30-31, 220
jurisdiction, 8

Katz v. United States, 39
Kawashima, Takeyoshi, 6
Kelly, James B., 31, 77, 214, 220
Knight, Jack, 8-9
Knopff, Rainer, 31-32, 41, 69, 77, 135-36, 219-20
Knox Contracting v. Canada, 184
Kourtessis v. Minister of National Revenue, 103
Kritzer, Herbert, 136, 142
Kurtz, Glenn S., 131, 142

labour board rulings, 167-69(t), 173, 175(t), 178(t)
La Forest, Justice Gerard: behaviour in civil rights and liberties cases, 119(t), 121(t), 123; behaviour in criminal cases, 74(t), 76, 78; behaviour in economic cases, 158(t), 160-61; ideology of, 20, 48-49, 55(t)-56, 76(t), 81(t), 121(t), 124-25(t), 160(t), 163(t), 202(f)-208; majority opinion authorship, 74(t), 119(t), 158(t); patterns of activism, 78(t), 123(t), 161(t)
Lamer, Chief Justice Antonio, 230n5; behaviour in civil rights and liberties cases, 116-21; behaviour in criminal cases, 72-76; behaviour in economic cases, 157-61; ideology of, 20, 48-49, 55(t)-56, 76(t), 80-81(t), 121(t), 124-25(t), 159-60(t), 163(t)-64, 206-208; on "judge bashing," 30; majority opinion authorship, 15, 73-74(t), 118-19(t), 121(t), 152, 157-58(t), 210-11; as opinion follower, 157, 210; panel striking patterns, 36, 117; patterns of activism, 78(t), 123(t), 161(t); task leadership, 15-16, 72-73, 76, 112, 118, 121(t), 152, 210-11

criminal cases, 72-75; in economic
cases, 155-58, 160
OPSEU v. Ontario (Attorney General), 147
"outsiders" on the Supreme Court, 16-17,
20-21, 72-73, 75, 118, 122, 157,
159, 190, 210-12

Packer, Herbert, 28, 199
panel assignment power, 25-26, 35-36,
42(t), 117, 212-13, 226
panel size: in civil rights and liberties
cases, 116-17, 152, 212; in criminal
cases, 70-72, 112; in economic
cases, 154-56, 189-90
parliamentary oversight of judicial
appointments, 35, 217-19
parliamentary supremacy, 23-24, 26-27,
37, 40, 42(t), 220
party of prime minister measure:
connection with activism, 78-79,
122-23, 162, 232n4, 234n1;
correlation with civil rights and
liberties votes, 64; correlation with
criminal votes, 64; correlation with
economic votes, 64; correlation
with other measures, 59-60, 228n1
(Ch. 3), 229n3; in criminal cases,
230n4; in economic cases, 18; in
equality cases, 127, 133-34, 138,
215; in free speech cases, 140-41,
144-45, 149-50, 215; as indicator of
judicial ideology, 15, 47-48, 51, 59;
in right to counsel cases, 84-87, 91-
92, 215; in search and seizure cases,
100-102, 107, 215; in tax cases, 179,
182-83, 187, 215; in union cases,
165, 169-70, 173-76, 215; validity
of, 59-61, 63-64; weak predictor of
ideological voting, 16, 18, 63-65,
86, 92, 106, 134, 144, 193, 214-17,
234n14

payroll tax deductions, 179-80, 183(t)-
84
Peck, Sidney R., 6
*PIPSC v. Northwest Territories (Commis-
sioner)*, 234n3
plots of ideological consistency, 194-
205; limitations of, 197; scoring
method, 197
police deception, 83-84, 87(t), 91(t)-
94(t)
political implications of findings, 213-
14, 217-20
political speech, 141-42, 145(t)-47,
149(t)
Power, John, 6
precedent, 4, 39, 47, 209, 228n4; in legal
model 5-6, 8-9; vertical allegiance
to, 47
Pritchett, C. Herman, 5, 45
Privy Council, 23-24
probable cause, 97, 101(t), 104, 107(t)-
108, 111(t)-12
property tax cases, 185
PSAC v. Canada, 172
public opinion, 32

Quebec *Charter of Human Rights and
Freedoms*, 1
*Quebec (Deputy Minister of Revenue) v.
Nolisair International Inc.*, 235n6
*Quebec (Human Rights Commission) v.
MakSteel Quebec, Inc.*, 232n5

R. *v. Andrews*, 148, 151
R. v. Collins, 97
R. v. Dyment, 96-97, 102
R. v. Elshaw, 92-93
R. v. Feeney, 105-106
R. v. Garofoli, 105
R. v. Golden, 102, 105-106
R. v. Grant, 103

191, 198(f)-202(f), 204-208;
majority opinion authorship,
73-74(t), 118-19(t), 158(t); patterns
of activism, 77-78(t), 160-61(t), 213
Wilson-Smith, Anthony, 35
Winters v. Legal Services Society, 90
Women's Legal and Education Action
Fund. *See* LEAF

Wood, Sandra L., 230n5
Woodward, Bob, 236n3
workers compensation benefits, 166-67
wrongful dismissal, 166, 169(t), 172,
175(t), 178(t)

Ziegel, Jacob, 217-18

LAW AND
SOCIETY

Margot Young, Susan B. Boyd, Gwen Brodsky, and Shelagh Day (eds.)
Poverty: Rights, Social Citizenship, and Legal Activism (2007)

Rosanna L. Langer
Defining Rights and Wrongs: Bureaucracy, Human Rights, and Public Accountability
(2007)

C.L. Ostberg and Matthew E. Wetstein
Attitudinal Decision Making in the Supreme Court of Canada (2007)

Chris Clarkson
*Domestic Reforms: Political Visions and Family Regulation in British Columbia, 1862–
1940* (2007)

Jean McKenzie Leiper
Bar Codes: Women in the Legal Profession (2006)

Gerald Baier
*Courts and Federalism: Judicial Doctrine in the United States, Australia,
and Canada* (2006)

Avigail Eisenberg (ed.)
Diversity and Equality: The Changing Framework of Freedom in Canada (2006)

Randy K. Lippert
Sanctuary, Sovereignty, Sacrifice: Canadian Sanctuary Incidents, Power, and Law (2005)

James B. Kelly
Governing with the Charter: Legislative and Judicial Activism and Framers' Intent (2005)

Dianne Pothier and Richard Devlin (eds.)
Critical Disability Theory: Essays in Philosophy, Politics, Policy, and Law (2005)

Susan G. Drummond
Mapping Marriage Law in Spanish Gitano Communities (2005)

Louis A. Knafla and Jonathan Swainger (eds.)
Laws and Societies in the Canadian Prairie West, 1670–1940 (2005)

Ikechi Mgbeoji
Global Biopiracy: Patents, Plants, and Indigenous Knowledge (2005)

Florian Sauvageau, David Schneiderman, and David Taras, with Ruth Klinkhammer and Pierre Trudel
The Last Word: Media Coverage of the Supreme Court of Canada (2005)

Gerald Kernerman
Multicultural Nationalism: Civilizing Difference, Constituting Community (2005)

Pamela A. Jordan
Defending Rights in Russia: Lawyers, the State, and Legal Reform in the Post-Soviet Era (2005)

Anna Pratt
Securing Borders: Detention and Deportation in Canada (2005)

Kirsten Johnson Kramar
Unwilling Mothers, Unwanted Babies: Infanticide in Canada (2005)

W.A. Bogart
Good Government? Good Citizens? Courts, Politics, and Markets in a Changing Canada (2005)

Catherine Dauvergne
Humanitarianism, Identity, and Nation: Migration Laws in Canada and Australia (2005)

Michael Lee Ross
First Nations Sacred Sites in Canada's Courts (2005)

Andrew Woolford
Between Justice and Certainty: Treaty Making in British Columbia (2005)

John McLaren, Andrew Buck, and Nancy Wright (eds.)
Despotic Dominion: Property Rights in British Settler Societies (2004)

Georges Campeau
From UI to EI: Waging War on the Welfare State (2004)

Alvin J. Esau
The Courts and the Colonies: The Litigation of Hutterite Church Disputes (2004)

Christopher N. Kendall
Gay Male Pornography: An Issue of Sex Discrimination (2004)

Roy B. Flemming
Tournament of Appeals: Granting Judicial Review in Canada (2004)

Constance Backhouse and Nancy L. Backhouse
The Heiress vs the Establishment: Mrs. Campbell's Campaign for Legal Justice (2004)

Christopher P. Manfredi
Feminist Activism in the Supreme Court: Legal Mobilization and the Women's Legal Education and Action Fund (2004)

Annalise Acorn
Compulsory Compassion: A Critique of Restorative Justice (2004)

Jonathan Swainger and Constance Backhouse (eds.)
People and Place: Historical Influences on Legal Culture (2003)

Jim Phillips and Rosemary Gartner
Murdering Holiness: The Trials of Franz Creffield and George Mitchell (2003)

David R. Boyd
Unnatural Law: Rethinking Canadian Environmental Law and Policy (2003)

Ikechi Mgbeoji
Collective Insecurity: The Liberian Crisis, Unilateralism, and Global Order (2003)

Rebecca Johnson
Taxing Choices: The Intersection of Class, Gender, Parenthood, and the Law (2002)

John McLaren, Robert Menzies, and Dorothy E. Chunn (eds.)
Regulating Lives: Historical Essays on the State, Society, the Individual, and the Law (2002)

Joan Brockman
Gender in the Legal Profession: Fitting or Breaking the Mould (2001)

Printed and bound in Canada by Friesens

Set in Giovanni Book and Futura by Artegraphica Design Co. Ltd.

Copy editor and proofreader: Francis Chow